Robert Barlow McCrea

Lost Amid the Fogs

Sketches of Life in Newfoundland

Robert Barlow McCrea

Lost Amid the Fogs
Sketches of Life in Newfoundland

ISBN/EAN: 9783337340759

Printed in Europe, USA, Canada, Australia, Japan

Cover: Foto ©Thomas Meinert / pixelio.de

More available books at **www.hansebooks.com**

LOST AMID THE FOGS.

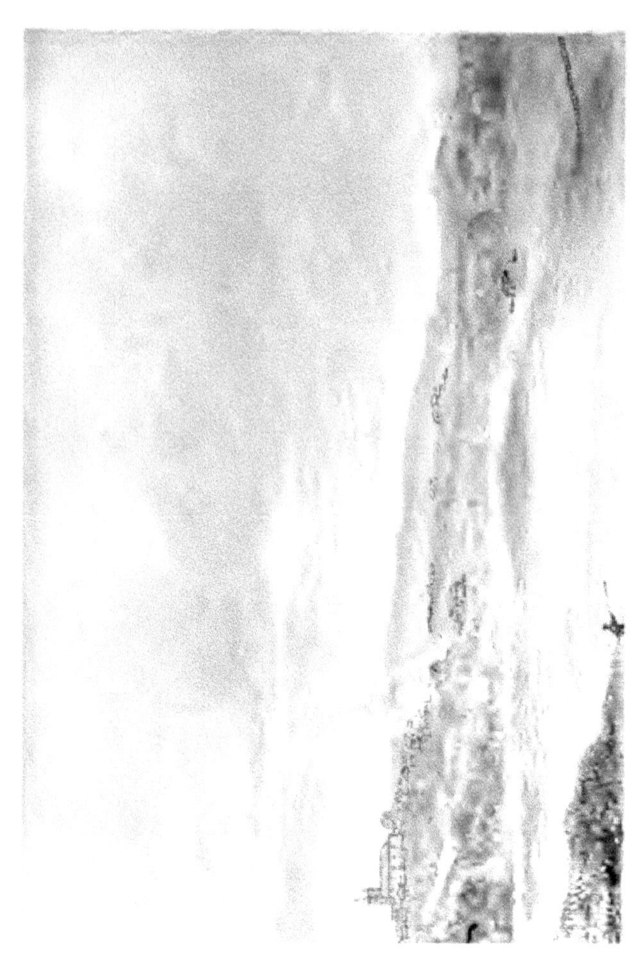

OST AMID THE FOGS:

SKETCHES OF LIFE

IN

NEWFOUNDLAND,

ENGLAND'S ANCIENT COLONY.

BY

LIEUT.-COL. R. B. McCREA,

THE ROYAL ARTILLERY.

"O Thou!
Who sittest far beyond the Atlantic deep,
Amid the sources of thy countless streams,
A newer page
In the great record of the world is thine:
Shall it be fairer? Fear, and friendly hope,
And envy, watch the issue; while the lines,
By which thou shalt be judged, are written down."

LONDON:
SAMPSON LOW, SON, & MARSTON,
CROWN BUILDINGS. 188 FLEET STREET.
1869.

EDINBURGH:
PRINTED BY BALLANTYNE AND COMPANY,
PAUL'S WORK.

		PAGE
INTRODUCTORY,	. . . .	vii
CHAPTER I.	THE HOME DESTROYED, ...	1
,, II.	"ON THE SAD SEA WAVE,"	9
,, III.	HALIGONIAN, ...	30
,, IV.	INTO THE BREAST OF WINTER, . . .	41
,, V.	UNDER THE BUFFALO ROBES, . . .	55
,, VI.	THE FIRST LIFTS OF THE FOG—THE HOME RESTORED, ...	72
,, VII.	CREDIT AND DISCREDIT, ...	91
,, VIII.	MARTIAL AND POLITICAL, ...	105
,, IX.	THE KNELL FROM CATHEDRAL HILL, .	123
,, X.	THE LAST DUEL IN NEWFOUNDLAND, .	136
,, XI.	THE ANGLICAN BRANCH OF THE CATHOLIC CHURCH, ...	161
,, XII.	SPRING—THE ARGONAUTS OF THE NORTH,	182
,, XIII.	THE HARVESTS OF THE OCEAN, . . .	204
,, XIV.	AUTUMN—THE FIRST DAY OF THE SEASON,	227
,, XV.	AUTUMN—A "WITLESS" EXPEDITION,	249
,, XVI.	"THE ODD TRICK AND THE RUBBER," .	269
,, XVII.	FAREWELL, ...	291

INTRODUCTORY.

VOYAGERS in the great ships, hourly passing between England and America, sight about the sixth day out a black desolate headland connecting two strips of high scarped coast, which from this point fade away towards the distant horizons of the north and west. This is Cape Race, the southern extremity of Newfoundland, famous for telegraphic signals and awful shipwrecks. Beyond, there lies inland a vast stretch of barren, bog, forest, river, and lake, of a total area much about that of Ireland, and stocked with herds of deer preyed on by bears and wolves. Beavers are not extinct; grouse and wild fowl abundant; salmon and trout in places to be found in any quantity. Once these were the happy hunting-grounds of the Red Indian and the Mic-Mac.

The former has entirely disappeared, and the latter will probably soon follow the inevitable law of race.

One European only has traversed this pathless interior from coast to coast. Could we but take a *coup-d'œil* of what this man saw in months of toil, the map beneath would reflect at least one-third of water back to our gaze: while the remarkable feature would also present itself, that with lakes and connecting streams absolutely countless, not a single navigable river could anywhere be found. The cause of this phenomenon lies in the enormous coating of moss spread over the whole region. The masses of descending moisture are always first absorbed by this vast sponge, which slowly yields the produce to the lower levels. Great periodical floods, which would ordinarily deepen the channels of rivers, are therefore almost impossible; neither have the streams from this cause strength to force the barriers of the hills and unite their waters.

Numbers of fishing settlements dot the coast, wherever indeed nooks, bays, or creeks afford shelter. Passengers ask few questions about the country, seldom receiving satisfactory replies, as little is known about it. Men button up their peacoats with a shrug, and thank their stars they are passing on to more genial climes. The impression, if any thought is taken on the matter, is that the place may be half-rock, half-wilderness, reeking of unsavoury fishy smells; that little good ever went to it; that nothing good ever came out of it. Whether civilisation has ever dawned upon the fishermen; whether their religion be Christian or Pagan; whether the fashions be those of the present day or of Eden; whether the folk eat raw or cooked meat; are subjects of indifference to the brighter, busier world outside the Fogs. My own ideas, before receiving the sudden order to penetrate the girdle of mists, and make myself a citizen of the world within, were not unlike; my ignorance of all concerning it, profound.

I know now that ignorance alone has militated against an interest in the affairs of England's Ancient Colony. Widely different were the facts and bearings of life there to what I had supposed. My lot has been cast in almost every colony of our vast dominion. Not even excepting dear old Corfu, have three happier years than those (perforce at first, and very willingly afterwards) in Newfoundland, been ever spent abroad.

Our duties, pleasures, and troubles there, are briefly described in the following pages. They aim at nothing greater than to present an idea of the social and political condition of the colony, with the general tone of its society. Would that in attempting so much, I had the gifts and talents of the *chef* of the —— Club, the grave white-bearded Bartoletti, to whom the faintest sketch of your intended hospitality sufficed for a perfect result. "Bartoletti," said Batty of the Royal Incidentals, "I 've a few friends at dinner to-morrow; I should like" —— "Take iced champagne, sir?" said the *chef*. "Certainly." "Very good, sir; will you have a little hock in after the fish?" "Quite so." "Very good, Captain Batty, I understand: you will have a very good dinner." The guests of the following night had never reason to complain that he had not picked up the tone of the intended spread quite correctly.

Little is said of the early settlements of the colony; for of history or story in this respect there is absolutely none to tell of. What its political future is likely to be, is hazardous to venture a guess at under the changes now progressing in the British Possessions of North America. As yet the Ancient Colony has wisely refused to link its fortunes to the new Confederation of the provinces, than which, it is possible, a more unsound or impolitic scheme was never promoted. England, unable to defend, with so distant a base, her possessions from the attack of a neighbouring people (who have unexpectedly acquired the knowledge of forming a strong military despotism at short notice, with little scruple in using it), wishes to retire from the chance of seeing the Union Jack lowered from the ramparts of Quebec. But the means adopted under her guidance, in the hope of avoiding an almost similar catastrophe, will probably prove futile. A nation, like a poet, *nascitur non fit*. It may spring (like the tree from the acorn) from a little nucleus until it becomes in time great and powerful, with the prestige of old traditions and glories to bind men's hearts together in a common cause; or it may acquire its liberty from bondage in a baptism of blood, equally cementing between man and his brother man. But it cannot be made suddenly out of various heterogeneous particles having nothing in common. What do the farmers of Upper Canada care for the fishermen of Nova Scotia one thousand miles away? or the lumbermen of the roaring Ottawa for the amphibious folk of Gaspé? The scheme is nothing but a rope of sand, which the first breath of adversity will disunite and scatter. The inevitable Yankees want the St Lawrence for geographical reasons. We lost our opportunity for dividing the balance of power on the American continent when Lee, Jackson, and Beauregard made their imperishable renown. Before many years we shall have to pay the penalty.

Still, with the loss of continental territory, England, for the sake of her commerce, must keep her chain of ocean videttes intact; and desperate ought to be her efforts in extremity to retain possession of such places as Halifax, and St John's Newfoundland. The strength of Quebec, in its capability for long defence, has probably been over-estimated; but St John's might be made invulnerable, the extremity of a chain stretching across the Atlantic from the Cape, linked together with St Helena, Bermuda, and Halifax. Within a few years from this, we may see its snug little harbour (holding securely one end of the great ocean alphabet) bristling with batteries and torpedoes, sufficient to uphold our flag, if driven there, like Moore to Corunna, in defence against all attack.

Loving that flag, and wedded to its fortunes, who could not wish that towards it the loyalty of those over whom it waves were warm and cherished. Yet here, if indeed in any of our colonies now, it can hardly be so estimated. Men's hearts are not disloyal—they are only indifferent. Nothing is offered to warm the feeling in those hearts, and the fire naturally dies out. Talents, and services brilliant in proportion to the situation, are rendered to the State; yet very little recognition ever reaches the labourers. Year by year passes, and nothing, absolutely nothing, occurs to arouse the love for the prestige of the old country: no honours, no message of interest, no royal visits, or gifts, or prizes for merit, to keep alive feelings worth all else in the moment of danger. How truly experience has proved already the shortsightedness of this policy! "Why look, yer honner," said a Paddy in Canada, "if the Quane would jist be ordering them to build her a cuppil of pallisses in Oireland, for hersel and the little Quanes about her, and be giving the boys good wages durint the job, it's little ye'd hear of Faniism." In a common-sense view, Paddy was near the mark. A pint of beer served out to each soldier of the British army on Her Majesty's birthday, to drink Her gracious health, would be worth more than the cheering done by order at the annual review. Schools, hospitals, good-conduct badges, gardens, libraries, nay, even the suppression of the abominable stoppages, are all capital in their way; but they are not that fillip to loyalty and affection which men in the gap will think of, when the inevitable time for guarding the flag against tremendous odds looms darkly in the future.

The true interests of Newfoundland and England are linked together: long may they so remain! Many would mourn with me should the day come when the old flag waved no longer from the heights of Signal Hill. Even as I write, the fair landscape from my window is every now and then blurred over, and a vision of memories, very dear, revolves distinctly out of it. I see, instead of the sunny and brown, the cold grays and blues of a rocky coast; instead of the smiling harvest-fields, long stretches of barren and lea, fleckered by the rising covey, or by patches of fruit, God-given freely to all! Instead of the river laden with the riches of Hindustan and foul with the refuse of a vast city—chain upon chain of lochs and streams of sweet sparkling waters, ruffled by jealous rocks, and dimpled everywhere by disporting fish; instead of the noble crowns of oak and elm—the pointed cones of the firs and larches cutting sharp against the northern sky; instead of the balmy air of a semi-tropical summer evening—the glorious Aurora arching itself as a crown over the throne of the King of winter, whence innumerable angels spread themselves by battalions in battle array over the heavens, moving ever and deploying in front of some foe unseen by us; instead of the Dundrearys and conventionalists of the old home,—the honest faces, clear eyes, and warm-pressing hands of unforgotten, busy, hard-working friends. To them I send the following feeble descriptions of their lives and adopted country; regretting if there should be ought to offend; and glad, very glad, if these in any measure recal the times and places wherein we talked or worked, rejoiced or sorrowed together.

LOST AMID THE FOGS.

CHAPTER I.

THE HOME DESTROYED.

WHAT a miserable day it had been: and how cheerily the fire sparkled as I lay back in my easy-chair one memorable evening in December 1861. My wife, chatting and working, was sitting opposite; the cat, blinking at the merry blaze, purred on the hearth-rug; the kettle, the sweetest lecturer on social science in all England, was unburdening its views upon the hob; and on that low but genial throne of love I lay back comfortable and happy. Perhaps the more happy inasmuch as I was tired, not with idleness, but good hard work. All that afternoon I had been assisting a day-labourer to clear and tidy a pocket-handkerchief of a garden which my predecessors had left planted with bricks, blacking bottles, old shoes, and such other savoury sorts of rubbish. They evidently would have looked with intense scorn on all our digging, clearing, trenching, and manuring; and would have thought it far cheaper to have stopped the greengrocer's cart each morning for a modicum of faded greens, instead of laying in the hope of fresh-cut Brussels sprouts as we did then. Only the week before it had been clearly established by all hands as a sure and ascertained fact that our brigade would not go abroad for another year at least; and although the news about the *Trent* outrage, as the papers called it, was fanning up a very pretty breeze throughout the country, yet somehow or other we all thought it would soon blow itself out. So much had it become the fashion with our rulers to accept kicks on behalf of the old British Lion, that we never expected him to growl and lash his tail on this occasion. So I closed the bargain with my landlord for the house, hired the gardener, laid in a good stock of coals, and sent for a sister from the Channel Islands to see us well through Lent. I thought of this while the tea was drawing, and very comfortable and cosy it all appeared to be.

There was a hurried knock at the door, and the servant brought in an official letter. I hate an official letter at any time, especially before meals. One may receive a good many without the appetite being a whit improved. But this one, I perfectly remember, I opened with great nonchalance, although I might have thought that it was an unusual time for that kind of missive to arrive in. But had I not made my preparations, built my little barns, stored them with good things for the future, and, above all things, planted my Brussels sprouts? What, then, cared I? Without a shadow of concern I sprang the envelope and read—well, there are some sensations in life one never forgets.

"Thou fool, this night"—it flashed through my brain quickly enough. It was worse to tell my wife, who was pouring out the tea, and calling Tom to drink his saucer of milk.

"What is it, Rob? Anything to worry you?"

Well! I forget how I told her: the remembrance ot the next half hour is all dizziness. I think she came at last to peep over my shoulder to see what that "stupid official" contained, and then she read in the adjutant's handwriting—

"My dear Sir,—The colonel has just come from the Horse Guards;—telegraphed for by D. A. G. this afternoon. A great deal more shine about that *Trent* job than we thought. We are all ordered off for Canada. You are told off for Newfoundland, and sail next Saturday in the Liverpool packet. Parade to-morrow at ten for inspection; all hands. Thought you would like to know as soon as possible. Excuse haste.—Yours, &c.,

"J. C."

"Sail on Saturday for Newfoundland! and this is Wednesday night!" As I wrote before, what we said or did that next hour is all a blur and dizziness. I hope we remembered that it was all ordered well and right; but I am sure that the taste for that pleasant tea was gone, and that the kettle sang any longer in vain for us.

There was indeed no time to be lost, and fifty hours of crashing and smashing succeeded. Household treasures were crushed in boxes or scattered to the four winds of heaven; when, ah! when to be re-collected? Even in handing over the Brussels sprouts to my neighbour over the paling there was a sharpish pang, and a hearty confounding of Captain Wilkes's impudence. Then, far worse, came the tearing of the heart's fibres at the parting moment: the wife to go back to her maiden home, the sister to her father; and I on to a new world, where Home to Englishmen is still an unknown word.

> "'Twas winter then, and as we parted
> The dry brown leaf was rustling on the ground,
> Making the sadness sadder, and the cloud
> Of the long farewell deeper in its gloom."

In the meanwhile, hastily going backwards and forwards, here and there, to and fro, in hurried trips to London and down again; in railways, steamers, shops, private houses, and libraries; I had been vainly attempting to discover something, no matter how indefinite, about Newfoundland. It appeared really to be what its name imparted, and not the oldest possession of the Crown, for scarce a syllable could I glean respecting it.

"Newfoundland?" said one of my friends. "To be sure; know all about it. Fish, you know: tremendous place for salt fish!"

"Newfoundland?" replied another travelled monkey. "Oh, yes! certainly; know it very well. Banks, you know—tremendous banks of mud, and awful fogs. Take care of yourself—cold, cough, bronchitis, eh?"

"Newfoundland?" ruminated a third, more honest; "never heard anything of it except they cook everything in cod liver oil! Rather not go there myself. Good-bye; God bless you."

Then there was a fourth and a fifth, ay, a twentieth, who knew only that it abounded in fish, fog, and mud banks. The picture was, however, sometimes completed with ice, icebergs, stunted pines, seals, whales, and other familiar items of the Arctic picture.

At length, wearied of fruitless inquiry, I turned into a well-known chart and map shop in Charing Cross, where they profess to have plans of all the civilised countries of the globe.

"Newfo*u*ndland?" said the shopman, laying the accent heavy on the *middle syllable;* "certainly, sir. American, I think; Northern or Southern? Oh! British colony, is it? Then we shall find it in this lot."

His index-finger travelled down a goodly list, but no, he didn't seem to hit it. He gave a sort of sheepish, hesitating glance round the ample shelves of maps, and said—

"I'm half afraid, sir, we have not any maps of Newfoundland. I really don't think it has ever been inquired for till now. But stop—by the by, perhaps this will do." He pulled out, from an immense flat drawer full of charts, an Admiralty Survey of the coast line about the great banks, with the soundings marked by hundreds all about it. What with the meridians and parallels, compass marks and tracks of ships, it looked as if a spider had dipped his legs in the ink bottle and travelled leisurely about the paper. Moreover, it was a very likely thing to be useful to any one desiring a knowledge of the interior of the country: very!

"Ah! well, sir," he said, "we've nothing more. I am sorry I cannot accommodate you." It was clearly of no use going further to ask for a "Murray's Guide."

So this is all I could scrape together of my future home, with one other little matter that may as well be told. There was an officer's widow, a lady of mature years, who lived on the outskirts of our great garrison town, attached by long association to its unbucolic habits and sounds, which possess often but little fascination for many, condemned, *malgré eux*, to live by them. I remembered somehow or other, many years back, when a subaltern under her husband, hearing her talk of Newfoundland, and just thought that I would run up and ask her about it. It was the last card, and it certainly did not turn out much of a trump. She laughed at my calling it New-foūndland, and said:

"Newfŭnlan'? oh, yes; I was there several years. Colonel C—— was a captain then. It was when we first married."

"Indeed. And did you like it?"

"Like it?—well, yes, very much. I was very happy there."

"And what did you do?"

"Do?—well, I don't think we did anything."

"I mean, how did you amuse yourself?"

"Oh! there are no amusements. It's quite out of all that sort of thing, except when the letters arrived once a month or six weeks."

"H'm! Are there good roads?"

"No. Scarcely any roads at all that can be called roads; but then in winter you may drive where you like in the sleighs."

"And the food?"

"Well, the beef was not bad, and the bread good."

"Any fruit or gardens?"

"Oh, no; nothing of that sort. Indeed, the summer is too short, except for early vegetables. The cabbages, I remember, growing in the ditch of the old fort, were splendid."

There was a grain of comfort then, thought I, remembering my unfortunate spec in Brussels sprouts.

"Well, but is there nothing else?"

"Yes; there's plenty of salt fish, and pork, and snow, and wild ducks, and Irish Papists. Oh! I remember now, it's an awful place for wind"——

"Wind?"

"Yes. It blows terribly, and it was always blowing. We were often and often obliged to walk out tied two and two together."

Mercy on us! thought I, as I went away quite full

of valuable information; and this worthy lady told me she had been very happy there, and yet she can remember nothing of the place but salt pork, wild ducks, snow, Irish Papists, and wind! none of which, to the minds of common men, contain the essential elements of happiness. It was very clear that her happiness consisted in the home which she formed for herself and its secret inward joys; and I thought none the less of her for the sweet truth she had unwittingly betrayed, but yet had never spoken in sober fact or word.

But what was I to make of it? Why, nothing—really nothing. The spider's legs over the Admiralty chart were just as explanatory; and I knew no more if I was to take out flannel shirts or strawberry jam, railway books or Victoria druggeting, than I did before. People do not usually travel about with barrels of salt pork, so a knowledge of the superabundance of that delicate viand by no means assisted or refreshed my musings. So this is why, the reason why, that I, having now experience of the things wherein the first Fish Colony is a sealed book, an unknown land, a country almost undiscovered, at any rate on the shelves of Mudie or the parlour tables of English homes, have taken pity on future voyagers, to tell them what they will see, and taste, and hear within the rocky barriers which frown upon the white sails hurrying across the misty banks of black, inhospitable-looking Newfoundland.

CHAPTER II.

"ON THE SAD SEA WAVE."

THE decks of the noble Cunarder, in which we were ordered to embark in Liverpool, were crowded with officers and soldiers, together with the few male passengers who had secured their berths before the Quartermaster-General pounced upon the accommodation. Boots it now very little to tell of the thousand phases of farewell and tender lingering looks of affection, or of last words hurriedly scratched off amid the din and medley of the saloon tables. Yet even here one could not see with indifference the sad sight of a sobbing girl; sobbing over some great unconquerable grief. The sounds came from amid a little group gathered near the top of the companion stairs, near to which several of us lingered, partly in sympathy, and partly in idle curiosity.

"I do assure you, Miss," said a female voice, breaking my reverie quite sharply—"I do assure you, Miss, there is no room. It's quite impossible as how you can come this voyage; nor you, Miss, neither."

The voice was that of the stewardess expostulating

with two young ladies, who had pinned the worthy sea-abigail at the head of the stairs, and resolutely refused to take "No" for an answer.

"Both married this week," whispered Ensign Sharp to me; "isn't it a pretty go?"

The ladies were pretty at any rate, and not the less interesting from the fact conveyed by the whisper. The younger, who could barely have counted seventeen, leant against one of the painted panels, her hands crossed in front, and her blue eyes suffused with tears. She had evidently given up the fight, and was reflecting how she should best reach home again. But the other was made of different stuff altogether. Some two and twenty summers had ripened her into one of the truest and fairest types of the Anglo-Saxon woman a man might meet with in a very long day's march. Nor was it difficult to see in the fixed expression of that deep-set hazel eye and compressed lips, a meaning which might be interpreted, "If you think I have gone through all this and come so far to turn back again, you are preciously mistaken."

"Are you sure, stewardess, that the ladies' saloon is full?"

"Oh! full! Miss," (the lady tossed her head just the merest little,) "I do assure you—turned upside-down intirely. The strictest orders was given, and we was told as how no ladies was coming, and Govinment has took up everything."

"But they said at the office I might come if *you* would find accommodation."

"I 'm sure it 's quite unpossible, Miss," (another little toss), "and so many gentlemen a-board."

"Then I must take Captain T——'s berth, and he will sleep on the floor."

"But, Miss," (spoken this time a little doubtfully,) "the gentlemen is all doubled up together in the cabins," said the poor mystified woman, trying to make a side-move down the stairs.

Clank, clank, ring, ring, clank, clank, ring, ring, ring, the second bell for starting. "Who 's for the shore?" cried a hoarse voice at the gangway.

The lady fixed her lips still more firmly, and more brightly flashed that hazel eye. Bending forward to the stewardess, she said, "Then I will sleep on the saloon floor, unless you will let me purchase the right to your cabin."

Triumphant! by all that is holy in love. Amphitrite, grown gray in Neptune's service, was not deaf to the value of earth's yellow dross. She hesitated, stammered, appeared to think, and was lost. "Come," said the happy bride, "go, like a good creature, and get it ready; we shan't quarrel about terms. Charlie," she continued, turning to a young officer who approached her with rather a woe-begone face, "go quick and speak to the agent, and tell Captain C—— to do so too. Don't be afraid," she added, again approaching her weeping weaker sister, (a stranger, as it turned out, until that morning,) "depend upon it we shall find plenty of room."

And so they did: for that evening, by the clear, bright

starlight, I saw them pacing, arm-in-arm, up and down the hurricane-deck, turning wistful looks now and again towards the eastern horizon, below which home was rapidly descending. The pleasant voices of the happy brides were as the old shoe flung after us in our exile, and an omen of another home to be recreated in the land to which not choice, but stern fate had wedded us.

Is it too old a story to talk a little of these great floating-hotels with which the skill and genius of a Liverpool man has linked the two continents together? Men who have travelled much about the world are enabled to make comparisons of the good and bad—or perhaps it may be more courteous to say, of the good and better—arrangements both of this and of other great transatlantic lines; to note on one side, in the midst of much that is admirable, blotches of meanness, dirt, and disorder plainly visible; while in other cases, strict attention to cleanliness, order, and liberality conduce vastly to the comfort of the voyagers and to the welfare of the proprietors. It is not to be supposed that all arrangements for ocean-travel have been perfected—that the *ultima Thulé* of order in sea-going ships has been reached; but at any rate it was marvellous to see, in the midst of the wide expanse of water, our tables covered four times each day with such a quantity and variety of well-dressed food. Nor even if it has been described before in brighter pages, these shall not omit a word of praise upon the manner in which our meals were served—a point which enhanced by a vast deal the general comfort of all on board. The tables ran along the whole length of either side of the saloon beneath the hurricane-deck, leaving a broad passage between for the use of the waiters. These, a large body of respectable-looking young men, all dressed alike in dark blue, ranged themselves, at the first sound of the dinner-bell, in a line, dressed as truly as at a parade, reaching from the pantry-door to the head of the saloon. From the moment the cloths were spread by a few of them, every dish, or plate, or bottle was passed from top to bottom of the row, hand over hand, like monkeys are said to steal cocoa-nuts from enclosures. We will suppose the passengers seated, and the tureens of soup at the head of the various tables. There is a sound of a bell,—one,—and instantly, from the parade of silent, marshalled waiters, there steps out each sixth or eighth man, and, with two paces, advancing together, the hands are simultaneously placed on the covers, a glance at the head of the table, where the captain sits, and at once the fragrant steam of a dozen tureens is released. This is the signal for the parade to break, and for a minute, while the soup is being distributed, the centre aisle is all apparent confusion; but the warning bell sounds again, the parade instantly reforms, the appointed men come and lift off the tureens on the starboard side, which are handed down the line to the pantry. The bell sounds —two—the signal for the whole line to face to the right-about, and the "port" side is cleared in like manner with the rapidity of thought, instantly to be furnished with fish and side dishes, and "right-about" all together to the starboards. Then a short double-shuffle down the centre, a tinkle, and the whole line rapidly forms up for the third set—joints and vegetables. The sweets, cheeses, dessert, and coffee complete the full figures of this prandial quadrille, which, with its intervening mazes, is danced to the music of popping corks and merry laughter of some two hundred guests, for whom this amusement is provided four times a day. The most remarkable feature of the whole ship to me was the silence, order, and regularity with which all this heavy work was done. Each man knew his place well, and it was said that to neglect or leave that place was tantamount to quit the ship and the service of the company.

It was in truth a merry dinner always, in spite of the cold; and there was a good reason why it should be so. On account of the somewhat exceptional nature of the voyage on this occasion, the captain had drawn the three senior officers apart and told them that the officers might call for what liquors they chose; and that, so long as they kept within moderate bounds, and did not greatly exceed the Government allowance, no accounts would be kept. "You are very good," replied the colonel, "and we are much obliged to the company; but I think it would be prudent to say nothing about it now, for there are no less than twenty-seven young assistant-surgeons among us." The captain laughed with a merry twinkle in his eye, and said, "In that case it certainly would be prudent." However, the news leaked out, and consequently the dinners were none the less noisy and merry; while the fish, if there were any in these icy waters, or Mother Carey's chickens in our wake, must have been astonished at the number of champagne bottles tossed among them. If a universal earthquake or deluge take place hereafter, burying the present abodes of men, and lifting up the bottom of the Atlantic as the future home of, perhaps, a superior race of beings, how will their geologists account for the multitude of bottles which, like the flints in the present chalks, will be found in regular layers or strata in the tracks of the great steam lines from England to America and India? Perhaps they will found their future theories of the habits of the former animal man on this circumstance among others; and with what result in their speculations, or how far their guesses would be from the truth, would be amusing and interesting could we but know them now.

One day when nearly off Cape Race, either the corks had flown faster than ever, or there was some unusual reason of merriment at the captain's table, just above ours, causing even the waiters, in the grave figures of the grand quadrille, to bend forward to listen and indulge in furtive giggles. The infection spread from table to table, and we soon found out what it was; though at first all down the starboard side, round the stern, and up the port side again, one could distinguish nothing among the babble but "boots" and "bet," "dollars," "Yankee," and such few prominent words. However, we had it all complete at last. A New York gentleman laid a wager with the captain, of a bottle of champagne, that he could not give him a correct answer within a minute to the following simple question—

"A Yankee rushed into a bootmaker's store in Broadway, 'Here, look sharp!' cried he—'just off for California—ship sails in half an hour—want a pair of boots—look alive!' Down tumbled the boots off the shelves, from which he was soon fitted. 'How much?' 'Five dollars.' 'Give me change for this fifty-dollar bill—sharp, quick!' The bootmaker, not having change, rushed to a money-changer. 'Quick, give me change for this fifty-dollar bill—passenger just off to California;' and in a few minutes away ran the Yankee with his boots—off to California, of course. In about an hour afterwards the money-changer came down to the bootmaker, 'Holloa! sir,' quoth he, 'this is a bad bill; pay me down fifty dollars at once,' which the poor fellow, much disgusted, had to do. Now, how much did the bootmaker lose?

"Come, captain, quick! answer; no thinking about it."

"Eh, sir? how much did he lose? Why, one hundred dollars, of course."

There was a shout of laughter round the table, and cries of "Right," "Wrong," in all directions.

"Why, you forget," cried one, "that the boots were paid for."

"What's that to do with it?" said another; "didn't the Yankee carry them off, and was not the bill bad?"

"Of course it was," said his neighbour.

"The captain's right."

"Bet you a sovereign he's wrong."

"Done. What do you say it is?"

"Why, fifty dollars and the boots. Am I right, sir?"

But the New-Yorker only laughed, and the chorus with him became louder. The question spread from table to table, right down, round the stern and up the port side, "What did the bootmaker lose?" until our ears were deafened with the answers and bets.

At length it reached a great big Boston man, who had set up among us as a sort of oracle; for he wore long, straight, black clothes, of a clerical cut, and above his grey head and huge flapping ears a monstrous shovel hat. We had all taken him for a superannuated bishop, until his friends let out that he had been at the head of a great insurance office all his life, deep in all the mysteries of policy and premium; so that verily it was thought assurance indeed when a pert ensign said—

"Now, I'll tell you what, old buck; bet you a bottle of champagne you don't tell right off, 'What did the bootmaker lose?'"

"Sir," said the big man, with much gravity, "I decline the bet; but I shall be happy to answer your question if you will put it."

So he was told, and then the pert ensign said again: "Now, tell us—quick, old boy—'What did the bootmaker lose?'"

"What did he lose, sir? Why, sir, he lost, of course, fifty dollars, on the one hand, which he returned to the money-changer, and forty-five dollars which he gave the rogue. He lost, sir, of course, ninety-five dollars, and the boots."

But, alas for the bishop-looking broker! A ludicrous shout of derision from some who had found it out greeted his reply; upon which he rose with a heavy frown, and went on deck.

Then again rose the cry, "What did the bootmaker lose?" from all parts of the table.

"Fifty-five dollars," cried a venturesome guess. "Forty-five," cried another, equally confident in his reasons. But the New-Yorker only smiled and laughed with all, telling us to give reasons for our answers.

The very waiters carried it into the pantry, bake-house, and galleys, whence it went to the second-class passengers and the forecastle; until all round the ship, in a circle from the red-hot funnel, where mostly we did congregate, was heard the familiar cry, "What did the bootmaker lose?" Reader, what was it, and why?

It really did one's heart good to hear those hard-working waiters crack their jokes on it in the recesses of the pantry. It is the best sign in the world, and the safest guarantee for the comfort, either of home or public life, to hear the fellow-creatures on whom we so much depend laughing and singing about us; and, further than this, one may be certain of the true calibre of our neighbours or companions in the scale of gentle-men or gentlewomen, in observing the manner of their address to their inferiors. To many men (like myself) it were far better to have no servants at all, than to be waited on in gloom, sullenness, dirt, or incapability, whether from ill-health or ignorance; and for this reason it might devoutly be wished that the order observed in this line were the rule on other great lines of steam-communication. I well remember one night, some three or four years ago, when running down before the trades, and just off that fatal rock islet of Sombrero, the vidette of the great Antillean group, that at a sudden disturbance kicked up at the small hours by some wild young ensigns, to my astonishment the waiters appeared on the scene, at the very beginning of the row, all fully dressed. The next day I called my cabin steward, rather angrily, to tell him "that again there was no water in the jug," and blew him up for his everlasting carelessness, when his forlorn, toil-worn, greasy look went to my heart; and I happily remembered in time my own easy lot with his hard measure of bondage.

"Where did you," I asked, "spring from last night in the row?"

"Spring from, sir? Why, nowheres, 'cept under the table."

"But you can't sleep there; you were dressed, the same you now are."

"Well, sir, begging your pardin, we do sleep there; and, in course, we 's never undressed."

"What!" I exclaimed, petrified with astonishment, "do you mean to tell me that you and the other waiters have never undressed since you left England!"

"Not that I knows on, sir; we ain't got no cabin, nor no place."

"No berths or bunks?"

"No, sir; none. When we are empty we gets berths; but they takes them away for passengers whenever they are wanted."

The thermometer was 90° in the shade, sometimes hotter; and we were now nineteen days from home. He rolled away with a languid step to fetch the water, and I, folding my arms in my bare shirt-sleeves, had a quiet minute or two to think over this miserable revelation, made on board one of the finest ships of a great steam company in the year of grace 1858. And this was the reason why the poor fellows died like rotten sheep at St Thomas. The man who spoke to me himself is dead since of yellow-fever there; he was gradually sickening for it as he gave me the tale. What! slavery not in Europe, or in English ships? and all this misery caused to swell the dividend a miserable sixteenth per cent. each half-year? What wonder the superstitious fancied that an avenging Heaven struck hard at such an iniquitous system, and sent their noble ships to split on rocks, or self-consume in withering flames; their bows once turned away, never again to point or bring back their ill-gotten gains to Old England's shore. Here and there, on the deserted coral reef, their iron ribs are cankering in rust, like the skeleton of many a poor English slave thrown on the sandy strand to rot, while wife and little ones are still dreaming of the good things "when father comes back again." Alas! all they will hear is from the boatswain's rough voice, telling them that he died of Yellow Jack and he "don't know any more about it."

Here is the story: never, I venture to say, more touchingly told before:—

"Sailing away!
Losing the breath of the shores in May—
Dropping down from the beautiful bay,
Over the sea-slope vast and gray!
And the Skipper's eyes with a mist are blind;
For thoughts rush up on the rising wind
Of a gentle face that he leaves behind,
And a heart that throbs through the fog-bank dim,
Thinking of him.

"Far into night
He watches the gleam of the lessening light
Fix'd on the dangerous island height
That bars the harbour he loves from sight;
And he wishes at dawn he could tell the tale
Of how they had weather'd the southward gale,
To brighten the cheek that had grown so pale
With a sleepless night among spectres grim—
Terrors for him.

"Yo-heave-ho!
Here 's the bank where the fishermen go!
Over the schooner's sides they throw
Tackle and bait to the deeps below,
And Skipper Ben in the water sees,
When its ripples curl to the light land-breeze,
Something that stirs like his apple trees,
And two soft eyes that beneath them swim,
Lifted to him.

"Hear the wind roar,
And the rain through the slit sails tear and pour!
'Steady! we 'll scud by the Cape Ann shore—
Then hark to the Beverly bells once more!'
And each man work'd with the will of ten;
While up in the rigging now and then

The lightning glared in the face of Ben,
Turn'd to the black horizon's rim,
Scowling on him.

"Into his brain
Burn'd with the iron of hopeless pain,
Into thoughts that grapple and eyes that strain,
Pierces the memory, cruel and vain!
Never again shall he walk at ease
Under his blossoming apple-trees,
That whisper away in the sunset breeze,
While the soft eyes float where the sea-gulls skim,
Gazing on him.

"How they went down
Never was known in the still old town;
Nobody guess'd how the fisherman brown,
With the look of despair, that was half a frown,
Faced his fate in the furious night,
Faced the mad billows with hunger white,
Just within hail of the beacon light,
That shone on a woman sweet and trim,
Waiting for him.

"Beverly bells
Ring to the tide as it ebbs and swells!
His was the anguish a moment tells—
The passionate sorrow Death quickly knells;
But the wearing wash of a lifelong woe
Is left for the desolate heart to know,
Whose tides with the dull years come and go,
Till hope drifts dead to its stagnant brim,
Thinking of him."

Six days away from England, battling with the fierce winds and storm-tossed waves to make our way boldly into the midst of the wide and misty Atlantic. The south-west, from out of a murky bank, had risen in all his vast impetuous strength and plunged us headlong into misery and turmoil; that is, such of us, and we are legion, who like the sea in fair weather passably enough, but are worse than useless mortals in a gale of wind—useless to ourselves, nauseous and troublesome to those about us. The great waves, swelling into liquid mountains along the horizon, tossed the good ship like a cork on their surface, and would as equally have tossed the *Great Eastern*, or anything which the hand of man could manufacture. It was an appropriate thought now—when, leaning over the bulwarks, clutching tightly to the shrouds, and watching the rise of successive mountains of water over the dark line where earth and heaven mingled imperceptibly—of man and all his belongings! How apparently insignificant they appeared to the terrible powers which hissed through the distended rigging, and contemptuously dashed the salt spray over and over the gallant vessel defying their utmost powers of destruction. It is something to think at all in such a moment, and it cannot be done for long. The brain becomes too addled for philosophy. One may look hastily, think briefly, conceive the beauty, power, and glory of the appearance, and then sink back at once into the realities such conflicts produce in the discomfort of the inner man. It was dirty, gloomy, muggy, wet, sticky everywhere. Even down below in the cabins the moisture ran off the walls, and daylight was but a mockery of the name. Four days of terrible unrest and weariness before the fierce storm passed us by, or, in nautical phrase, the wind chopped to N.-E., with smoother seas, and then to N.-W., with sleet and snow, and piercing, bitter cold. Each hour, as we approached the American shore, the cold became more and more intense; the voyagers in greater numbers crowded to the lee of the hot, red funnel, and asked each other wonderingly the figures of the thermometer, or betted or hedged upon the chances of peace or war with the Yankees. Then two or three would link arms together, and stagger, with heads down, along the deck until forced back for heat and shelter again; while, ever and anon, the ship would lurch heavily, and come back upon her roll with a sluggish thump, from which a shower of salt spray would tower some twenty feet above her bows, to fall back upon the deck and shrouds a mass of broken, glistening, crystal ice. Perhaps it was all a joke to Arctic voyagers, and that Sir Leopold M'Clintock's crew would hardly have buttoned up their pea-jackets to face such a trifle as a keen nor'-wester at 27° below zero; but to us, unaccustomed to it and unprepared, it was three days of real misery, which few would care to pass again, and which many did pass in their berths entirely, huddled tight beneath the blankets. One might envy the cook in his warm, comfortable galley, and linger about the little iron door, almost wishing to volunteer as assistant, until the close smell, and the heat, and the oil from the engine-room close at hand, combined with the quick, unsteady motion of the ship, drove all loiterers up to face the blast, and crouch again behind the red funnel for shelter. But all miseries have their end; and, on the morning of the day before we reached Halifax, the fierce destroyer had passed onward, and a raw, damp wind from the southward had taken his place upon the mighty plains of ocean. But, look! what wonder, what marvel is this? The ship is literally hung with diamonds! Each mast, and rope, and shroud, and stay coated with transparent ice, inches thick, upon which the rays of light, breaking ever and anon from behind the mists, resolve themselves into a million points of prismatic, inharmonious colour. The sailors are knocking off the ice from ropes, and shrouds, and yards, whence, like showers of broken glass, it descends crashing on the decks. From our shelter behind the great, red funnel we watch them sweeping it, by great shovelfuls, overboard, and wonder what they would give a barrel for it in Cairo, where the hot blast of the sirocco dries the very tongue and throat to leather. If one could only sink distance, it would literally, as in many other riches of earth, be throwing silver overboard by the bushel.

"Such terrible waste! isn't it, dear?" said a sweet, soft voice close at hand. "Don't you wish, dear, we had it all for our poor old folks down at the lodge?"

It was the voice of the brave young bride, who was leaning near the gangway on her husband's arm. Well, thought I, a curious wish indeed; maybe my face expressed the thought, for she nodded, and said—

"I was thinking what a pity to see so much good stuff thrown overboard. Oh! so very sad! such terrible waste!"

"But it's not of much use," I replied, deferentially;

"and the old women in England would scarcely care for it."

"Ah! indeed you 're mistaken,' indeed you are; we could pick out all the good bits, and there appear such a quantity thrown away."

"But surely they would find little nourishment in ice?"

"Ice!" she exclaimed,—"ice! I don't mean the ice;" and she laughed a merry peal of cheerful sounds. "Oh! dear, you surely did not think I meant the ice; I was talking of the great basketsful of remains from the cabin-tables which I see thrown overboard. Now, wasn't I, Charlie, dear?"

"Chatting nonsense of a parcel of stuff, eh, Carry? I dare say."

"I 'll pinch your arm if you say that again, sir; I will, Charlie. I wasn't talking nonsense of a parcel of stuff. Perhaps you have not seen the great baskets of provisions thrown overboard," she added, turning again to our group.

"No, indeed, I could not have supposed it; perhaps it 's the mere rubbish."

"Indeed it is not rubbish. You can have no idea what is in those baskets which are turned into the sea three times a-day. I saw legs of fowls, and wings too, great bits of turbot, slices of beef and mutton, mince pies, cheese-cakes, biscuit, bread, ham, and fifty other things all muddled together, enough to feed a whole village, if properly cleaned, and put on one side. Oh! it 's so sad to think of such waste, indeed it is!"

"But, my dear Carry, you don't suppose it's done on purpose; depend upon it the steward would make something of it if he could keep it."

"Let's ask him, Charlie; there's a dear: it makes me quite unhappy."

"Very good, little woman; anything to satisfy you: come along."

So slipping and sliding along the hurricane-deck, down the corkscrew-ladder, and beyond the bar, we solicited an audience of the great functionary within, and had the gratification of seeing him smile complacently, though withal not without a touch of pity when our request was made known.

"Bless you, ma'am!" he vouchsafed to reply, "we've a tried it scores of times, both a winter and a summer; and it isn't to be done. When we first started, the most particular orders were given by the owners to save all the good scraps for the poor at Liverpool and New York; but the whole mass of it fermented, and smelt, and moulded; and there was such a quantity that there was no place to keep it; and, in short, there was no help but to pitch it away, and overboard it goes."

"It's very sad," said the tender-hearted girl, "to see such waste."

"So it is, ma'am, so it is; but where's the help?" Here's some nice, hot, smoking currant buns, just out of the oven. Please help yourself, ma'am; I thought they'd be just the thing for this miserable day."

And thus the chief of the stewards dismissed his petitioners with their hands full of cheery, hot brown cake, fragrant with fruit and candied lemon-peel. The young wife ran off with a handful down the cabin-stairs for her sick friend, the old stewardess; and before one could count twenty she was walking with her husband up and down the icy deck again, and exchanging pleasant words all round. A very queen among us she had been the few days of our companionship together, and worthily had she sat upon her throne. There was nothing wonderful in the homage paid her by a large mixed set of officers and travellers; how one ran for a stool and another for a shawl; how all waited for her to take her place at dinner, and rose at our end of the table when she gave the signal; or brought her books to read, and gladly took a lesson in cribbage and backgammon when the candles were lighted. Nothing wonderful in all this, nothing; for a woman at all ages may command or take it. She was young, but it was not that; she was fair to look on and comely, but it was not that; she was sharp, and quick, and clean, but it was not that: it was, that she was kind, and cheerful, and gentle, and, withal, strong in good common-sense, supported by a total absence of prudery and affectation. Womanly as a woman, she sat among a mingled mass of men who were her servants at any moment, and proud to do a little service at her bidding; men who knew instinctively that such a woman was able and willing to do them a service should necessity arise; a woman weak and pliable in sunshine and prosperity, yet one who would arise a lioness under the trials and adversities of a Saragossa or a Lucknow.

"Pass we the long, unvarying course; the track,
Oft trod, that never leaves a trace behind;
Pass we the calm, the gale, the change, the tack,
And each unknown caprice of wave or wind;
Pass we the joys and sorrows sailors find,
Coop'd in their wingèd sea-girt citadel—
The foul, the fair, the contrary, the kind,
As breezes rise and fall, and billows swell—
Till, on some jocund morn—lo! Land! and—all is well."

Next day we were off-and-on the port of Halifax, waiting in a dense fog for a pilot; guns firing each quarter of an hour, the captain pacing the bridge impatiently, and heavy wagers rapidly passing among the ensigns and assistant-surgeons relative to the momentous question of peace or war. Suddenly, about midday, without warning, the pilot was alongside, and hailing for a rope. There was a rush to the gangway and a cry for news. "Is it war?—Is it peace? Oh, pilot, speak, I do entreat you, speak!" And so entreated, that oracle squirted a mouthful of juice upon the deck, and most poetically replied—

"The skunks have gived 'em up. I knowed they would."

There was a groan and a shout of dismay among our junior comrades as their vision of glory melted into air. "Who'll buy a revolver?" cried Ensign Sparkles, "going cheap;" and in another hour we were alongside the Cunard wharf at Halifax.

CHAPTER III.

HALIGONIAN.

STAFF officers by dozens on the wharf, and indescribable confusion everywhere for about two hours; at the end of which time some two hundred officers had received orders for their various destinations, and we had been transferred to the *Tuscaloosa*, lying at the orders of the Quartermaster-General, in the harbour. To see the men settle down in their new floating-barrack was the work of another hour, when, as the wind had risen to a contrary gale, and the *Tuscaloosa* had scarcely any coals on board, the captain decided that he could not start till the next day for Sydney, Cape Breton, where he was to replenish his stock of fuel. This ascertained, a party of us went on shore for the night, partly on business, partly to see the place, or rather so much of it as peeped out of its mantle of pure white, whereby we could count the steeples against the sky, and note here and there patches of dark wood on the hills around. At such a season as this there is little else to be enjoyed, for the snow is no respecter of nature's features; be they stern or soft, beautiful or tame, varied or monotonous, it covers all alike. But in the bright, gay summer-time, as I saw it after, Halifax has its own share of beauty. Built on the slope of a hill, facing the neck of a magnificent harbour, with abundant room to expand in all directions landward, and deep water for ships along the wharves seaward, with a fine climate and large trade, the stranger has a right to look for a city with the visible marks of prosperity on its face. Nor is he disappointed. For he can walk some miles through streets with fair houses and good shops, sprinkled here and there with buildings of more important pretensions and better style of architecture. He will observe the streets to be well laid out, and increasing in breadth as they stretch toward the country; that there is a style about the greater part of the well-to-do houses bespeaking the substantial comfort of the English home within; and, lastly, that many of the streets are lined with noble trees, which, not only in the balsamic fragrance of their blossoms in spring, but afterwards in the flickering shadows thrown across the highways, add much to the enjoyment of the citizens. Standing on the crest of the parapet of the citadel, and taking a traveller's glance at all beneath; the city sloping to the water's edge, with its thirty thousand inhabitants; the busy wharves crowded with ships; the lines of broad road stretching on all sides like a giant network into the distance, entangling in the meshes farms and villas often half-hid by wood or thicket; the blue harbour, island-guarded from the sea, and expanding, as it recedes landward, into a noble basin; or, lastly, as the eye follows the wake of the little steamer to its landing-place at the pretty suburb opposite, and notes the villas and farms concealed upon the hills, as they undulate and deepen in the distance—all is to the outward eye prosperity and advancement. No doubt, as in other human lots, there are cankers within, but the impression gleaned from the surface glance leave pleasant things for the memory to dwell on.

A large place now, yet the nucleus of a mighty city, the capital of the England of the New World. Yet it is not so long ago, little more than a century, that Lord Cornwallis laid its foundations, and foresaw the progress of an emporium commenced within the shelter of such a noble harbour. With a climate fit to work in to the greenest old age; in which the fruits of the earth ripen abundantly; with its coasts swarming with fish; with a position commanding the commerce of two great continents; with shelters and estuaries in which old ocean ebbs and flows, with daily invitation to build the ships which ride his bosom; with timbers and cattle, and the bed of the earth replete with coal and minerals beyond all calculation; with a free government and equality for all religions in the commencement of its career, it is in truth hard to calculate to what state of civilisation and grandeur such a country might in years upon years advance. The world has never yet seen such a commencement with such advantages. This is the true England in the New World. Let us hope she may be worthy of her progress and position.

Little did I think, as I made these reflections on descending the hill of the citadel, what an unwilling opportunity I was about to have of seeing the country in its whole length, and, alack! present dreariness.

It so happened that, on leaving the ship for the shore, I had brought a favourite cat for a run or a little lovemaking with the blue-nosed feline beauties, as Tom might happen to find it. How it came to pass that we two were fellow-travellers through this hard world was in this wise.

Five years before this time it was my fate to be quartered at that delectable hole, Port Royal, Jamaica. Built at the extremity of a long sandspit running into the sea, with a nigger town on the interior side, and beyond that a huge burying-ground called the "Palisades," with neither food to eat, books to read, nor people to speak to, with the thermometer at 84°, and swarms of sandflies at intervals,—dissolution, disgust, and dreariness, are but feeble names wherewith to describe the existence we submitted to. Now and then there was the sharp shock of an earthquake, often serious enough, as history can tell, in these parts; but the enemy we dreaded was like the Almighty of old, neither in the wind, nor the earthquake, nor the fire, but in the still small voice which ever and anon whispered each morning of death, sudden death to the strongest as well as to the most feeble of our little band of exiles. The archangel who so terribly brooded over our destinies was the fatal yellow-fever of the American tropics. At the moment of which I am speaking, there were living in the barracks facing the little parade thirteen people. Of these, within three weeks, we buried seven, two went to England more dead than alive, three recovered, and one escaped attack altogether.

Among those who died was the doctor's wife, the kindest creature and the tenderest nurse to all about her. This bereavement, together with the fatigue he underwent, broke the poor doctor down; and he was ordered to England on sick-leave. I saw him off by the mail-packet one morning at daybreak, and as I looked into his face, I saw in it that unmistakable yellow-leaden hue, too well known as the forerunner of the fatal messenger. I pressed the hand of a dead man in wishing him good-bye. The packet, on its return, told us that he was struck by Yellow Jack the next day, and died the following evening, after a brief twenty-four hours of intense suffering.

A month, and the scourge had passed. I was writing in the afternoon, when suddenly along the verandah I heard the cries of a cat mewing piteously. In another instant a large white-and-gray Tom entered the room, keeping up his cry with increased fervour, and looking at me with unabashed confidence, just as if I was an old acquaintance. And so I was, for I recognised my visitor as the doctor's favourite, who used to sit on the breakfast-table between him and his wife. Now he was a scarecrow, and mewing away at me for his very life, as much as to say—

"Look at me, your old friend Tom, deserted by his

friends—nothing to eat; isn't it shameful? Give us something, for pity's sake."

I wondered at first, until I thought of his trials, that the doctor had not found a home for him. Then I sent out my black boy for a little milk, and breaking up some bread into a saucer, put it before Tom. It did me good to see the fellow eat it. Then up he jumped on the table, looked at me steadily, as if to say, "You'll do for me;" and, quite regardless of my ink and paper, set to work to lick himself all over, which being accomplished to his satisfaction, he curled up on my blotting-book for a good nap. From that moment he never left the premises, and at the end of a week we were the best of friends.

However, at that period the health-officer of the port paid me a morning visit, and no sooner did he spy Tom, asleep, as usual, on the table, than he exclaimed, "Why, there's our cat: the doctor gave him to my little Lucy, but he bolted two days after, and we've never seen him since; we thought he had gone back to his old quarters and died."

I was in great hopes the little girl would not claim him; but in an hour a little black negress came running in, crying—

"De missy him beg de buckra for her pussy." So poor Tom was forcibly collared and carried off.

It was a week after this again, somewhere about the middle of a scorching hot night, when I was tossing about panting for cool air, half asleep and half awake, that, all of a sudden, I was startled by a low noise near my pillow, and immediately felt something very soft and very warm rubbing gently against my head. Just as I was about to give a shout to startle the intruder, it happily flashed across my mind that it was the cat, who had found his way back; and a cautious glance across the dim light revealed this to be the fact. There he was behind my pillow, bending forward his great bull head and purring to himself as he butted it upon mine. "Here you are; I've found you again." Then he turned his head the other side for another rub. "I'm so glad to see you; say the same to me." So he rubbed and purred away until tired. When quite satisfied with his proceedings, he stepped gingerly down to my feet, curled up, and fell asleep.

Flesh and blood were not proof against this, though hitherto I had never felt any peculiar marks of affection for the pussy tribe. But it matters very little what it is, whether a child, a dog, a cat, or any other pet; what the human heart demands for its love is confidence, and confidence in itself soon begets love. Tom, this strange cat, deserted by his old friends, by death also, had shown extraordinary confidence in me, and I determined we should not part in future. So I made a doll-bargain with the young lady, and soon rejoiced in undoubted ownership of the little animal. He accompanied me to England and to twenty different quarters therein; and when we had to pay the penalty for Captain Wilkes' bombast, my wife said, "Take Tom, and he will amuse you on board." So he did; forming an especial friendship with the purser's steward, who vowed, with the execution he performed on the rats, that he "earned his grub and worked his passage well, he did."

Thus it happened that, afraid to leave Tom in a strange ship, where, unknown, he might be ill-used, perhaps chucked overboard by the steward's assistants, I brought him ashore to my friend's house, where the children gave the old fellow a most humorous welcome, feeding him up to the eyes, and pulling his ears and tail in strict proportions to their hospitality. So we were both of us well entertained, and went to sleep once more on shore rejoicing.

The next morning the gale blew more furiously than ever; and when at ten o'clock my servant said the captain had come ashore and declared he was not going to sea, we all prepared thankfully for another pleasant day together. The misfortunes began by the children running in to say that Tom had gone outside to take a walk, and spying a great hole in the ground had bolted down it. We found that he had gone into an open drain in search of game, and far away underground we heard a faint, pitiful "miew," the only answer all the calling and coaxing could elicit. The weather was bitterly cold; the thermometer below zero, and threatening to snow hard.

"If the snow blocks up the mouth of the drain he'll perish to-night," said my friend. "I'll see if I can find a man to dig him out."

The pickaxe was well into the ground, when right behind us, from the middle of the harbour, the boom of a gun caused us to turn round quickly.

"Why, it's from the *Tuscaloosa!* What does it mean? She has the Blue Peter flying."

"What! it's only an hour ago the captain sent to say he was not going to sea, and it's blowing harder than ever."

The man plied the pickaxe into the frozen ground well; but, alas! poor Tom was frightened with the noise, and retreated into channels as we advanced, the pitiful "miews" becoming fainter than before.

Bang went another gun from the *Tuscaloosa.* I began to feel very uneasy.

"Oh!" said my friend, "I'll tell you what it is: it's a *ruse* to get her sailors off. I daresay they were on leave last night, and are drunk about the town."

"It's impossible he can be going to sea; it's blowing a hurricane dead against him." And again we set to work on the release of the little prisoner.

It was beginning to snow, and threatening heavily from the north-west. I encouraged the man with promises of reward, and well he worked for nearly half an hour. We had almost forgotten the *Tuscaloosa,* when the boom of a gun down the harbour made us turn round again, and we saw the report proceeded from the side of a frigate from which a signal fluttered as well.

"Look!" cried W——, "the *Tuscaloosa's* answering; and, halloa! what's this? she's got her steam up. 'Pon my soul I think she's going to sea after all."

Could it be possible? Heavens! what should I do? Why should the captain send such a message? Another gun from her side, and the paddles took a few revolutions forward to short-heave the anchor. W—— dashed to put to his horse, while I rushed for my carpet-bag and desk. In ten minutes we were down on Cunard's wharf, and thence saw the steamer slowly steaming down the harbour.

Not a boat was to be seen; and in a minute she could barely be distinguished through the whirling, blinding snow. I was horror-struck at the situation—men, baggage, command, all gone away, off to Newfoundland, and I left on shore here. I groaned loudly, and consigned the captain freely to Gehenna.

"It 's not the captain's fault, I can assure you," said a cheery voice behind. We, turning round, beheld the pleasant face and goodly form of William Cunard, omnipotent in all these matters in Halifax.

"Not the captain's fault!" I exclaimed, in vehement heat; "why, not two hours ago, he——"

"I know," said the merchant-admiral. "I know all about it. It was the frigate there, which came in about two hours ago, did it. Her captain, who is an awful Tartar, saw the *Tuscaloosa* lying there ready for sea, and ordered her out at once. There was a tremendous scramble on board; and I suspect others are left behind besides you."

"And are there no means of catching her?"

"I doubt if even you could have got off now," he replied; "but I'll tell you what you do. She was to go to Sydney in Cape Breton to coal for England. She'll be a week coaling. The mail starts overland to-morrow morning. Take a place, and you 'll catch her there."

A good straw, indeed, thrown out to a drowning man, and gladly I clutched at it. There was only the proper explanation to be given at headquarters, and obtain leave to carry out my scheme. It was, of course, necessary to express great regret at the misadventure, and receive the general's reprimand. These matters officially are always, and very properly, measured by their success or results; intentions or accidents not being taken into account. However, all 's well that ends well. I made apologies and peace, obtaining leave to go overland to Sydney and rejoin the *Tuscaloosa.*

Before reaching my destination I found the penance to pay was amply sufficient. Nearly two hundred and fifty miles in an open sleigh across the boundless tracks of ice and snow, with a temperature far below zero! Most travellers describe countries which they pass through in the prime of summer; and here I have an opportunity of reversing the medal, and presenting the bleak side to view. Bismallah! let us see it. *Che sara sara.*

CHAPTER IV.

INTO THE BREAST OF WINTER.

THE journey from Halifax across the length of Nova Scotia really commences from the little town of Truro, some sixty miles from the capital, to which a rail winds through a level country, round the head of the noble harbour; through pine-wood clearings, little lakes dammed up; past farms, sawmills, and the solitary charcoal-burner's hut: all sparsely scattered here and there, as signs of a country still but partially occupied by man. These died gradually out as we left Halifax, and commenced again on our approach to Truro. The town itself appeared to be a collection of wooden villas and cottages, of unpretending architecture, the abodes of well-to-do people, by whom the blessings of religion, judging by the various spires dotted among the houses, were by no means neglected. There was a large open square at the end of the street, with the little inn in the corner from which the mail-cars started, and about which—best of all signs—not a single beggar gathered. Looking about, we saw the sign of rural prosperity in this little township; one day, perhaps not far distant, to become the more considerable market-town and emporium of the produce of the great plains which surround it. It needs but to look at the well-featured, sturdy men, and well-dressed women, who gather round the doors of the inn to hear the news from Halifax, to speak with confidence of an approaching time, in which, under their hands and the hands of their children, this country shall rise in its own greatness, a check to the ambition of its overgrown neighbour. A comely race, in truth, they were, pleasant to behold and pleasant to hear, with a speech unempoisoned by the easy, ready-lying brogue. Brown hair and beards, blue eyes, huge fists, and strong Yankee hatred, were the leading tokens which a stranger rapidly gathered of this people; good signs—none better—of future strength and freedom.

This is all I noted in very truth. Can a man passing rapidly through a township half-buried beneath the white morsels of heaven, do much more while waiting for the horses of the mail-car to be buckled to? Less than an hour sufficed to do this, when the driver invited us to be seated on the sleigh; an article about a foot off the ground, looking much like a slice clipped off three pews of a modern Methodist church. Stout buffalo robes covered the passengers well over the breasts; the luggage was strapped behind; the driver, a cheery young man, jumped up on a little flat perch on the corner of the front pew, shook up the reins, cracked his whip, woke the bells of the four horses into a merry peal, and we dashed through the embryo square of

Truro, up a side street, across a bridge, and away into the open country, guided by the rough picket fences stuck along the snow. It was a capital start, and if we could have kept it up, should quickly have covered forty or fifty miles. But soon after we left the shelter of some little pine woods a few miles out, the snow became very thin upon the road, and the runners grated dismally on our ears. The driver was off and on to his perch like a bird every five minutes, coaxing the poor brutes to struggle against the tremendous friction of such a load. At length Jehu pulled up.

"I'm very sorry you must jump out, please, and walk this bit. I'm most afraid we shall have the same thing all the way."

"It snowed hard yesterday," observed a passenger.

"So it did; but there's been a smartish wind all night, and drove it all up against the fences. We shall make but poor travelling of it if this goes on."

Go on it did all day, and long after nightfall; but it had this advantage, that it warmed the feet, which otherwise had sad times of it. Twice we stopped at shanties along the road side, built by new settlers, as the clearings from the forest close by appeared to indicate. Perhaps they should be called small farms, and not shanties; for although things were in a rough-and-ready sort of style inside and outside, still there were three or four apartments to the house, and outhouses for the cattle into the bargain. We found at each place ready, roughly laid out, with very primitive cutlery, steak, eggs, toast, tea, and potatoes. It would be hard to call the preparation breakfast, inasmuch as it was furnished for lunch as well; again for dinner, and again for supper, without the minutest variation. But for all that there were several little things worthy of notice. The good woman, to my surprise, not only summoned us to meals, but sat with bare arms fresh from the stove at the head of the table, pouring out the tea, yet receiving the first attentions from the toast and steak, and sharing in all respects the repast with us. Though but a rude farmer's wife, still she was our hostess, and a lady then and there in her own undoubted right. The same principle prevailed everywhere, as I found afterwards, in these colonies; and when the lady was young and pretty, as happily was sometimes the case, the custom was not amiss. At any rate, it never proved unpleasant or inconvenient, and in its primitiveness was entitled to respect.

The driver, too, took his meals with us at the end of the table; yet it was to be observed, when all the passengers took a "nip" just before re-entering the sleigh, he invariably, though pressed, refused. "Don't ask him," said one good woman; "they never touch: they are sworn not to do it when on duty with the cars." To make amends for this abstinence, good meals, at regular distances during the day and night, are provided. It is, no doubt, a wise precaution; for the journey at this season, as we shall soon see, is not without its dangers, requiring a cool head and strong arm at sundry times; the more necessary for the safety of travellers almost helpless themselves at such sudden moments of trial.

Thus we sped through the bitter day, crouching beneath the "buffaloes," jumping out to walk over the "bare," and munching steaks with tea dilutions whenever we changed horses. Great slices of the country were cleared for the farmer's use; and the heads of the picket fences projecting above the snow told us of fields which, when awakened from their winter sleep, were gay with green and gold and crimson, or bejewelled with the fat kine, now cooped up in gloomy stalls, and wearying for these joyous pastures. True, the features of the country now were, as Elizabeth Barrett grandly says—

> "Looking equal in one snow;"

but the undulating hills, falling and rising here and there, spoke plainly of beauty when the winter shroud was gone. Grandeur and sublimity of scenery there was not; yet, again, the little forests, thick with hemlock, pine, and birch, through which the many sparkling rills, bursting through the matted copses, ran to join the prouder stream of the deeper valley beyond, sent back the thoughts into summer and autumn, with pleasant visions of much loveliness. Easily could I credit that it was a country in which the hard-working man could live at ease and be happy.

So sped on the day: the clear sky, across which siffilated the keen north wind, deepening gradually into darkness. As the light fled, so grew the cold, and more crisply each moment sounded the hoofs of the cattle upon the crystal road. We were yet many miles from our first halting-place, when suddenly, on the crest of a hill, the driver pulled up and looked well ahead, lost apparently for the minute in reflection. Before us, at the bottom of a steep decline, lay a wide frozen streamlet, across which a tressel-bridge, unguarded by side rails, stretched its spidery arms. Like the road, the bridge was a mass of glare ice, the polish of which, with the mercury at 26° below zero, was as dangerous as it was perfect.

"You must walk over this, if you please, gentlemen," said the driver; "the bridge is too narrow, and a slue might be dangerous."

Out we jumped, and no sooner out than down went another passenger and myself on the ice, whence, in spite of all our frantic struggles, it was impossible to rise. There is no word in the language that I know of to express the smoothness of glare ice at a very low temperature. However, we stood the laugh at our misfortunes from the others, who had sparrables in their shoes, or creepers underneath.

"We 'll help them over," they cried to the driver; while he, gathering his reins short, and waking up the nags, went smartly down the hill, over the bridge in a canter, and was on the crest of the opposite side before we could count ten.

"Now, then," said our Samaritan friends to us cripples in the ditch, "lay on your backs, and give us your hands, and we 'll cross you over."

Bumping, sliding, laughing, just like a dead bullock I was dragged down in the wake of the car. As they tramped over the planks, we could hear beneath the frozen surface the torrent roaring as it fretted across the hidden rocks of its bed. Well they laughed at us going down-hill, but groaned as they went up the incline; we, chuckling inwardly, now hoping they enjoyed the dead pull of two hundred pounds up an angle of thirty-five degrees. By the time we were all up at the top, and they had propped us against the face of the hedge, it was hard to say who had had the best of it; but the chorus of merriment broke the ice among us effectually, and thawed us into capital friendship for the rest of the day's journey.

This, at any rate, cannot be described further than that, with the mantle of night overhead, and the mantle of winter underfoot, blotting all nature entirely from sight, at about ten o'clock we arrived at the little town of New Glasgow, and pulled up before a small wooden *auberge*. On the principle of any port in a storm, the stuffy little parlour was an agreeable change to travellers more than half frozen in the strictest sense of the word. Yet, when the driver came to tell us that the roads were so bad, he would not go on until the morning, so uncomfortable was the prospect that I felt half sorrow for his decision. The place was engrained in dirt. It was not the fact of what is called "roughing it" which made the thing disagreeable. To that I had been well accustomed. But to foul air and filth, dust-tracks over the chairs, saharas in filth on the cornices, piles of half-stupified flies, spiders' webs, and spittle in all stages of evaporation, I entertain a mortal objection. When was the den purified, or the holey carpet swept, or the dirty table-cloth, which the maid sprawled over the table, washed? Maid! it is a profanation to use such a term connected with the brawny-armed slattern who jumped about and slapped the things down as a savage might have done. But the cause soon received explanation. At a joke which passed between two of the passengers, the creature paused in her work, and, to my amazement, placing her arms against her hips, burst into a hoarse laugh, which shook the very rafters over our head.

"Oi, oi, oi, oi, be the blessed! but that's thrue for ye, mister; oi, oi, oi, oi!"

The creature was Irish of the lowest type, and so was the mistress, who soon after, with the steak and eggs, toast, potatoes, and tea, came in to preside. The house was Irish; not that that is altogether as a necessity a bad recommendation, yet it certainly is when it belongs to the less-refined class of that restless nation. Worse luck, for the food too was dirty; the forks indescribable. Hot tea one was obliged to swallow; then I munched some biscuits, and asked the creature I had irreverently called a maid "If I could have a bed?"

"Oi 'll see," quoth she.

"And if so, could I have a fire?"

"Is it a foire?" quoth she, again; "begorra, it's more than oi know."

However, in half an hour she showed me up a narrow stair into a room, which, to my unutterable disgust, was so full of suffocating coal smoke that one could not distinguish her figure when she was a yard inside the door.

"The divvil run away with the fireplace," cried she; "it's the thrick it's always behaving with me." One way of accounting for it certainly, considering that it was a register stove, and when she lighted the fire she forgot to open the register in the chimney. They certainly are right in the *Times* when they say in the advertisements, "No Irish need apply."

She slammed the poker up the chimney, and burst the windows open, advising me to go back to the parlour for half an hour. This I did, and when I returned and shut the windows down to keep out a temperature of 35° below zero, no pen could describe what the state of that room was. It suffices to say, that the coarse sheets and blankets upon the bed were frozen hard as boards, and that the possibility of rest was gone. There was nothing for it but to return a third time to the cobwebbed parlour, roll my cloak well round, and lie down alongside the stove till daybreak. This was nothing in itself; but with eight or nine snorers in a dirty den ten feet square, it was something to be endured. Faugh!

The cold at daybreak culminated to its highest point during the journey. As the sun rose in the heavens, cerulean and cloudless, we saw that we travelled through a country bound under a mighty spell. The streams no longer ran; the woodman's axe was silent in the woods; both kine and poultry in the farmer's yard had sought the shelter of the stables; and not a human being or a sleigh did we meet for many consecutive hours. During the short continuance of what is called "a cold snap," every creature with warm blood in the veins, for dear life, seeks shelter. Happily there was no wind. Had there been, it would have been impossible to travel. This we felt whenever we lost the shelter of the pine woods and the road wound to face the north, for then the current of air caused by our motion seemed to concentrate the bitterness of the frost upon us. Coat, hair, whiskers, moustaches, were all hung with icicles; so, crouching beneath the "buffaloes," we had naught to do but to wish for the end of the day's journey, which, to all appearance, was as likely to pass along as free from adventure as it was miserable.

We were, however, early in the afternoon, rapidly and sufficiently roused from our lethargy. The road wound along the edge of a deep, thinly-wooded ravine, in which, some two hundred feet below, we could see the tops of the pines and birches fringed with drooping feathers of snow; on our left the high bank, the continuation of the side of the gorge, out of which the road had been cut. Turning suddenly a corner, there lay before us a carpet of glare ice, caused by a little stream which overflowed the road at this point. Necessarily it sloped towards the ravine, and no sooner were we on it than the sleigh gave a jerk to the right, then another. The driver, seeing the danger, shouted to the horses; but, with a tremendous slue, the vehicle swung round as on a pivot, and hung over the edge of the brink. Bursting the "buffaloes," out jumped the front passengers, but our wraps, tightly packed, would not yield an inch. Horrible was it to hear the scraping and yielding of the horses' hoofs, as the increasing weight of the unsupported sleigh overpowered their strength. It was but a moment of agony, shouting, and suspense; when over, over, over, yielding inch by inch, backwards we slipped into—destruction! No, as it mercifully happened, we were caught, just as the hind feet of the leader was at the edge, by a stout fir tree, which, had we missed, we must have gone headlong into eternity. A branch stretched within reach, across which, in ten seconds, with bumping heart, and blood suddenly revivified, I was sitting surveying the wreck.

Sharp and quick as the cracking of his whip came from the mouth of our driver orders on the crisis.

"Unbuckle the traces—stand to the heads of the shafters—keep 'em down—run, if you please, straight ahead, not half a mile—call the miller—bring ropes—sit still in the sleigh—for God's sake, sit still—if she moves off you 're gone."

In less time than it has taken to write it, the traces were loosened, and the leaders released; while the shaft horses, happily bogged tight in snow and brushwood, were also made powerless to struggle. There was a little barrister from Sydney, now travelling homewards who proved himself a trump at the moment of difficulty, cutting in and out about the horses' heels with the confidence of a Rarey. He now sat at the heads of the shaft horses, and in reply to the pitiful entreaties of the two passengers still in the sleigh, he said—

"Now, I tell you what it is, this ain't a joking matter; if you attempt to get out I'll let their heads up, and you'll be in 'kingdom come' in less than five minutes."

What an agreeable announcement to the poor devils, hanging by their eyelids over an unfathomable precipice for thirty minutes, which in this world they will never forget. At the end of that time we heard the joyful sound of approaching help, soon realised by the presence of the miller and his three stout sons. With ropes fastened round our waists, we were soon dragged on to the road; the traces were cut, the sleigh fastened to the trees, and the horses released as well. Then quickly were hauled up the boxes, and lastly the vehicle itself, smashed well in behind, with shafts cracked short as carrots, and the iron runners burst below. Till now, not a word had passed between the miller and the driver, but when all was safe on the road, the latter, taking off his hat, and wiping a brow over which rivers of perspiration flowed—

"Ah! the de'il mend ye, Jock—the de'il mend ye!" cried he, shaking his brawny fist; "it's come at last, and might hae cost us a' our lives. Is this yer promise, which ye hae made fifty times, to cut the trees along the edge? The shame on ye, Jock—the shame on ye, Jock!"

"Now, Sandy, man, what's this ye're saying?" replied the miller, "talking thus, when ye oughten to be giving praise that ye're off so well. Maybe I am to blame, but the snap last night came on so sudden."

"Sudden!" said Sandy, in a voice more mollified, for they were old friends.

"No matter, Sandy; we're all wrong sometimes: let 's get the sleigh down to the mill, and we'll soon put you to rights. Jamie, take the axe, and lop down three or four of those trees, and lay 'em along the edge. I'm very thankful it's no waur, Sandy, God be praised!"

And as Jack, the miller, lifted his hat in speaking, the last words echoed in many of our hearts I believe, though not spoken aloud. Sandy stretched out his hand and grasped that of his friend. We soon heard the roaring of the mill-stream at the end of the pine wood, where lived and ground his corn this jolly and sensible miller. His mill lay snugly in the middle of a little hollow, through which wound a mountain stream, now crystalled in its winter sleep; while very picturesque against the white hills stood the red-tiled roofs, the brown old wheel and bridges. Gaily the miller peeled his home-spun coat, and called his sons about him, bidding them light the forge, run out the anvil, blow up the furnace, and strike stalwart blows with him upon our broken vehicle. In less than two hours the runners are spliced, the baggage is repacked, and Sandy, the driver, is yo-ho-ing his flock together.

"Weel, Jock," cried he, stretching his hand to the miller, "I'll no say but ye ha' dune us a gude turn, forbye it was yoursel that——"

"You'll just be saying naething about it this time; I'm glad to work, and wish it were better."

"Shall I no charge it, then, agen the maister, Jock?"

"You'll just charge naething, Sandy; and let us be thankful my over-forgetfulness came to no waur." So the brave miller lifted his hat, wishing us God-speed; and again the sleigh bells rang sharply through the frosted air, until at ten o'clock they ceased for that day before a clean little hostelry in the biggest street ot Antigonish. There we took off our numberless wraps in the parlour, to see the table spread with the everlasting steak and potatoes, eggs, toast, and tea; yet, marvellous difference! neatness and cleanliness were visible everywhere; and when the hostess took her seat at the tea-tray, one felt, from the tone and texture of her attire, that a good bedroom and night's rest was a possible perspective. Nor were we disappointed; the less so when, after the sweet clean sheets hot from the kitchen-fire were spread upon the bed, the tall Scotch landlord, himself a pensioner and *olim* an officer's servant, brought up great jugs of boiling water, a bath, and abundance of towelling. The night thus passed in the thriving little town, with the queer old Indian name, must indeed be marked with a red letter in the diary of an unwilling winter traveller in Nova Scotia.

CHAPTER V.

UNDER THE BUFFALO ROBES.

WILLINGLY could a traveller, weary and half-starved with cold, have indulged in a long snooze under that clean Scotch roof; but an early knock before daybreak summoned us down to the discussion of "the inevitable steaks and eggs, the toast, potatoes, and tea." A long journey was before us; the Gut of Canso was to be crossed before night, requiring, at this season, a favourable opportunity. Dismally sounded the bells as the sleigh hurried us through the streets of the little town, still hushed in sleep. Bitter was the cold as we lost the shelter of the houses and breasted the hills; on the opposite fall of which, far, far away, lay the sister colony of Cape Breton. Nothing to see but one eternal snow; nothing to do but to shrink beneath the "buffaloes" as far as possible, and let fate do its worst.

However, we had a little diversion at noon, which roused us up for a few minutes in a droll sort of way. We had stopped for lunch at the little inn where the horses changed, and were seated round a rickety table, discussing "the steak and eggs, the toast, potatoes, and tea," when, without a shadow of warning, the man on my left lifted his arms high above his head, gave a yell which in any other temperature would have turned the blood cold, and, tumbling backward with his chair, lifted the table reversely with his legs, of course upsetting the concern with a stupendous crash. For the first instant of astonishment little could be heard save cries and oaths, as the various parties were saturated with hot liquids, grease, or milk; then the little barrister, escaping from a bath of gravy and onions, ran to the fallen passenger, exclaiming—

"My ——! the man has an epileptic fit."

So it was; and dreadful was the struggle for escape of the soul within—the foaming lips, the fixed staring eyes, the life-rending convulsions—to behold. Poor fellow! he was quickly lifted to a sofa, neckcloth loosened, ice rubbed on his face, hands chafed, and salts applied to the nostrils, until he gradually acquired a kind of half consciousness, in which state he was lifted again into the sleigh, and propped with coats as best we could under the "buffaloes." Then the little barrister whispered that he was a Scotch engineer, travelling down with another of our party to pump water out of the Sydney mines; that, on arrival at Halifax, he had ran loose for a week or so, going to bed "mellow" by night; and now, during the journey, refreshing by a solid "nip" whenever the sleigh stopped. This I had observed, but seeing it had no effect on him, thought nothing of it. But Nature will not be denied altogether. Had he got drunk daily all would have been comparatively well with him; but his constitution acted differently. The fiery spirit heated the blood to fever-point within, and the bitter cold condensed it from without. There was no safety-valve left: so the fire, flying to the brain at last, overturned the cauldron of its wrath upon the most vital point.

Still we travelled on, over the crest of hills where beyond on the horizon lay the broad St Lawrence. As we wound down lower and lower we could see nothing of the bright blue waters of the gulf; but far as the eye could range it was white with ice, and differing only from the land in the angular form of the great blocks piled along the margin.

Down, lower and lower, from the heights of the hills, through gaps wherein the track ran round in great circular coils towards a distant village; crack went the driver's whip, crack, crack; and very busy were the bells as we rattled down the slope. The little barrister was turning anxious glances towards the west, where a great bank of indigo was darkly looming. "Surely," said he at length to the driver, "it's not so cold as it was."

"No, sir; but I hope we shall cross the Gut before that snow-storm breaks on us."

The boatmen, standing at the entrance of the shanty at the foot of the hill, shook their heads as we jumped from the car. The Gut was full of floating ice, passing rapidly through; and no boat was safe in crossing the narrow stream which, passing through a cleft in the hills about a mile in breadth, divides Nova Scotia from Cape Breton. We followed the driver to where the margin of the water should have been, and certainly the prospect was not inviting. On either side, fringing the land for the width of quarter of a mile, the ice was blocked solidly; while between the shores, in the open water, we could see the great blocks sweeping down the channel. A boat nipped between them, or even struck, would be cracked like a walnut; and, as a warning, standing sharp against the white hills opposite, were the tall masts of a ship, wrecked in a snow-storm two days previously. "No," said the driver, "it ain't to be done; we must bide the slack of the tide."

Slowly and sadly we turned to wait two weary hours in the shanty, where, save the excitement of drinking bad spirits and water, there was nothing to be done. An hour must have slipped away, during which the noisy voices had sunk into torpidity, when, happening to kick a bit of old newspaper with my foot, I picked it up as a godsend. It proved to be part of a fresh American journal, and, among other items, contained an account of the death and burial of the Prince Consort. There were extracts from the English papers in great variety. Just as we left England, many articles in the magazines, from gifted pens, had touched the fame and virtues of the wise and prudent prince not unworthily; yet I did not remember having seen anything which surpassed in beauty the thoughts in the ragged scrap of the Yankee paper on the floor of the boatmen's hut at Canso.

It may be some in England would like them as well, so here they are:—

"THREE LITTLE WREATHS.

"When the royalty of England was engaged in the solemn duty of burying the dead of the palace, a few weeks ago, among the ceremonials which fittingly attended the entombing of a prince, nothing was so touching, nothing so profoundly suggestive, as the laying of those three wreaths of moss and violets on his coffin—the simple token of a daughter's love. It has been remarked among thoughtful persons that, in the numerous accounts we have had of the last hours of Prince Albert, nothing has been said of any religious ceremonies; nor is it known whether the earthly prince was reminded, or was able to be reminded, of the fact that he was about entering a presence where the forms of earthly courts do not exist, and where the garments to be worn are neither of the purple of human royalty nor of the pattern of human approval. It would have been well to say of him that he died in the Christian faith, and to leave on record, in connexion with his last hours on earth, something whereby we might gather how the English nation regard the death of a prince in his descent to the level of human nature. But, from aught that appears, no one seems to have thought of him as anything but a dead prince, to be embalmed and buried with the royal dead of England.

"No one except those children, who, in the presence of the grim monarch, forgot their own line, its prerogatives and power, while they laid on the coffin of their father the token of undying love, the emblems of resurrection and reunion hereafter.

"It is the smallest but most meaning incident in the funeral story. A thousand years hence it may be that some explorer will be searching among the ruins of Windsor for relics of the ancient days. Should he find that vault, where the kings and their children lie, he will wonder at the splendour of the gilded coffins, at the trappings which adorn the solemn repose of the dead; but if he should, by chance, find on the coffin of Albert some wreathed moss, some petals of dead violets, they will create in his breast more tender emotions, they will carry him back with more of the sense of common blood and common destiny to the long past years, than any carved stones or monumented brasses. It is in the affections, as in 'the common lot' of men, that princes and beggars are equal.

"There is something interesting in the fact that, in all ages, and almost all countries, flowers have been strewn over the dead and laid on their graves, as tokens of love that reaches through the darkness. We remember to have seen an Egyptian mummy's case opened, in which lay the embalmed body of a priestess or princess of early days. How many thousand years her body had reposed in the Theban mountain, undisturbed by the fall of empires or the crushing chariot-wheel of time, no one could tell with accuracy. Doubtless she lived before the Parthenon was founded, before Rome was. The monuments of human greatness had been created and had crumbled, the memorials of kings and warriors had been decreed by senates, carved by sculptors, admired by generations of men, and had gone to dust under those chariot-wheels, while the repose of the Egyptian girl remained calm; and when it was at length broken, we found around her head a wreath of braided leaves and blossoms, unbroken even in their delicate tendrils. Thus, a token of affection, a simple weaving into a wreath of these memorials of human love, had outlasted the most elaborate work of man in honour of his dead heroes. So the love they typify outlasts all earthly measurement of duration.

"It will hardly be that those wreaths will long continue in the atmosphere of an English burial-chamber. But they speak of a love that overlooks the changes of time—that reaches beyond the confines of life. The prince who has now been laid there had many qualities that endeared him to those who best knew him, and is mourned by a widow who finds little consolation in her royalty, and by children who find a mournful pleasure in gathering moss and violets at Osborne, to make wreaths for his coffin."

"Now then, gentlemen, if you please, we'll make a try," said the driver, putting his head into the door of the hovel; "sharp, please: just an hour before dark."

Following his lead, a few minutes brought us to the land edge of the ice, usually the shore of the sea. The hills loomed high on either side of the narrow channel, their summits black with snow clouds. "Come on," cried the driver, as he looked at the ominous sign, "Come on quick, gentlemen!" and so saying, he dashed among the ice-boulders, which lay for three hundred yards between us and the water. It was all very well to cry "come on," but to us with smooth shoes it was next to impossible. If any one who reads this will upset a basin of lump sugar upon the table, and watch the struggles of two half-drowned flies upon it, they might then better understand our miserable plight. With terrible tumbles which hurt seriously, with rolls along the smoothest blocks, and bolder creeping over the rougher, we managed at length to reach the boat at the edge of the ice, which pushed off instantly into the channel. There was little need to row, for the tide set us rapidly down, and steering alone would bring us diagonally to the opposite shore. The grand thing was to avoid, with the boat-hooks, the great blocks whirling round past us, so placid in appearance, but a squeeze from which would have sunk us instantly. It was not a pleasant position, for the chop sea lopped us up and down deridingly, and the snow falling thickly seemed to close a sort of doom upon our frail cockle-shell of a bark. It came to its crisis when a cry of agony from the little barrister, at a heavy lurch, grated on the nerves like the sharp risp of a file.

"Oh! my G—! Oh! my G—!"

He was grasping the seat with clenched hands, as pale as death, and with chattering teeth. It was horrible to hear him shriek, for at the next lurch he cried again—

"Oh! save me, save me!—We are drowned!—My G—! save me, save me!"

We tried to soothe him—him who had been so smart, and had shown such presence of mind in difficulties on shore. The boatmen shouted roughly to him to be quiet. But he cried the more helplessly, for his nerves were quite unstrung at being thus suddenly thrust upon a new danger out of his own element.

"Save me, my G—!—save me!" until the echo of the hideous yell was mockingly sent back by the side of the hill we were rapidly approaching; and, in a few minutes after, with thankful hearts we jumped upon the opposite blocks of ice, and scrambled bruisingly over them to dry land.

There we were very soon in a pretty fix. "Follow the track up the hill for about half a mile and you'll find the inn," cried the driver. "Come on," said the little barrister, all cock-a-hoop again, "or the snow will shut out the road." We hardly thought who followed us, but at a turn of the road I saw that the only creature near us was the drunken engineer. At that very moment, without an instant's notice, this wretched man fell backwards in the soft snow with a terrible yell, struggling and foaming worse than in the morning. Of course we flew to his assistance; and for half an hour laboured to bring him back, but only to a state of unparalleled violence. With the greatest difficulty we kept him down, and avoided the blows which he struck about him. It was a serious business; darkness had fallen upon us, and the snow upon the tracks obliterating all traces of the road. Neither of us, in the confusion, could tell again even the direction to go in. We shouted; there was no answer; and the pleasant conviction of being soon buried and frozen in the snow-storm began to loom strongly in the present.

"Shall I try to find the inn," said my companion, "and bring assistance?"

"Impossible! Even if you could do it, you might never find us again."

"Shout! for heaven's sake, shout!"

We shouted to crack our lungs, but not even an echo replied. Another half hour passed, the most anxious thirty minutes of my life, when, in the distance, the bells of a sleigh faintly tingled. How we shouted needs no telling; and at length, joy unspeakable! we heard a faint response. It was a woodman's sleigh; and very much astonished was the man to find us. We had still heavy work to do. The poor brute, who was nearly frozen on the snow, refused to move, and struck wildly at us when we tried to lift him. We made some great efforts, and several times had nearly reached the sleigh, when he broke away, and threw himself headlong down again. The man proposed to drive on and get more assistance, but we besought him not to go, on account of the heavy drift rapidly increasing. What was to be done? It was impossible to abandon a fellow-creature, but yet our own lives were in risk.

"We must stun him," I said, at length, "to save ourselves; will you consent?" and I drew out the heavy wooden hand-guard of the sleigh, ready to strike.

The woodman said "yes," but the barrister would not.

"D—— un!" cried the former, "I'll choke un." It was a bright idea, though less merciful than mine.

We dashed at him again, and in spite of his kicks and bites the woodman secured a black silk handkerchief round his throat. A Thuggish twist of his fingers, and the wretched man gradually fell back insensible. To loosen the grip, place him flat upon the boards of the sleigh, and throw ourselves on him to keep him down, was the work of an instant. The driver sprung up, and lashed his horses. The struggles of the poor fellow to get away were dreadful, but we kept him down for the five minutes we had to run. At the end of that time we reached the inn-door exhausted, torn, and bruised. We had saved the life of the miserable man, and that was one consolation. Yet what a life to save. It was as sad a sight as needs be; the poor wretch, with his purple face, trembling hands, and foam-dropping lips, all crouched in the kitchen chimney the whole evening, eagerly watching the chance of a dram, which it was a mercy to give him. We protested against his company any further, as far too dangerous.

Boots it little, indeed, from this point to tell the adventures of the next three days through the wide white wastes of Cape Breton. How we crouched miserably beneath the buffaloes, peeping out only in the shelter of the woods, where birch, and beech, and pine, and hemlock, bowed their snow-laden branches mournfully as we passed. Or how, at night, we lodged a few brief dark hours at shanties, where civility invariably atoned for luxuries; and, as usual, the eternal steak, and toast, and potatoes, and tea, and eggs, were dispensed to us under the immediate auspices of the pleasant landlady. Did I say civility? It was more than that; it amounted always to kindness. On one occasion, at a poor place in a little valley on the borders of the great lake of the Bras d'Or, where we stopped for dinner, in spite of the keen air, my limit to the maceration of tough steak, after thirty meals of that ilk, had arrived. This the good woman saw, and, beckoning to her husband, said, "Jamie, gae doun and crack the ice a wee bit in the burnie; and see, man, if ye canna pu' out a pair o' trout." As luck would have it, in half an hour he returned with three splendid fish, not one of them less than three-quarters of a pound. Not long was it before, split and fried, their deep saffron flesh lay invitingly before us. This was, indeed, to eat the fresh-water produce in perfection; and, if only on account of the welcome change, those golden mountain trout are to be remembered as some of the most delicious morsels that ever crossed the lips of a now very weary anxious traveller.

Weary, yes; yet anxious still more: and the more yet, as we traverse the miles towards the end of the journey, whether I should catch the steamer at Sydney after all, or (horrible to think of) have to make this useless journey back again to Halifax. I told this to the little barrister, when, to my joy and surprise, he replied—

"Do you know, I think you could find out all about

it soon. There is, I remember, a telegraph station close by, and you can ask the question."

We were then not far from St Peter's Bay, with the shores of the Bras d'Or Lake on the other hand; and in less than half an hour, in a little clearing close by the edge of a pine wood, we came to a solitary hut. Entering, we saw a well-favoured woman, busy at some needlework; a table with a couple of telegraphic hammers, a clock, some writing materials, and a fire, where a pot was, no doubt, cooking a little humble food.

"Can we send a message to Sydney?"

"Certainly," she replied; "will you write it there."

She took the paper and read my earnest request to the captain of the ship not to sail till the next evening; and to my surprise, turning round, said—

"You need not be at the trouble to send this; the *Tuscaloosa* will not have finished coaling till to-morrow night, and will sail the next day for Newfoundland."

"Are you sure?" said I, with a heart leaping towards the good news. "How could you know it?"

"I knew it, because the captain telegraphed this morning to the senior naval officer at Halifax, to tell him so. This is a check station on the line, and as I sit at work I listen to the click, click of the needle, and understand all it says."

Marvellous power and advance of science, never before to me more forcibly illustrated. Here was a woman at needlework, in a hovel in the backwoods, understanding, by a noise which might be mistaken for the scratching of a mouse in the cupboard, the thoughts of men distant hundreds of miles from each other. The medium of writing, and therefore of sight, cast utterly on one side, and that of the ear alone employed. Will the power of man over the material world ever go beyond this, annihilating distance by touch, feeling, sympathy, taste? Who would now dare to say no?

It was the evening of the next day that my hopes were realised, by seeing across the frozen harbour of Sydney the double funnels of the *Tuscaloosa* cutting sharp against the sky. It was a long drive round the frozen harbour, some fifteen miles, I think; the weather was again bitterly cold, and when the sleigh stopped at the wharf, we were so benumbed as to be scarcely capable of motion, A woman was standing close at the door of a decent cottage, and ran out to ask us in. Bless her Samaritan heart! she was not satisfied by setting us by the blazing fire, but concocted hot ginger-tea forthwith, for our great rejoicing and comfort. Would that I had remembered her name, that I might the better have recorded her kindness, even though it be but another sample of that benevolence which among a simple pastoral people had followed us throughout the long journey, over the boundless wastes of their winter-bound and otherwise inhospitable land.

Yet I saw it afterwards, when its wintry mantle had fallen, and its full bosom, turned lovingly to the sun, had revived under the light and warmth of the great comforter of nature. The tender tops of the pines rivalled then the emerald of Ind; the cattle wandered over meadows half green, half golden; the blossoms of the plum and cherry, as they fell thickly, deceived the eye with the threat of a mimic winter; while above them blushed triumphant a thousand apple orchards, to restore a belief in the reality of approaching summer. It was hard to believe this very Sydney the same place, seen now beneath a leaden sky and shrinking cold, and then bathed in floods of light and colours manifold. It was, indeed, to share the beautiful with Nature itself to stand upon the crest of the rise beyond the little coal-carrying, shipbuilding town, and watch the road, fringed with copses and woods, dotted with cottages, wind round the blue harbour stretching far intò the distance landwards, a sapphire set with a girdle of cinnamon stones. Across the harbour opposite there are farms and cottages, a church or two, and little woods where haply partridges still hide; while on a little spit of sand running shallow into the sea, a flock of curlews are very busy, probably with fish spawn, for the seas about, we are told, are actually alive with cod, herring, and mackerel. There are white sails sprinkled on the main, a boat with flapping canvas stranded on the end of the yellow spit, and the blue smoke of the distant town of Sydney proper curling over a woody hill, perhaps an island. It is just a bit of water-colour a sketcher would love to work in. Ay, more, it appears a wondrous place for a poor man to settle in. True, now it is little more than a village, but with such a harbour, climate, and fisheries; with such enormous resources in coal, to say nothing of other minerals, what will land be worth here one day, when the world increasing makes greater demands upon its wealth?

But we must close this pleasant little slide of summer sunshine, and turn back the revolving disc for a space to the dreary winter. Comforted by the ginger-tea, I struggled on board the *Tuscaloosa*, thankful, indeed, that the misadventure had so happily ended. Two mornings afterwards I came on deck early to catch the first glimpses of our new home. We were within three miles of the coast, and the captain, with a powerful pair of glasses, was searching along an iron ridge of bleak lofty cliffs for the narrow entrance to the port of St John's. As we approached, the white-capped margin rose more boldly from the sea, to the height of some six hundred feet, and where it touched the highest, a little flag, bright with the rays of the morning red, indicated that we were already seen. It was a signal also for us to steer on, for no break in that great black wall was visible until we were close in-shore, right abreast of the opening. Then, indeed, they parted for a hundred yards or so, to reveal a narrow passage, guarded by bristling batteries. Very slowly we steamed through the dark portals, looking up with wonder at the lofty crags almost perpendicular over the decks. Beyond the innermost neck, the passage expanded into an open basin, landlocked, hill-surrounded, and entirely hid from the sea. This was the harbour of St John's, along the edge of which, facing the entrance, were built its fishing wharves, and beyond, upon the rising hill, the fishing city itself. Crash through the layers of ice encrusting the still waters of the basin, and which formed instantly again behind the wake of the great ship, went the ponderous anchor to the bottom; and a wild cheer from the soldiers forward announced the journey ended.

CHAPTER VI.

THE FIRST LIFTS OF THE FOG—THE HOME RESTORED.

WELL, if before leaving England no person could be found who knew anything worth mentioning about Newfoundland, really the view from the deck of the steamer was hardly more enlightening. There was just about as much information visible as a bride might obtain of the happiness of her future life, from looking at the cake on the wedding breakfast-table. The oval basin of the harbour, surrounded by grand white hills, but now in itself all frozen over, dull-looking, and opaque, save where round the ship it was cracked like a broken mirror; and little wreaths of smoke, soiling the shroud of the snow-buried city on the slope of the inner hill; were the chief features of what cannot be called a landscape. For the matter of life, activity, or business, there was a man, apparently a boatman, on an opposite wharf strapping his hands across his shoulders to keep himself from absolute petrifaction; and down away where the smoke hung thickest beneath the hill, the ear could just catch the hum of human traffic and daily existence. "Wish you joy of the prospect," snarled the captain, with a grin, as he dived shivering beneath the hatch. It was as much as one could do not to send a nameless word or two after him.

A piercingly cold day, without life and bustle to keep the blood warm, and the brain from stagnation, what a misery it is! Here we were at the end of our voyage, within two hundred yards of the shore, yet actually at a dead lock how to get there. No boat could cut through the ice, and the pilot said he doubted if it were quite safe to walk on; at any rate, though close to his own snug house, he did not go home in that fashion, which was a pretty good proof of what he thought about it. The sailors forward paced to and fro, silent and moody, or shuffled about with the ends of stiffened ropes, which refused the best skill of the coiler. They were all asleep on shore; we were all sulky on board, cold, and miserable. There was nothing to be seen but the white hills, the flat harbour, and the hazy sun: that was the position for four wretched hours, each minute of which some one cried through his chattering teeth, "Eugh! it freezes harder and harder."

Up and alive again! for all miseries end at last. Just as the mid-day gun was fired from the battery on the high cliffs above the entrance, a snort of defiance issued from the pipes of a little saucy steamer amid the wharves and masts a quarter of a mile down the harbour; and inch by inch we saw her emerging from the confusion of ships and spars, to force her way into the open. Before her iron-sheathed bows the brittle ice cracked and sprung up into sparkling splinters; and when, after backing and charging here and there, she turned fairly towards the *Tuscaloosa*, it was pretty clear that our deliverance was assured. All hands came crowding up the hatches; the cheery bugle sounded the "fall in;" the captain ceased to growl; while, in the bustle of hoisting up the baggage, the thermometer fell, fell, fell, down to zero, and far beyond, yet no one noticed it any longer.

Yet at first we found the exchange from the black, greasy deck of the steamer, to the white, slippery surface of *terra firma*, but a poor one after all. Great was the amusement of the big-limbed loafers and apple-cheeked damsels collected round the Queen's wharf, to see the new soldiers come ashore, when in succession each made a jump from the paddle-box, to slip, slide, stagger, and then come "heels up" helpless on the ground. But it was all good humour and fun, with many a hand held out to set the amazed tumblers on their legs again. It was up and down, down and up, groans from the fallen, shouts from the rabble, all the way up the hill that quarter of a mile to the barracks. Not a very cheery prospect even there,—if we except deal tables and iron bedsteads, those bare empty rooms, looking without fires, oh! so dreary and comfortless! The iron-bound visage of the stiff, grim barrack-serjeant, redolent of defects and damages, with his pencil and note-book, is not a refreshing sight at best of times; least of all when men are in a hurry to light their fires and make their beds. To examine nail holes, or Queen's cracks in the windows then, was quite beyond the patience of a man who had no sensation left either in feet or hands; so telling that worthy functionary I would trust all things to his honour, I dragged him to look up my own abiding place, where a vision of tea and snugness already floated up as a mirage of comfort again.

Whew! what a change! the wind, long threatening by its sullen moans, as the sun declined, had risen in its wrath, bearing along in furious gusts volumes of blinding snow. It was really no fancy to suppose the white spilikins were striving in vain to escape from the torment of the pitiless pursuer; now in corners against walls or buttresses; now lying humbly on the ground, or concealed beneath the bushes; now flattened against doors or windows beseeching shelter; now hiding in holes or gutters, in comforters or pockets of travellers, or in any possible chink that could be found. No, no; rest for such a handy plaything to the fierce voyager from the vast barrens of the North-West there was none. Dashed here and there, and everywhere about; heaped up for one second in gigantic cones, and scattered the next broadcast for roods around; tossed and whirred and hunted; what a game it was to look at: but mind, to look at under shelter, behind double windows of a snug room or of a warm conservatory; but no fun to watch it now, and quite enough to do to follow the serjeant's back, as he tacked across the open square.

At length (I was nearly blind, and only knew by it stumbling on him,) he prised himself against a door in a wall, and forced it open with a grunt; when, across somewhere else, up a couple of steps, into a dark passage groping, and a sharp turn to the right, brought us to the desired haven. Haven! home! it makes me smile now when I think of the desolation of the picture as it was then. A large dome-like chamber, with a vaulted ceiling, dimly lighted by a ration candle, upon whose miserable combustion the breezes, entering freely by many holes and chinks, were playing the same riotous game as outside. My servant, who was tugging at the frozen cords of a valise, looked up, just as if to say, "I wonder what the master'll think of this?" I dare say he might have hazarded the remark, had not a huge puff of black smoke curled out of the fireplace, and effectually cut short his sympathy.

"I can't make head nor tail of this here stove, sir; it's awful."

It was, as we afterwards learnt, one of those charming Yankee contrivances for giving heat at the expense of every other comfort, called a "Franklin," very common in former days in the western hemisphere. Projecting a long way into the room by a connecting pipe to the flue, the heat by it circulated through the apartment was not to be doubted; but the smell of the sulphur and heated iron, together with the everlasting watch required, we soon found to be quite beyond endurance. When the blower was off, out went the fire in ten minutes. *En revanche* with the blower on, the roar of the furnace inside exhausted our fuel at a terrible rate.

I thought my servant a fool at first, and set to work to manage the concern myself; but as soon as I had used up a day's allowance of coal in less than an hour, and made myself as black as a parboiled nigger, I acknowledged (to myself) that we were both sailing in the same boat.

At last he went to his tea in the barrack-room, and I sat down in the dark vault to watch the stove. Amid so much discomfort this was something to do at any rate; and further, while perplexed at the concern, I popped the blower on and off with alternate fits of freezing and thawing; with the mutton fat in my hand I sought out all the principal chinks around the room, and plugged out the snow and wind with dirty linen and paper. There was comfort too in the thought of the man returning with tea,—and in speculation as to the materials he could raise in such a wilderness for so civilised a meal; and I reflected how best I should manage to toast a sausage or a herring, my ideas as to the resources of the land being by no means exalted. Then I dragged the bed close to the stove, and, crouching close down, consoled myself with the thoughts that even this was a palace to a tent in the Arctic regions, in which, perhaps, many a better man was perishing at the moment. Then I wondered how the other fellows were rubbing on, and whether the winter was all like this in Newfoundland, and how many people were snowed up and starved annually. Then came softer thoughts of home, and—and—I suppose, at last, I must have dropped asleep.

At any rate, I only remember my name suddenly called out, and a stamping of heavy feet at the door. I could barely distinguish them; a huge mass, like half a dozen Newfoundland dogs rolled into one, shaking clouds of snow from its exterior. Beneath an otter-skin cap shone a pair of bright eyes enveloped in a mass of whiskers and beard, profusely sprinkled with sleet and snow.

"H'm!" said the figure, advancing; "how are you? don't you know me?"

The voice struck across the memory as that of an old friend, though its echo was but faint at first.

"Eh! don't you remember Wolfe at '*The Shop?*' I remember you very well. I command the Incidentals here now. I missed you on landing, and only just found out where you were."

Remember him! of course I did. Fellows who were cadets at "*The Shop*" never forget each other. But considering that Wolfe then was a thin slip of a smooth-faced youngster, it was hardly to be wondered that a recognition of this matured Polar bear, under the influence of a solitary government dip, did not immediately ensue.

But a leap of twenty years is nothing to old school-fellows. In less than ten minutes Wolfe knew the outline of my history since we parted, and I knew his. By this time the blower, which I had taken off to do due honour to his presence, required replacing. The flame of the candle flew at right-angles to the zenith, and the flap of the ragged paper on the walls reminded one of linen hung out to dry.

"H'm!" said my friend, "these quarters are not in very good order, I see."

"Confound you!" thought I to myself; "and whose fault is that?"

"It's the same all through the place," he continued, deprecating any remark; "I should be most happy to repair, but the money's the thing. They—will—not—give—the—money."

"Then why do they send us to do duty abroad?"

"Ah! that's not my business. But all I know is, of late years they have screwed and tightened things down in the Colonies to the very last turn. They seem to think new barracks will never be wanted. We have been 'patching up' and 'rubbing on' here for sixty years; and I should never be surprised to get an order cutting us down still lower. The fact is, they are afraid to ask Parliament for money for the Colonies."

"Am I to live here in this state then—this dog-hole?"

"H'm! well, no; not exactly. I'll see what money is left in the estimate—precious little I know. However, come over to my den, and dine with me, and we'll talk over that another time."

Leaving a line in pencil for my servant, and recklessly throwing on half a day's coal, we groped our way through the passage into the open air. Heads down, ram-fashion, we butted against the storm,—I following his figure, dimly seen through the chilling drift. His garden gate, about three hundred yards away, we reached sadly out of breath in about twenty minutes, and then expended several more in forcing it back against the fast-increasing pile of snow, happily still soft and yielding. The gale, too, fought stoutly at his house-door, and fain would enter with us. That last victory secured, the inner door opened on a bright vision of, to me, a well-frozen voyager, Paradise regained.

A pleasant, roomy hall, brightly lighted, with a staircase running spirally round one side to meet a gallery above, along which, and up and down the stairs, little children were chasing each other, with merry laughter. White muslin dresses, bare necks, and hyacinths in blossom, with such an atmosphere outside!—it was truly bewildering; when, to crown it all, just then a vision passed of an Anglo-Saxon, golden-haired lassie, with the neatest little cap, and cherry-ribbons to match, who tripped across the hall with a tray, and completed a picture which said plainly to the heart—"English home! English home!"

A rapid whisking with a rush brush, scattering the layers of snow and sleet, made us presentable in the fragrant room to which Cherry-ribbons pointed. I had fancied myself pretty well cognisant of barracks all over the world, and hitherto believed that the regulation fixings, chimney-pieces, paperings, and fireplaces, were pretty much of one pattern everywhere. There is an exception, no doubt, to all rules; and here I found it to this one amid a flood of light from gasaliers, reflected from varnished walls of creamy whiteness, upon which the flickering shadows, caused by a blazing fire, chased each other in merry, mysterious mazes. Pictures, flowers in full blossom, trickety tables, and stands in odd corners, spangled with little goblets and knick-nacks reflecting the dancing light in a multitude of colours, helped to fill in the picture of a pleasant contrast for the eyes of a man who had lived with the rudest externals of the world for many past days.

"Can this possibly be Newfoundland?" was my venturous remark on making the acquaintance of my fair hostess, and of several of her friends who were toasting themselves before the fire.

"Why, what did you expect? I suppose, like us, you could hear nothing of it in England, and thought it was all fish and fog!"

"Just what they said, with ice and wind into the bargain. And here there are heliotropes and hyacinths in blossom, and ladies with low necks in January!"

"Besides," I could not help remarking, as I observed Mrs Wolfe's eye taking a complacent survey of her pretty room, "this is quite a different kind of barrack to anything I remember seeing before."

"Oh!" she replied, with just a little stiffening of the head and neck, "this is not a barrack; this is the quarters of the Royal Incidentals—his official residence! which—is—quite—a—different—thing."

"No doubt of it!" I added, meekly; "I only wish we were all Royal Incidentals."

"Yes, indeed," chimed in another lady, with a merry laugh; "and I should have my room cured of smoking!"

"And I," said her neighbour, "would have a sweet, little greenhouse built. Oh! I do so love flowers!"

"I'm sure I should like a lovely white and gold paper, too," added the third lady of our little party.

"Dear me!" cried the hostess, a little bewildered by the variety of the attack, "I'm certain it's not Captain Wolfe's fault about the smoke; he's always trying to doctor those dreadful chimneys."

"I think I could cure them," replied her fair persecutor. "I'd put in a lovely American grate, like this one;" and her little foot, in its black satin case, pointed slyly to the glowing furnace before us.

"Oh, dear! but you know it would be so expensive to put these grates in quarters, so Captain Wolfe says. This, you know, my dear, is a residence for the Royal Incidentals."

"And—quite—a—different—thing," we all cried, in jocular chorus.

"And pray, may I ask, where does the commandant of the garrison live? Has he a residence?"

"Oh, no! He lives in quarters in the barracks like the rest. I think," she continued, with another complacent glance at her domain, "the whole of his rooms would go into this; and he's a dreadful grumbler about the smoke, too!"

"Well! but he's a full colonel, and at Waterloo before Wolfe or I was born! I wonder he does not try and turn you out of this little palace, and take it himself!"

"Turn us out!—turn us out! the residence of the Royal Incidentals!" gasped the good lady,—"out of this lovely house, with our farm, and garden, and fields, and dairy——"

"H'm, my dear!" said Wolfe, with a little cough, as he entered the room—"H'm, my dear! are we going to dine to-day? Twenty minutes late."

Another American stove half-blinded the eyes as the folding-doors were at this moment opened by Cherry-ribbons, and a goodly table laden with substantial blessings brought to view. Our hostess caught my expression as I wandered from the brilliant chandelier to the brighter hearth, thence to the crimson curtains festooned upon the walls. Nor did I fail to catch hers, and understand by its arch smile how she intended to imply "Don't you, my poor fellow, wish *you* belonged to the Royal Incidentals?"

Perhaps so; but never mind that now, for she gave us a capital dinner, which, since I had been assured there was nothing to be found eatable in Newfoundland but codfish, I may as well enter into a little fully. Palestine soup, of first-rate quality, heralded the repast; and greatly did I wonder in my heart as to where the rich cream and Jerusalem artichokes, which clearly formed a main part of its ingredients, came from. I wondered still more to perceive there was actually no fish to follow. But we had a pair of roasted fowls, plump and tender—taken, as Wolfe explained, out of a box where, with many others, they had lain half-frozen for weeks. A Bath chop, smoked to a flavour and quality which left no reasonable doubt of its being home-cured, aided the discussion of the poultry. Then followed a boiled leg of mutton, with French beans preserved in salt, nearly as good as if just picked out of the garden: mashed potatoes and a grouse-pie, with kidneys and mushrooms. Ye gods! what a perfume rose to the nostrils of a hungry man when the lid of that pie was lifted! Talk of codfish, boiled or salted! Why, it was a dilemma how to dine, and that was the truth; a dilemma, moreover, rapidly increasing as we proceeded. For the Gordian knot of the first course was cut only to be at once reravelled with gooseberry-tart and clotted cream—actually clotted cream, as good as Devonshire ever boasted of—fig-pudding, jellies, and tipsy-cake. The interlude of a Stilton, accompanied by the crispest of celery, is hardly worth recording, compared to my surprise at the dessert which followed. A green Spanish melon, a pine from Porto Rico, a dish of the incomparable Pomme-Gris apples from Montreal, oranges from Havannah, olives, figs, and crackers! I ventured, after the first glass of port, to observe—

"I think there is no fear of an everlasting surfeit of salt-cod, as I heard of in England."

"Oh! so did we," rose in a general chorus round the table; "we all heard there was nothing else, in winter at any rate."

"But it's all off our farm, every bit of the dinner," said Mrs Wolfe, exultingly.

"What! has the Royal Incidental residence got a farm, too?"

"I should think so, indeed! the Incidentals——"

"H'm! my dear!" cried Wolfe—"eh? Shall I ring and see if the fire in the next room wants stirring? Not a farm," he continued, turning to me, "a mere paddock—a little field—nothing worth mentioning."

"And the garden, Willy, dear!" cried the lady, who understood no such mysteries or depreciations of her glory; "and the poultry-yard, and the sheep-pens, and the stables, and the outhouses, and the kennels,—do you call that nothing? The Royal Inci——"

"My dear—h'm!—that fire will be out. Oh! surely you are not going yet?" So the folding-doors smoothly closed upon the ample crinolines, and Wolfe said, with a smile—

"Now, draw your chairs close to the fire, and we can make ourselves comfortable. Hark! how it blows still!"

"Upon my word, you seem to have fallen on very snug quarters here, to say the least of it."

"Oh! my dear fellow! I admit, so-so—very comfortable. I admit it—wife's geese are all swans, that's the truth of it; but it's a good quarter, a capital quarter on the whole, and very few of the fellows in England know anything about."

"No botheration, I suppose, or worry—official, I mean?"

"Very little; and above all things, a healthy climate. So with what my wife calls a little farm, h'm! (which makes me smile), we rub on well enough."

"Yes," he continued, giving his moustache a ruminating turn, "there's another blessing for which we cannot be too grateful."

"No General Officer in command, eh?"

"You've hit it; and a telegraphic message to Halifax and back costs thirty-six shillings. What a comfort! Why, at one of our big camps, life was not worth having, literally not—worth—having. Four mails, besides expresses without end. From sixty to one hundred official letters every morning, and telegraphs every quarter of an hour. Orders and counter-orders without end, with litter and confusion everywhere. The office floor was carpeted each morning with envelopes two inches thick. A pretty life of it, and neither thanks nor extra pay, though the work was extra in every way. Oh! it's a delightful service at a large military station at home, with a telegraph attached to it! Thank heaven, the mail only arrives here once a month in winter, and once a fortnight in summer. The women complain of it, so do the merchants; but it's quite enough for me. Help yourself."

"Well, these are blessings in this out of the way place to make up for other deficiencies. It certainly is a grand thing to be five hundred miles from the general and his staff."

So we filled our glasses, and laughed over many old stories of younger days, dug up out of memory's retrospect of the old "shop" the first time for twenty years. Coffee came, was discussed, and though we heard the buzz of the drawing-room through the folding-doors, we still sat to conjure up the almost sacred scenes of schoolboy-days. It was a long vista to travel down before we arrived at Newfoundland. But as we rose at the second summons, conveyed through Cherry-ribbons, "That tea was growing cold," Wolfe said—

"Now, don't be afraid; you may find this place a little heavy at first, on account of the season, but you will like it very well by and by. The people are kind and social, and the summer very pleasant. Fishing good, shooting first-rate, climate healthy, living good, and not too dear; take it all in all, it's a capital quarter, and you'll see if I'm not right."

His wife confirmed all he said over a cup of tea, all the better for standing under the "cosy," as a thick crimson nightcap made to envelop the teapot in these parts is called. Yet we were well scolded for sitting so long, as Mrs Wolfe said—

"Over your wicked days, I'm sure, before you became good, steady, married men."

"Oh!" we replied, "we assure you, we have been listening quite meekly to the praises of the Royal Incidentals."

"Then," said she, laughing, "I forgive you. They cannot be praised too much. They are the cream of the service, I think."

"And we poor fellows, then, what are we? the dregs, or skim-milk, or what?"

"Oh! I don't say you are anything. All I know is, *they are* the cream of the service to me. Come, I've another cup for you."

Well, she had a right to her opinion, and a good opinion it was in the bargain. She had drawn a prize in life's lottery, and had the good sense to know it. Such honest, true-hearted pride was worthy of all respect. Thank God, when good women feel such pride, from the Queen on her throne to the humblest fisher's wife in the wide realms of England; to whom might be offered vainly all the estates and riches of the world if, without husband and child, they were to be held and possessed.

Eleven sounded on the pendule. How quickly the time had fled amid the harmony of pleasant voices, music, and rustling silk. "Well," said my friend's wife, as we shook hands, "I am glad you have found out that Newfoundland is not such a barbarous place after all. I'm sure you will like it when you put matters a little straight." Thought I to myself, in milder weather, perhaps, but certainly not now; for the plunge from the bright porch into the dark, snow-driven night was anything but a joke. The wind howled avengefully, the sleet slapped bitterly in the face, and the drifts caught me artfully in their deep, soft traps. There were but three hundred yards to go, along a straight road, but that was the work of half an hour. It was a series of clinging to the fence, with half frozen hands, pitching headlong into the drift, or pausing to listen for the chance of a guiding sound. It came at last, just as I reflected on the chances of being found, like Lot's wife, at break of day. A picket of soldiers, dragging a drunken comrade by the heels, came roaring round the corner. Stumbling after them, I scrambled through the gates, and groped a way into my den. The stove was all but out, and the place so thick with smoke that one might have cut it with a knife. What matter? by this time I was hardened and desperate, and had, moreover, found out, pleasantly enough I admit, that I did not belong to the "cream of the service." I was soon well under the pile of cloaks spread upon my camp bed, and glad to be there. The words of the great commandment rose before my conscience, and thinking of my own unbounded blessings, I fell asleep.

Sometimes remembering that miserable night, and many others which followed while that dirty Government hole remained as I found it, I would look round with a smile at the contrast it now presents. After hammering at the study door of my good friend's official conscience, little by little, inch by inch, as the means came to his hand, he was able to mend matters up. A good grate, a clean paper, a little paint, a stopping up of rat holes here and there, created a marvellous change for the better. True, we have never aspired to an "official residence," or to a farm, or paddock, or cows, conservatories, gas, white and gold paper, or such other choice luxuries. These are left, no doubt quite properly, to the "cream of the service." At any rate so think the fair ladies who represent that favoured corps in all quarters of the world. Nevertheless, we drink our tea with plain milk very happily. The bird sings in the corner, the plants in the window are in full blossom, and old Tom, rescued from the drain, and sent on by special express in the mail-boat, purrs before the brightest of fires. Best of all, a little woman again chats and laughs over her work, every note of her cheerful voice seeming to whisper, in a gentle refrain, "Home is home, even amid ice and snow and every gloom; all is bright within, and, God be praised, home is home!"

CHAPTER VII.

CREDIT AND DISCREDIT.

"A SPLENDID day, sir," cried my man, stamping the snow off his boots, as he entered about eight o'clock next morning. "A splendid day, sir, as ever you saw. You 'd hardly know the place again."

"Cold?"

"Froze up, sir, as hard as a gravestone; but there ain't any wind."

Up I jumped to realise these blessings, and found them not exaggerated. Mother Earth was bedecked with a garment of the purest white, so dazzling as to force weak mortal eyes to turn for peace to the soft cerulean blue above. Not a breath of wind, nor a sound but of the distant sleigh-bells, and the crisp, musical crackling of the blanket beneath the feet—a proof that it was freezing sharply. So it continued—a real Canadian day, as should not be lost without a ramble. Two hundred yards away, outside the gates, Wolfe was standing with his dogs, yet I could fancy he was close to my side when he shouted—

"Will you come for a walk through the town?"

Off we went, slipping, sliding, tumbling down the glacis. The dogs, two large handsome setters, in magnificent condition after the shooting-season, came bounding after, thoroughly enjoying the sport the heavy fall of snow afforded them: now buried together in their wild play in a drift, now casting up a volume of mimic spray, now scratching it away in eager rivalry for a bone snuffed beneath the surface. It was "stand clear," as the noble brutes came bounding after us at Wolfe's shrill whistle. Turn round and fend them off with a friendly guard, or up you go,—cut off your feet in a twinkling, they miles ahead again before one had time to protest, either with tongue or stick.

So on we went, dogs and friends together, past one or two minor streets, straight in their line, yet poor in their build; and down a steep, rocky descent, which, although in the very centre of a large town, was still untouched by the hand of man. It led us straight into the main avenue of St John's,—Water Street,—which, formerly built of wood, was destroyed in a terrible conflagration in 1846. A grand opportunity for rebuilding a fine street, which certainly, in any other community, would have been seized with avidity, was then sadly lost. Stores and houses of all sorts, according to the purse or fancy of the proprietor, were run up on the alignment of the harbour; the whole, in its snakelike twisting, for nearly a mile and a half long, presenting, to the eye of the stranger, a commonplace, yet substantial appearance. Behind the buildings, on the water side of the street, project the wharves for the ships and stores; and, while the lower basements of the houses are appropriated to the retail-shops (as good as one may meet in any third-rate town in England), the merchants live above: for the business of the merchant here combines both the wholesale and retail styles. He deals in thousands in one minute with his right hand, and will sell you in the next a packet of pins with the other. Moreover, his retail is not confined to pins alone,—that is to say, one article of trade, or even to a dozen or a thousand. His wide stores contain an *omnium gatherum* of most of the necessaries and rubbish of civilised life. The same system, it is true, prevails generally in most of our colonies, but not to the extent it has hitherto done here. Where else is there (with the exception of Taylor's, in Corfu, of everlasting memory) any shop where one might purchase a crape-bonnet, a ham, a chimney-pot, a wedding-ring, and a bottle of Radway's Ready Relief? This, however, is more correct of the big stores on the south or aristocratic side of the crooked street. In justice to the proprietors of those on the opposite face, it is but fair to say that apparently the whole of the shops there, with scarcely an exception, dispose of but six articles—old crockery, apples, lucifers, herrings, stale buns, and rum; and the greatest of these is rum. Never has it appeared before what became of those old-fashioned chimney-ornaments, in outrageous gilded china, of those bronzed teapots and jugs, the admiration of a past generation at home. Here they all were, enjoying the worship of the youth of another race. It was really quite startling the first glimpse of that big china long-eared spaniel, with a snub nose, the type of so many thousands of his fragile race, adorning the windows of every shop all down the length of the north side of Water Street. It was to take a great leap back of thirty years at least, and to pass a gentle hand across a poll but thinly-sown now, ere the rusty links of a remembrance of a nursery-acquaintance with him were tightly snapped together.

So it became clear, as we passed along to the river head, at the top of the harbour, that every shop on one side of the street was the emporium of the merchant dealing in all the commodities here in demand, and every shop on the other was, speaking generally, a grog-shop. A stranger to the style of business might pass along with the commonplace reflection that, under such circumstances, the principles of trade, on the one hand, were conducted still in a rude and primitive style; and, on the other, that the labours of the disciples of Father Mathew had not been very successful in the community. He would be right: but there would be yet much more to be learnt, leading at last to the conclusion, that the gambling and drinking shops, lying contiguous and cheek-by-jowl, were meet and well-placed companions. The merchant is really no merchant here,—that is, no fair speculator, under the usual and proper understanding of that term in trade; he is simply a great commercial gambler. The planter or middleman imitates his superior on a smaller scale; and the ignorant fisherman follows suit as a matter of course. This system of trade, between the supplier and supplied, began in the first days of the settlement as a fishing-colony, when goods, only to be procured from a few rich merchants at the summer-stations, were necessarily taken in advance by the fishermen; and, unhappily, the same plan of barter still exists, to the detriment of the morality and prosperity of the community. In short, the workman eats his bread before it is earned by the sweat of his brow; and it is not difficult to arrive at the result of such a plan. The merchant, with his stores full of provisions, clothing, fishing-gear, and household goods, like a spider in his parlour, awaits the approach of the hungry fisherman, his legitimate fly. In the spring, before the seal-fishery commences,—in May, when the cod are coming in,—in November—no matter whether the season has been favourable or not—the fisherman must have supplies for his family; his children must be fed. The merchant, once embarked in such a business, has no choice but to continue, or lose all. He must, therefore, charge awful profits, to remunerate himself against such an awful risk. Accordingly, while he sells a barrel of flour to the cash-customer (when he gets one) for 30s., he books it to the fisherman (who may or may not pay him) for £3, 10s.; a pair of boots worth, perhaps, 17s., are put down £2, 5s.; a gridiron, worth 2s. 6d., is noted at 9s.; a Jersey, 7s. 6d., at 25s., and so on. This is but a moderate estimate of this iniquitous barter; it being by no means an uncommon thing, when the risk is greater, to book the same barrel of flour at £6, and all other things at a thousand per cent. in proportion.

Iniquitous barter, be it well understood, on both sides;

and let us see how it acts. The fisherman, in the majority of cases, little he cares on the matter. The system descended to him from his fathers; they rubbed on and lived under it, and so will he. So he travels home with his goods, eats and rejoices, caring nothing for the evil day of reckoning, which comes when the fishing is over: the fish delivered at so much on one side of the ledger, and the outrageous credit he has taken balanced on the other. Rarely, indeed, is there a residue in his favour, but enough still owing to bring him back to the spider's parlour again, and, in most cases, keep him in the meshes all his life. The consequences to the man and his family are easily understood. Economy, order, cleanliness, education, prosperity, are practically to them unknown. As he gains his money in a chance-like, gambling fashion, so he spends it recklessly, without a thought for the morrow. Let us look at the results which bad fisheries, for a few consecutive years, engendered. Latterly, no less than one-third of the whole revenue of the colony has been spent in pauper-relief, failing which a great part of the labouring population would have perished. And, traced back to the origin of this outlay, this enormous sum was simply a tax or penalty, paid by the whole public, on the pernicious system adopted by the merchants in their business transactions.

There is yet a worse evil than this. The fisherman looks round, and sees in the ocean a great gambling-pool, from which he may, perhaps, in some very favourable season, without great trouble, draw a famous lottery-ticket. On the other side, he sees round his door abundance of land, which, with toil, will yield him sustenance, in turnips, potatoes, hay, barley, fodder, and garden-stuff. But is it in poor, ignorant, human nature to labour and sweat, when—oh! so easily—all its wants can be supplied without the toil?—when the simple credit at the merchant's enables all to eat to-day, and to pay when Providence is pleased to send the fish? So the patient earth is left, year after year, untouched; and the greasy fisherman, leaning idle, in the precious spring-time, against the merchant's store in Water Street, hugs himself with the cherished idea, that his ticket this year in the great fish-lottery will surely turn up a tremendous prize. Thus slow and sure, against chance and luck, have little hope of winning. But it must be understood that this is a way of existence eminently suited to the Irish character, luxuriantly developing the richest traits of that unstrung nationality, which forms the majority in this most ancient, yet still untilled, offshoot of the British crown.

There is something to be said on the other side of a question involving such lamentable consequences to the welfare of a people. There is some truth in asserting that the merchant of the present day cannot help the mischief; that he does his best with the disastrous legacy of his forefathers; that he could not begin a new and healthy system without the concurrence of all his compeers, involving the risk of immediate collapse to many of them. He is obliged to charge the fisherman exorbitantly for his credit, for the risk is tremendous—out of all proportion to anything else known in trade—not only on account of bad seasons, but also from the bad faith of the men to whom he has given supplies, year after year, with scarcely any return, yet waiting, hoping, praying, believing in an eventual turn of luck. Yes, luck!—the whole business of the colony is absolutely concentrated in that word. At last the prospect of a brimming year arrives, and all looks hopeful. The merchant hears great accounts of the catch and of the quality of the fish; indeed he sees, here and there, his neighbours' wharves begin to groan with ocean-fruit. He begins to hug himself with the belief that, at last, his books are not only to be balanced, but that large profits will enable him to realise the dearest wish of his heart—a country-house near Liverpool or Greenock. But, alack-the-day! to his intense disgust, many of the fishermen begin to come to his office with long faces and tales of *bad* luck; to be turned away with threats and curses, of little avail, indeed, for he understands only too well the lying lips the ill-taught fellows open. How is the enigma to be explained? for fish in abundance there is, without a shadow of doubt. It is all sold, as soon as caught, for *cash down*, to other parties. The fisherman, on the Banks, with his boat loaded to the brim with fish day after day, makes a simple reflection, that, if he sends up too much of his labour to the merchant, it will just be wiping off old scores, and be paying for bread eaten long ago. So, in the gray of the morning, it happens that a fore-and-aft schooner comes booming along, the skipper of which, backing her sails among the little crafts, soon fills up his venture, at a moderate expense, when away he bowls to Halifax or Boston, to join the Yankee or blue-nosed cuckoo-traders in growing fat over the helpless sparrows of Newfoundland. Up go the iron shutters before the warehouse doors and windows; and one hears, every now and then, of £20,000 worth of book-debts sold by auction, in the Commercial Rooms, for £20, and at another, of £15,600 for a five-pound note!

The signs of these things are about us and around us as we walk on. The success or failure of mercantile speculations cannot be altogether hid behind the baize-doors of the counting-house. The prosperity or poverty of a British city must be, at any rate, stamped plainly on its face; for British merchants, when fortune smiles, button not up their pockets; and, from within, their good-will, loyalty, pride if you please, but honest pride withal, pour forth large blessings on all around. In their own homes of plenty they pluck freely of the fruit and flowers, and scatter them generously abroad. Yet, could any stranger, knowing this, traverse this great commercial city from one end to the other, and not draw the conclusion that something at the root of its business was wrong and rotten,—some trust, which had failed to establish itself between man and man,—a want of faith between employer and employed? He will be told, on the one hand, that, in proportion to its inhabitants, a larger business is done here than at any other colonial city; and he will look about, on the strength of this, and see not a trace of that pride to which the honest citizens of the great marts of earth point with well-founded satisfaction.

Wolfe and I, talking of these fishy things, slid and slipped and stumbled adown the whole length of Water Street; past the wharves and ships; past the bridge of boats which spans the neck of the harbour, past another mile or so of straggling houses in the suburb, before we turned our backs to the bitter westerly wind. And yet, in all this, the principal part of St John's, aligning the whole length of the bright, hill-surrounded harbour, not a trace, not a sign, of a public building, or of a monument, or ornamental fountain, or anything to denote a love of country, or patriotism, or good-feeling to one's fellow-men, could be noted. From this point we struggled homewards through the snow, by narrower streets leading to the upper parts of the city; past the Roman Catholic cathedral, so proudly and admirably perched on the highest crest, to command the harbour, the Narrows, and many miles of inland country round; beneath the statue of the Baptist, at its entrance, with the scallop in his hand, so truly emblematic of the everlasting cry of the Chief Fisherman—"shell out, shell out;" and so on, past the big stone Government House, and past the whole outskirts of the other side, towards the east and north. It was ever the same. The houses were principally wooden erections, straight up and down in pattern, without a particle of superfluity or ornament, and mostly mean of their kind, as the residences of British merchants. But few of them had, upon the margin of the pretty lakes which fringe the city, country-boxes for the summer, preferring the dirt and dust and cod-oily smells of the fishy town; not for economy or meanness, but in the belief that, in the gambling nature of their business, each year would turn up the ace of trumps, and prove the last of exile.

No athenæum, or rink, or library; no town-hall or museum; no greenhouses, conservatories, or parks. Nothing, absolutely nothing to be seen but the bare, cold, unappealing necessities of life.

The sun was just setting as we concluded our first walk round St John's, at Bakehouse Corner, opposite the little fort; a convenient spot, where roads meet and converge, and where the folks lounge about and chat.

"Wait half-a-minute," said Wolfe; "I hear the farmers going home. It's worth while to see the style of driving here."

In less time than he named, merry bells and loud voices were heard rapidly turning the corner at the foot of the glacis. On they came in succession, five or six sleighs, or lumbering catamarans. The occupants, drivers included, were lying full stretch across the bars, backs to the horses, shouting, laughing, or swearing jocosely at one another, as the mood of the instant took them. It was a procession of bacchanalians, foolish, half-screwed, yet intending no harm or mischief. The leading catamaran was going at a heavy trot, right in the centre of the track, the reins dragging through the snow by the side, and the owner flat across the bottom of the concern, face up, and most likely asleep; while his legs, perched across a flour barrel, hitched upwards like a pair of pistons at every forward jerk of the horse. Not one of them was watching the road, yet they followed the leader in the narrow track as skilfully as a London cabman could have done. On they went—on, on—past the crest of the hill down to the little bridge spanning the river at the head of the lake, till we could see them no longer, or hear the music of the bells discordantly mingled with the half-drunken human laughter.

"Well," said my friend, "what do you think of that?"

"Think of it? Why, that there will be a frightful accident before these fellows reach home. Look at the leader! no one guides him! suppose he drowns the whole lot of them?"

"No fear; that horse is going to a farm six or seven miles across Windsor Lake, and he knows every foot of the road; and besides that, his master is dead drunk. He'll carry him home quite safe, and the wife will lift her old man off the sleigh, and put him to bed. Valuable horse that, eh?"

"What brings all these fellows into town at this season, through all this snow?"

"Why, these are some of the best in the country, half-fishermen, half-farmers. They come in for supplies for their families, mostly flour, tea, and molasses. You may thus see the advantage of the arrangement of our principal street at a glance; the flour barrels from the merchant's stores on one side, and the rum from the grog-shops on the other."

"Great facility for business, certainly; but what

will happen to people or sleighs meeting that drunken lot?"

"That's their look out, as you will soon find, in the shooting season especially. It's *you* must get out of the way; *they* have nothing to hurt. But it's only when the farmers come into town they get so 'cut;' generally in the country you will find them sober enough. A rough lot in some respects, but uniformly kind, obliging, and civil. Come home to tea."

Willingly, though first we had to run the gauntlet of a mimic snow-fight in the little quadrangle opposite the Governor's gate. There some of the college boys, having escorted so far their friends on their way home, took naturally to pelting the sentry, and then to have a few parting shots among themselves, or any passers by. Fast and thick the volleys flew, and a boy in front of us having missed a stinger with both hands, received it full smash in the face, to the intense delight of the opposite party. "Butter fingers! Butter fingers!" was the yell; and it did one good to hear the old English schoolboy word in so strange a place. Butter fingers! it carried one back to English playgrounds, and told us better still of English blood training here to rule, please God, with healthy tone and heart in the future. Oh! for the days gone by, when that dear old expressive term was pitched contemptuously at our diminished heads.

So ended our first walk in Newfoundland, the forerunner of many others. It was pardonable, indeed, if one felt by this time tired, for ploughing through the heavy snow was just the work of a ticket-of-leave man taking a turn at an amateur treadmill to keep his legs in practice. How dreary and blank it was outside, and how cheerful within, where my fair friend—if she still, most justly to herself, persisted in declaring that there was nothing to be named with the "cream of the service"—was a dead hand at brewing a fragrant cup of tea, richly garnished with that lubricant whose name she borrowed to express all that was best to her in the vast length and breadth of Her Majesty's military service.

CHAPTER VIII.

MARTIAL AND POLITICAL.

THAT body of military men, long known in the Army List as "The Royal Newfoundland Companies," was in these days at its very last gasp, destined soon after to be amalgamated with a more prosperous and important corps. The causes which led to this wholesome change, affecting largely the social and political bearing of the colony, will properly find a place in these pages.

First, a few words respecting the regiment itself; for, though called by an inferior title, a small regiment it had always been. It was principally made up of volunteers from regiments serving in North America; usually married men, who, with families, and weary of the routine of parades and knocking about the world, jumped at the chance of a more settled kind of life, half-soldier, half-colonist, pretty much according to the taste of the superior on the spot. It was, indeed, ordered that these volunteers should be men of established character; but this rule was little attended to, for the temptations to commanding officers in Canada and Nova Scotia to shunt their incorrigibles to the unknown regions of fish and fog land were too strong to be neglected; and, as a matter of course, when a call for volunteers was made, all the hard drinkers and other pleasant boys were shipped off to the unhappy commandant of Newfoundland.

Nor were the companies, in another sense, less of a refuge to the destitute, in regard to the gentlemen by whom they were officered. Very convenient, in those palmy days of old, were colonial corps, as asylums for fast young men, worn out young men, and young men without money; and again, as ladders, whereby to scramble into the service, to elderly young men, who could bring some Parliamentary lever to aid them up. It was usually appointed to control such mixed materials to some experienced yet hard-used veteran, whose office was but a hornets' nest if he attempted to enforce strict discipline, for which he might receive but scant thanks, as, under all circumstances, high efficiency was little expected. What was required at his hands was, by skill and tact, to keep things orderly, with a good outward military appearance. If he managed this, he had brought his experience to an excellent market.

So matters crept on for many years, the Companies falling under the command of one veteran after another; the officers performing the duties expected of them well and comfortably; not indeed emblazoning the colours with the titles of heroic deeds, but keeping up with the men a respectable semblance of martial order.

Until it so happened, during a political disturbance, when the force was suddenly called upon to act, certain circumstances brought its discipline into such questionable relief, that it was determined to expunge the Companies as a separate body, and by amalgamating them with another regiment, annihilate that local influence which had grown stronger than other less tangible fealties. What this storm in an oil-jar was, and how the soldiers came to be mixed up in it, must now be briefly narrated.

The great land of fish-and-fog has really no history, in the fair sense of the word, and has made no mark worthy of record on the great muster-rolls of the past. No battles have here been fought in which the liberties or rights of the oppressed have been wrested from the despot's grasp; no revolutions here have torn society asunder with piteous trembling in a midnight earthquake; no grand discoveries to assuage pain, increase the means of the poor, or the luxuries of the rich, ever claimed a birthplace here; no ruined, ivy-covered walls crowning the rugged heights above the harbour, point to feudal dignities of yore; no moss-covered graves, beneath the rugged elms, sleep within the hallowed shade of the village church. There are no such sacred landmarks by which the course of time and progress may be traced, yet it will be shown that the land, without a place in history, has not been without its blessings, and great blessings too; and its little story, unromantic for three hundred years, may be told in a very few words.

The first adventurers who touched these shores, in the fifteenth century, came back with marvellous accounts of the shoals of fish upon the coast; and represented the land (for, remember, they came in the bright summer time) as pleasant and fair to look on, covered for the most part with thick woods, or open plains, upon which luscious wild fruits ripened in extraordinary abundance. They spoke of numerous harbours and inlets indenting the high cliffs, into which the gracious streams from the hills poured their sparkling waters. A few aboriginal red men were seen, who hunted the vast numbers of deer, wolves, bears, and ptarmigan. Was not this the sort of land into which to tempt the adventure of Anglo-Saxon enterprise? Assuredly so; and very soon it happened that summer after summer ships brought out hardy men, who, dropping anchor in the sheltered coves along the deep watered shores, and lighting their camp-fires on the beach, caught fish, dried it in the sun upon flakes of fir boughs; fed gaily on choice fat venison; hunted the wolf, bear, and marten for pastime; and brought home in the fall of the leaf enough to turn into broad gold pieces, with something to spare for silk attire for the long-deserted wives. Increasing numbers necessitated at length the establishment of some law among the community; a point settled by their agreeing to nominate as their chief magistrate for each season the captain of the first vessel arriving, who hoisted his flag as Fishing-Admiral for the summer. To him, as to a dictator, all questions were referred for arbitration; and by his orders punishment, where imprisonment was impossible, was promptly dealt out by means of a post and a good stout cowhide. For many years, indeed generations, during which, be it well borne in mind, there were no women among the adventurers, this rough and ready sort of justice answered every purpose. But at length, perhaps tempted by the building of better ships, some bolder wives ventured out with their husbands, and naturally, when the first storms of winter set in, the terrors of a return voyage across the broad Atlantic with bad provisions began to prevail, and the thoughts of braving the winter in sheltered woods and nooks to expand into experiment. The bold experiment succeeding, the example quickly formed the first real settlement. It was composed entirely of fishermen, rough, illiterate, hardy, and oleaginous, who, in a healthy climate, quickly increased to thousands. At length the Government at home dignified the little settlement and its branches by the name of a Colony, and in process of time sent out a Governor, with orders at first to reside among the people during the summer, but afterwards permanently all the year round. Under these, for the most part able men, duly authorised magistrates superseded the ancient and honourable tribunal of the Fishing-Admiral, until gradually the usual staff of colonial administration, with its Executive and Legislative Councils, Houses of Parliament, and all the big wigs and little wigs, crept in under the wing of the great man, to help to cut and carve the annual colonial cake. For many years from the era of the baking of the first cake they cut and sliced at it pretty much as they pleased, with this proviso, that nothing could be eaten or taken away without the absolute consent of the Governor, or by a reference through him to the home authorities. This system eventually became a great bugbear. It was in truth an unutterable nuisance to Privy Councillors in England, to study and settle paltry questions anent the distribution of slices of stale colonial cake, even to the crumbs which fell (often furtively) beneath the legislative table. These impediments at length increased to that extent, combined with the difficulties of arriving at just decisions at such a distance, that it was determined to leave the more advanced colonists to cut, carve, and eat their own cake entirely as they pleased, under the awe-inspiring title of Responsible Government. This system began to be put into practice at the commencement of the reign of Sir Alexander Bannerman, who succeeded Sir Charles Darling as Governor, in 1857. Kings, Lords, and Commons, as the grand principles of the Constitution of the British Government, were forthwith inaugurated as a combined authority in the colony, on a scale, it is true, ridiculously small, yet not for that matter ridiculous in itself, provided the working element of strength in the governing and confidence in the governed existed. This unhappily at first did not; and why it did not requires a fresh turn of the colonial kaleidoscope to understand.

The first fisherman of this great fishing colony is, and always has been, the representative of the Holy Father. He is not, indeed, known in law as The

Bishop of Newfoundland, but in fact and custom, except by a small minority in St John's, his proud prerogatives to the title are indisputably accepted. He lives, as might be expected, in a big house, under the shadow of his big cathedral, on the top of the biggest hill, facing the harbour; and nothing that comes in or goes out, nothing happening, or likely to carry with it the most trivial influence, whether of public or domestic weal or woe, but is, in the general belief of the community, well known within its walls. Independently of the ordinary fees paid into his coffers, for the usual services and rites of the Church, his grand annual revenue is collected by the merchants (whether Protestant or Catholic) from their Roman Catholic subordinates, and no feudal lord of old ever received greater deference, or stricter obedience than he as to his assumed rights on this head. Gravely inconvenient would it be (as the worldly-wise merchants know to their cost), if, when all things were ready for the voyage,—vessels repaired and crammed with provisions, and the ice reported to the northward black with seals,—by some mysterious influence, not a man, save the scum of the streets, would embark on the perilous venture; if, indeed, the heretical firm, who should stiffly tell the Bishop to gather his own taxes, were silently tabooed by the brave yet superstitious fishermen. To them is to understand a nod, and to obey. They hear, as it were, the cry, "Great is Diana of the Ephesians and the statue which fell down from Jupiter!" and they ask no questions of the why and wherefrom of its influence.

This is the time of sowing; and then cometh the harvest, wherein not a ship comes back from the sealing, but the priest is duly advised thereof, and not a hatch is lifted until the Roman excise is strictly exacted. As soon as may be after the anchor is dropped, the holy man steps from the merchant's wharf to the deck of the ship, where the men, to whom half the profits of the voyage belong, with folded arms and reeking in grease, are lolling expectantly about the greasier decks.

"God save all here!" says he, with the sign of the cross, and a pleasant look around.

All hands are lifted respectfully to touch the shaggy caps at the holy salutation; though, if the truth must be spoken, the welcome is rather of a chilling character. Of this the priest takes not the slightest notice, but unabashed, and still more affably, says—

"Well, boys, glad to see ye all back again; and what luck?"

"Ah! but indade, father, sorra the much o' that."

"Well, now, I'll be saying, boys, that the blessing has followed ye all; I'll go bail there's seven thousand beauties under our feet now."

Hark to the howl which runs round the deck, and the men begin to gather round the priest.

"Indeed, then, we have na', father," cry a score of voices, "and that's the holy truth."

"Now, to think of that, boys, after all we'd heard of the craturs this spring. Say, then, six thousand five hundred?"

"Begorra, and nothing like it, father," shout the chorus again.

"To think of that now! Well, now, five thousand?"

"The divil a skin over four thousand in the ship, father, and by —— that's the truth."

"Well, my son, and a fine voyage too. The Lord be praised for it! You'll say the good word first, Pat O'Flaherty, for I know ye of old as an honest boy. What shall I write down to your name for the Church and the Blessed Mother?"

"Ah, father! be aisey wid me now. Sure ye know it's me that's badly off these three years with the wife and childer, and the praties all gone. You'll be putting me down a pound."

"A pound! ye villain! Is it a pound I'd tell his Lordship, and you the skipper of the ship? I'll put ye down three pounds, Pat; and if ye make me ashamed, I'll be settling myself for it. Now, Tim Nowlan, hold up here, my man; what shall I say for ye?"

"Ah, now, father! we've had the bad saysins afore say tin shillings, and the Lord bless ye!"

"Do—you—see—the—ind—of—that—rope, Tim Nowlan, I say? If it were not for disgracing my coat, I'd be after lathering ye meself. You're down for a pound; and little for ye, a single boy as ye are."

So, between threats and persuasions, chaff and dark forebodings, the clever ambassador tottles up his list, down to the boy who serves as cook's mate, and drops it at the counting-house of the merchant as he walks out of the premises. The rest of the affair gives him no anxiety. He is quite sure the amount will be deducted from the men's accounts, and a cheque despatched in due time to the Bishop's secretary. The merchant makes a wry-grimace at being thus converted into a Romish tax-gatherer; but no doubt his Lordship on the big hill enjoys this seasoning of the dish, reflecting on the pleasure and profit which results in thus constituting himself his own ecclesiastical commissioner among the prosperous yet graceless heretics.

Yet it is right, when thus speaking of the enormous influence of the priesthood, to show where it acts for good. Many an act of retribution is secretly prompted from the confessional, where the guilty man, revealing his spoilings and pickings, receives advice which conscience compels him to act on. One morning, when leaning against the desk of a merchant's office, a man came in, and, casting a sheepish look at the proprietor, said, "I'm come to pay up, sir; and here it is."

"Pay what up?"

"Wal, sir, d'ye mind the bit of a dust we had about five years back?"

"Ah!" said old Nic, the dawn beginning to break, "you were teller on the wharf then, and you cheated me; was that it, eh?"

"Wal, sir, we had a breeze about the fish, and that parted us; and, if I must speak it out, I did reckon up a little wrong, I believe. I've made it up as near as I can—'bout £80, I believe; and here it is."

"Hand it over."

"Wal now, sir," cried the fellow, as he tendered the

notes very reluctantly, "if you have overcharged me sometimes, as I daresay you have, by mistake, we might be quits, you see, 'stead of you taking the money."

"Not a penny," cried old Nic, bringing down his hand a clincher on the desk,—"not a penny. Here, Tom, carry this money over to credit. And you, my man, tell Father Kearney, with my compliments, he has done quite right, quite right; good morning."

Bravo! old Nic.

Thus of the seals, so of the cod, and the herring, and all the other smaller fry. Not a man goes out in a boat but knows that, of his labours, a part goes to Mother Church. That he need not plead ignorance, the Bishop takes good care to name a day, in the height of the season, upon which he ordains that all fish caught are scrupulously to be set apart for holy use. It would rather be more correct and fair to say, for the Church and for the glory of the Church alone. For willing testimony should be borne to this refulgent fact, that, not for his own luxuries, not to administer to his own pleasures, are these lordly revenues collected by the Bishop, but purely to promote the vigour of his own faith according to the light of his conscience. With his priests and other ecclesiastical staff, he lives in a certain state on the pinnacle of the hill in a palace, upon the external decoration of which but little of his taxes have been wasted; and the same may be said of the great cathedral itself, as well as of the nunneries, schools, colleges, workshops, &c., which, beneath that holy shade, form quite a little separate township, wherein his word and will are absolute law. Nor in the interior of his palace, fitted only for the residence of a plain, simple gentleman, has gew-gawgery, or decoration, been unnecessarily lavished. Truly, with the great means at his disposal, and considering the unquestioned manner in which his pleasure concerning them might be accepted, there is much in the absence of worldly ostentation which commands unfeigned respect.

But to turn the thoughts of men away from the true service of God to which they have immediately consecrated their energies, the tempter has more than one illusion to hold out. A man may shut up in his heart the seeds and roots of many mortal weaknesses, but a chink will ever remain open, out of which some will spring. If he trample down, in blindly outraging his nature, all domestic loves, another lust, that of power and place, will assuredly raise its rank, unfragrant head in that congenial soil.

It was upon this rock the worthy Bishop stumbled in his otherwise fair and even path of life. Had he looked behind and reflected on the experience of his predecessors, he might have avoided the obstacle, even by withstanding the devil in plain worldly wisdom, and escaped the terrible fall the arch-fiend gave him; which true men of all persuasions were grieved to witness. This is how it came to pass.

We have already seen that, for many generations, the simple people who composed the fishing settlements, even long after the seat of government had been concentrated at St John's, were contented with the institutions which they received at the pleasure of the mother country. But at length, as the city increased, an agitation sprung up for a representative legislature, at a time (more than thirty years ago) when Sir Thomas Cochrane was Governor, and the mitre of the Roman Bishopric sat on the head of Dr Fleming. Up to this, Protestants and Catholics had lived together on terms of brotherhood, untinged by the animosities which the differences in religion too usually engender. They had worked together to obtain the relief of the Catholics from all civil disabilities; and again in the demands which were urged upon the Home Government for representative institutions. But, alas! no sooner was the boon acceded, no sooner did the Governor pronounce the words which gave them a right to an opinion as to how their cake should be cut, then the cake itself, the whole cake—yea, every plum in it, petrified into a great bone of discord. Even this might have been arranged; but, tempted beyond his strength, the Bishop mingled his enormous influence with the elections. Political feelings have since banded men in parties together, separated old friends and families, and intensified their antipathies, as the party war-cries grew louder and louder at each election. So bitter did the strife become, so accursed were the gangrenous feelings engendered, that Sir Thomas Cochrane, who had laboured long (yet prematurely) in obtaining a successful reply to the demands of the people, and who for other causes was strongly entitled to their respect and gratitude, was actually hooted, hissed, and pelted by an enormous mob, as he embarked at St John's for England on the resignation of his government. Well may he have bitterly thought of the sad words of Wisdom, as he steamed through the Narrows seaward: "I looked on all the works my hands had wrought, and on the labour that I had laboured to do, and behold all was vanity and vexation of spirit, and there was no profit under the sun."

But a time of retribution came to the Bishop in his turn; and the weight of the terse adage which sums up in those common words the result of human glory, power, unrest, and every other blind search after earthly happiness, came home to him sorely in the latter days of life. The venerable prelate was a good, kind man at heart, and the reaction was therefore the more crushing. Stories are still told of him, how, while strength remained, he went alone and humbly to the doors of persons who had differed with him, or to whom he believed he might possibly have done injustice, to seek their forgiveness and reconciliation. Looking down into the black chaldron, out of which he had fondly hoped to refine the pure gold to regild the tarnished glory of his Church, and seeing there instead the abominations, the follies, the strife, the ugliness, which his labours had kindled, he bitterly repented that his hand had not been stayed, and mourned that the time when the English gentleman, whom his low and intensely ignorant rabble had insulted, ruled the land, could not again return. So he too departed, a Solomon, with the words of wisdom and repentance on his lips; and yet, as in the great story of old, his successor heeded them not.

Then cried they, when Dr Mullock ascended the mitred chair, "Ah! here is a wise man who will not commit the faults of the good old Bishop just dead. This one will not meddle in worldly things. He knows better than to compromise his position with the issue of political pastorals, and in exciting men's passions for party purposes. Now we shall have peace and quiet once more." For a while they were right, and might still have been so, were it not that those influences which impel the Roman ecclesiastic to the love of power are too strong for resistance; and to an able man, sprung originally from the people, and at length seated on that high eminence above the city, whither every breeze, laden with piscatory incense, wafted the knowledge of his power, the desire himself to move the secret levers of state became daily more unconquerable. At length he clutched them with a strong hand, and, with his own men and creatures in place, long wielded them at pleasure. Like the surface of a bog covered with bright green moss, but stagnant rottenness beneath, so for this time the authority of the Fish colony was handled ostensibly with success, while inwardly abuses and corruptions were sapping out its very vitals.

But now, having brought down our story to more recent times, another character appears on the stage, destined to exercise much influence over the fortunes of his fellow-men beyond the Great Fog Banks.

In 1857, his Excellency Sir Alexander Bannerman was appointed from the government of the Bahamas to that of Newfoundland. He had also been Governor of Prince Edward's Island, a colony not without an interest in the fish trade, and, moreover, as he hailed from Aberdeen, and had personally engaged, in his early days, both in the seal and whale fisheries, he brought to Newfoundland, together with a reputation for honesty, a character for ripe experience in the great ocean staple, and of being a good fisherman to boot in every sense of the term. At the time of assuming the reins of power, he was well advanced in years; his tall commanding figure, though apparently feeble to a casual observer, still retaining the great characteristics of the majestic proportions for which it had been conspicuous in youth; while the simple trust beaming in every expression of his face was a sure passport to the respect of all with whom he was brought in connexion. Age had, while making inroads on his physical strength, left his mind fresh and unimpaired; assisting it, moreover, with a memory which never slipped the minutest trifle from its prolific net. Extremely liberal in his political opinions during the many years he sat in Parliament, and moreover a coadjutor of O'Connell in obtaining the release of Catholic disabilities, he had another claim to a cordial reception from the most bigoted of the Irish community. However this may be, it was soon pretty evident to outside observers, that the "First Fisherman" of the colony, the able prelate on the hill, was little inclined to yield an inch of influence or position to any other fisherman sent here by authority; and that the question to be resolved under the shadow of the Cathedral was, how to make all inferior fishermen believe that the chief hook-and-liner still dwelt there, while the ostensible master of the State smack was drifting into an opposite channel. So having to deal with a man utterly guileless and unsuspicious of craft or cajolery, the Bishop steered the staggering skiff pretty much as he willed for a long time. Indeed, the two chief fishermen became quite cordial in their acquaintance, the Bishop being a frequent visitor at Government House, and well acquainted with the official mahogany. It is not known whether any thoughts or hopes of proselytising entered the episcopal ideas, but at any rate in those palmy days he presented the Governor with a large gold-clasped Douay Bible, which conspicuously figured ever afterwards, a mark of affection and respect, from his faithful and loving "✠John Thomas," on the drawing-room table of her Ladyship. The acquaintance may even have been said to have ripened into that stage which warrants a little badinage without offence; for on a certain occasion it is recorded that, on the Bishop complaining of palpitation of the heart, the canny old Scotch gentleman looked up and said, "'Deed, man, and I've been lang thinking you're right; an' it wouldna surprise me to hear ony day ye'd come doon, while stalking up that great big cathedral o' yours, like an auld pair o' boots." It must be confessed it was horridly familiar, and the

Bishop, before his chaplain, by no means relished it; but it is fair to add that it was spoken when the one great fisherman had become wide awake to the tactics and policy of the other; and just before the final blow up, which is now to be related. This will bring us back, as it were, in a circle to our original point of starting,—the share of the late Royal Newfoundland Companies in the programme of this mimic page of warlike history.

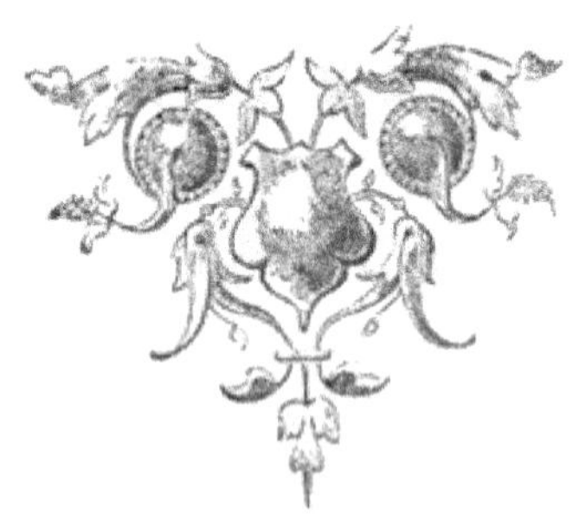

CHAPTER IX.

THE KNELL FROM CATHEDRAL HILL.

If there be one advantage greater than another which a liberal constitution, a free press, an encouragement of education, and a deep, inward cultivation of religion, bestows on a people, it possibly should lie in an under-current of general belief that, within such conditions and circumstances, the public weal must prosper, notwithstanding the blots and deficiencies which any particular leader might momentarily cause; so that, when the engine of State should work a little crankily, there is duly provided, by sound public opinion and its free expression, the necessary machinery for repairing it. But in this last principle lies the whole gist of the matter; for, strange as it may appear, with all the above advantages and safeguards, it still is possible to find a land in which, while the principal men are absorbed in the hope of the acquisition of rapid wealth, public opinion is either dead or stagnant—so stagnant, at any rate, as to view with indifference the liberties of the constitution long stifled by a power unauthorised and irresponsible save to itself.

Thus the puffing little engine of Fish-and-fog-land, working under *quasi*-responsible stokers and drivers for some five or six years, had become, in the year of grace 1860, so very rusty and cranky indeed, that, among the shareholders of the company, there was a general feeling of suspicion and distrust concerning it. The Chief Fisherman on the Cathedral Hill had long assumed the chair, and given his orders concerning it; but, about this time, it would not run smoothly on the grooves he chose for it, and it wanted but a little more pressure on the valve to burst and blow up altogether. This weight the irresponsible driver (determined that the engine should run where he listed, and nowhere else) supplied; and very unexpected by him, as to the rest of the shareholders, was the explosion which followed.

Fish-and-fog-land was, about this time, in a denser fog than usual. The supporters of the Bishop were discontented with themselves and their vassalage. Among them were able and estimable men, who, though tied down by the bigotry of their faith, were sitting restless and uneasy under an unlawful fealty, but still unable of themselves, or unwilling, to shake off the mediæval yoke. Murmurs, mild and respectful, rose here and there, which might have warned a more cautious usurper of the coming storm; until at length, though still mildly, the Government—his Government!—actually neglected or evaded carrying out certain legislative enactments upon which his Lordship's wishes had been promulgated. It was, indeed, high time for the mighty voice from Cathedral Hill to make itself heard; and soon, by one of those highly-seasoned documents ironically termed "Pastorals," the roar reverberated over hill and vale to the outermost fishing-cove of the colony. There was certainly no mistake about the language, nor ambiguity respecting the meaning of the Bishop to his flock. The present holders of power were condemned up-hill and down-dale for their shortcomings, their pilferings, their selfishness, and their misappropriation of the public funds. He painted them to posterity by the choice epithets of "State-paupers and locust-like officials;" and he called upon the electors of the country to look out for new representatives, and to hold themselves in readiness for another election, "the which," added the Bishop, "may be very soon."—! ! !

It would be no great stretch of imagination to realise the Bishop's satisfaction as he penned the above dignified record of his political opinions, whereby he had thus typically lashed the backs of the rebellious ministers, and which should convey a universal consternation throughout the length and breadth of Fish-and-fog-land. "Ah, ah!" it may be supposed, was the turn and drift of his inward chuckle. "Ah, ah! this will teach them to mind my words and wishes a little more; they will none of them like to risk their seats and lose their pretty pickings. Oh, oh! Sir Alexander thought I was coming down, like a pair of old boots, did he! He'll soon see there's a kick left in the old boots yet! They all want a lesson, and they shall have it." Can we imagine Cardinal Manning, under any circumstances (say when, even after dinner, the Pope's health is drunk before the

Queen's), announcing that he had made up his mind to dismiss the ministers, dissolve Parliament, and order a new general election throughout the country? If Sir Alexander Bannerman had had any private doubts before as to the person who was *de facto* Chief Fisherman in the fish-colony, this remarkable "Pastoral" must have completely satisfied them. But the churchman had wofully miscalculated the moral force which lay dormant beneath the usually placid and benevolent exterior of the old British gentleman, who very speedily showed that he was equal to the occasion.

> "He was a man that felt all chief
> From roots o' hair to sole o' stockin',
> Square set with thousan'-ton belief
> In his own strength, if airth went rockin'.
> Ole Sandy wouldn't stand see-saw
> 'Bout doin' things till they wuz dun with;
> He 'd smashed the tables o' the Law,
> In time o' need, to load his gun with."

In other words, the old Scotchman at once decided that he must fill his position, or resign, and had not long to wait before he had a favourable opportunity of showing his metal. The leader of the Government, an able man, but placed in a false position, so that he could no longer steer a course acceptable to his feudal lord whiie preserving his own independence with dignity, floundered in the House, until, by a few ill-advised remarks, he compromised his position personally with the Governor. First the minister, then the Parliament were dismissed, and a general election for new members called throughout the colony. "If," as no doubt his Excellency reasoned, "the good sense of the country returns honest men, with which the business of the Government can be conducted—well; if not, they must themselves be responsible for their own shortcomings. But it is my duty to sound the state of public feeling, and to leave no means untried whereby the hand of legitimate power may be armed and strengthened."

Now, to any one who has learned anything about election-times among a people of Milesian blood, it may easily be apparent what a terrible broil and commotion rose in the fish-kettle when the proclamations for the new election were announced. It was a question of life and death to the Bishop; or a loss of prestige and power, next to it. So he put forth all he knew; and his numerous staff of priests, scattered through the out-harbours, bays, villages, and fishing-settlements, laid their sacred shoulders to the political wheel as well. But all in vain. The Protestants, except in St John's, where they are outnumbered (six to one), have, in Newfoundland, a small majority still; and their spirit being as fairly aroused as that of the opposite party, in spite of intimidations and serious rows, which occurred in several places, it soon began to appear, as the election-returns arrived, that the Bishop's servants would be in the descending scale of the balance. One may easily imagine the dismay under the shadow of Cathedral Hill as this unwelcome result became more evident daily.

Still, so orderly was the conduct of the people, so friendly had been Protestants and Catholics one towards another for generations past, that it was never supposed but when the excitement of the elections had passed away, the new members would duly take their seats, and business be resumed without any difficulty. Riots and rows were unknown in St John's, and the organisation for their suppression was therefore practically non-existent. It happened, however, that there dwelt in St John's a citizen of good position, who, being a pervert from the faith of his fathers, was the more violent in his new opinions. He had held office under the Bishop's Government, and was resolved, *coute qui coute*, to hold a seat under the new government, and do valiant battle as heretofore for his Lord therein. He lost his election in the outharbours for which he stood, but, under cover of a lot of rowdies, suddenly, by his eloquence, forced the returning-officer to give a false certificate of his election. Hastening back to the capital, armed with this paper, he had the amazing assurance to force his way into the Parliament House on the day of opening, whence he was expelled with difficulty only just before the Governor and his staff appeared to inaugurate the assembly with the usual proceedings. *Hinc illæ lacrymæ*—soon about to flow.

A large crowd, mainly composed of sympathisers with the defeated politician, had assembled before the doors of the house. It need scarcely be added that they were gathered from the most ignorant fanatics of St John's. Not that there is anything peculiar in this, it is the same in all large cities; but it is not in every city, thank heaven! that a man of education, and who had already held an honourable position in the councils of a government, will stoop to make use of such tools for purposes of aggrandisement. Let alone, the people, though ignorant enough, are quiet, orderly, and kind; but even under such circumstances it takes but little skill to mingle together the foul elements of rapine, misery, and destruction. Human nature is ever too ready, in some shape or other, to prey upon its fellows.

So, no sooner had the Governor's carriage disappeared behind the gates of the official residence, than the mob, like the herd of swine with the devils in them, rushed violently down a steep place leading to the principal part of the city in Water Street. There, furious at the expulsion of their friend from the house, they commenced forthwith to plunder and destroy the shops and stores of persons who had taken a leading part in opposition faith and principles. For a considerable time they had all their own way, robbing and gutting in a way quite new to Fish-and-fog-land. In vain did several priests, hurrying down from Cathedral Hill, nobly try to stem a torrent which had been become by loot still more polluted with strong drink. Expostulation was all in vain. Such a horrid scene Newfoundland had never before witnessed. The roars and curses of her infuriated ruffians wanted alone the aid of fire to make her principal mart in its mimic resemblance to a little Gehenna complete.

This, no doubt, would have been, but was not to be. As the long spring day waned to its close, the handful of men who composed the Royal Newfoundland Companies were seen coming down the hill at the double from the barracks, led by an able and experienced officer, who, had he possessed the power, would probably have cleared the streets, without loss of life, in twenty minutes, at the point of the bayonet. But a commanding officer possesses no power to act, except at the instant command of a magistrate, an official who can scarcely be expected, at such a wild crisis, to form the clearest judgment upon life and death. So, in the middle of the principal street, on a point where, beneath the market-house, the place is commanded by a steep hill, the troops were halted, and there exposed, for two mortal hours, to the ridicule and stones of the mob, who paid as much attention to the Riot Act as they would have done to a snow-storm. They laughed at the notion of the troops firing on them: certainly not without reason. Three-quarters of the soldiers had intermarried with the people, and it was scarcely to be wondered that they reposed some confidence in their friends. At length, as twilight descended on a scene so strange in the Ancient colony, a shot, nobody knew how, and nobody could tell afterwards, was fired at the troops; and then, at whose immediate command nobody exactly knew, and nobody could tell afterwards, an irregular volley was poured at close point-blank upon the crowd, which instantly turned to flee with hideous yells of terror. At that moment—(O Bishop! why not sooner? You knew your power over the people! why let them loot, and plunder, and outrage humanity for half-a-day within a very earshot unheeded?)—the great bells of the big cathedral on the hill clanged and clashed an impetuous summons for assembly within the holy walls, and instantly the wretched tools, cowed and bewildered, yet foaming with anger, their oily garments bedabbled here and there with blood, swarmed up the ascent to hear the commands of the Great Fisherman. As that ominous knell reverberated over the city, the long aisle of the sacred building, its capacious naves, and the great square in front, became filled; until the iron gates closed like a net upon the human "school." A wondrous sight it must have been! The raging crowd pressing on each other, surging and swaying to and fro to get nearer to the altar; the priests hurrying in to don their sacred vestments; the servants struggling to light the lamps and candles; the cries for revenge, for a leader, for orders; and the earnest voice of the Bishop pleading, commanding silence, even to him long, long in vain! At length, falling on their knees at the raising of the sacred relics, they heard his commands solemnly given, that they should disperse and go to their homes in peace, nor leave them again that night, on pain of excommunication. The great gates were flung open, and in an hour the stars twinkled over a city where slumber and silence apparently reigned supreme.

But, in truth, it was not so. In more than one poor fishers' home there was weeping and wailing for the dead, and women were secretly staunching wounds as best they might, fearful to call in better aid lest it should betray to the avenging law complicity in the riots. Even under the very shadow of the cathedral there lay, terribly wounded by a rifle ball in the leg, a priest, an amiable and highly-respected man. Strange to say, he was the Roman Catholic chaplain to the garrison; and, doubly anxious to prevent a collision between the two divisions of his flock brought so suddenly into antagonistic bearing towards each other, he had thrown himself upon the rioters in earnest expostulation, and was unhappily struck down with the first volley. How many were killed and wounded was never known; though that it was far smaller than might have been anticipated may be understood when it was reported officially that next day, where the troops had stood in loading, bullets had been picked up, the which, had Yankees or Frenchmen faced the veterans, would have found a very different destination. A strange thing afterwards to think of, that the only volley the regiment ever fired in anger was the knell of its own existence.

It was all over, that storm in the fish-kettle; the winds and waves fell suddenly as they rose, and a great calm prevailed. The Bishop moreover received, very happily, his *coup-de-grace.* Frustrated in all political moves, and furious at the late occurrences, especially at the calling out of the troops, he went down in hot haste to the Governor, and vented his indignation in vehement accents. Sir Alexander, a veteran general in all such matters, received him much as usual, quietly and courteously; tapping the well-worn cover of his Scotch horn, while he listened to the angry ecclesiastic denouncing the actions of the authorities.

"I won't have my people shot, Sir Alexander; I tell you, I tell you, sir, I won't have my people murdered. I won't have my priests assassinated in cold blood!"

"What business had they there, Bishop? Why were they not in their proper places, my Lord?"

"I say, Sir Alexander Bannerman, I won't have them shot; I won't have my people murdered. There are eight thousand men with sealing guns, who swear revenge; and last night I had to produce the sacred relics to quiet them, or they would have come down and torn Government House stone by stone from the ground; and it's you, I tell ye, Sir Alexander, who may be thankful."

"Thankful for naething, Bishop; for I am weel sure that if they had thought of it, ye'd hae sent for Leddy Bannerman to the Nunnery, where they'd hae taken gude care of her."

It was a happy shot, and the last one fired at this remarkable interview, of which the substance by popular report can alone be recorded. A happy shot, indeed, which brought down the Bishop at last, as the Governor predicted, like "an auld pair o' boots." Lady Bannerman among the nuns! Lady Bannerman speaking her honest, plain, straightforward heresy among those reserved and sacred damsels! Horror of horrors! Better fifty priests be shot than that such an evil as this should be inflicted. For the Bishop well knew, from past hospitable experience, that the good lady was a woman little likely to blink at what she thought an erroneous state of things, but far more likely to do an incalculable amount of mischief (or good, as the case may be) by plain, heart-searching words in circumstances of honourable provocation. Lady Bannerman at the convent! a guest among the nuns! As soon would the Bishop had the city powder-magazine scooped out beneath his cathedral. So the curtain which rose to solemn tragedy fell on comedy and laughter; for we can easily fancy the arch humour with which the keen old Scotch gentleman told her Ladyship how he had discomfited the Bishop, and saved Government House from the sack of those awful eight thousand retainers, "all armed with sealing guns!"

It may not be out of place to quote a forcible passage from a book,* lately published in the United States, containing the most extraordinary record of faith, misguided enterprise, superstition, ignorance, self-abnegation, and unswerving courage amid unspeakable horrors ever brought to light.

"Holy Mother Church, linked in sordid wedlock to governments and thrones, numbered among her servants a host of the worldly and the proud, whose service to God was but the service of themselves; and many, too, who, in the sophistry of the human heart, thought themselves true soldiers of heaven, while earthly pride, interest, and passion, were the life-springs of their zeal. This mighty Church of Rome, in her imposing march along the high road of history, heralded as infallible and divine, astounds the gazing world with prodigies of contradiction: now the protector of the oppressed, now the right arm of tyrants; now breathing charity and

* "The Jesuits in North America," by Francis Parkman.

love, now dark with the passions of hell; now beaming with celestial truth, now masked in hypocrisy and lies; now a virgin, now a harlot; an imperial queen, and a tinselled actress. *Clearly she is of earth, not of heaven;* and her transcendantly dramatic life is a type of the good and ill, the baseness and nobleness, the foulness and purity, the love and hate, the pride, passion, truth, falsehood, fierceness, and tenderness, that battle in the restless heart of man."

This is the verdict on the Romish Church two centuries back. Is the picture in our own time so very different?

CHAPTER X.

THE LAST DUEL IN NEWFOUNDLAND.

HERE was yet another knell rung forth in that imperious peal from the belfry of the Catholic Cathedral of St John's, at eight P.M., on the night of the 13th of May 1861. Then jarred on chilled and awestruck ears the warning-note for the dissolution of the old colonial corps called the Newfoundland Companies. Their first and only action with their friends in the principal street of the city, compromising as it did, in some respects, the prestige of their discipline and efficiency, proved fatal to their own life and unity.

It was with the system and not with the soldiers that the fault lay, and the order for abolishing it was no doubt wise and well-timed. Yet it is not to be wondered at, when the news came which changed the scarlet into green, dispersing far and wide so many old comrades and acquaintances, there was deep regret among the class in which both officers and men had formed homes and kindred. Among their betters there were sighs and lamentations not few nor far between; for sage mammas, and bright-eyed innocents too, understand full well how far less valuable is the wandering officer, who to-day is and to-morrow is gone, to the man who must perforce make the colony his abiding-place and home.

But the fatal day arrived when the transport-pennant, fluttering on Signal Hill, heralded the Canadian Rifles steaming up the "Narrows," at the entrance of the lovely little landlocked harbour. There is nothing of this old delight left save a few scattered portraits in some gilt-edged albums, precious and to be loved until the bright eyes which bend wistfully over them shall with themselves fade with their freshness away.

It was said before, that, for all public purposes, Newfoundland had made no mark in history; so neither is it likely that the history of her martial corps will ever be historically handed down. Old stories of love, of virtue, and vice, in varied conflict together, are common enough in little towns as well as in big ones, at home as well as in the colonies. I put aside a crowd of such to pass on to one sad tale connected with the Old Companies, which, as illustrating better than much dry discursive talk the manners and customs of thirty or forty years ago in the great fish colony, and as belonging to a country so utterly untroubled with adventure or sensation as this, may well be preserved.

It is moreover the story of a duel; let us gladly add the last duel fought in Newfoundland. In those old times before steam had so rapidly shuffled mankind together, and blunted the rough edges of some of our vices, card-playing was much more of a business or important pastime than it is now. Men did not sit down in the long evenings of winter only, when a little unbending or excitement to assist a friendly intercourse is acceptable; but they played then summer and winter, spring and autumn, beginning in the long hours of morning and ending in the short ones of night. But, as will be supposed, it required something more than the sober rubber with a sixpenny point, the feeble amusement of their degenerate successors, to keep up the excitement for such a time; for when these men pulled off their outer coats and snow-shoes in the hall, they came for a good cut in at heavy stakes, with a long wind up at that rattling game the three-card loo, of Irish origin. If merchants, they staked nothing less than seal points and a quintal of cod on the rubber, and many a goodly ship with its costly cargo changed hands nightly on the turn up of a card. It was merely the usual excitement of their gambling style of business carried to perfection in a different channel than the counting-house and ledger. "Do you see that fine old gentleman," said a friend, in a mysterious whisper behind his hand, at the very first whist-party to which I was invited; "Ah, sir! that man's a wonderful fellow! He landed here from Ireland in an old pair of corduroys, with half-a-crown in his pocket, and carved his fortune out of pure luck. He won at three-card loo a lot of cask staves, and set up as a cooper; then he won some tons of seal-oil to fill the casks; then he won a schooner which he sent off to the seal-fishery, and she brought back a thumping trip; he staked this against a building yard, won it, played again for a parcel of oil vats, and won those. So he went on till he had made a hundred thousand pounds, sir! yes, sir, a hundred thousand pounds! and all the loose cash in the colony. Oh, sir! but he's a dead hand at 'five-and-forty;' and if you happen to have a few half sovereigns to spare, they'll soon find their way into his pocket. But for all that, he's a man risen on the wings of luck by his own industry, and has filled the highest posts in the Government with credit."

"He has a most benevolent countenance for all that."

"So he has; just the sort of benevolence beaming from it which suits a good tough official; smile and promise as much as you please, but precious little performance. Oh! his benevolence is the right sort you rely on it."

"You say he landed here a poor boy. He looks to me born and bred of a good sort."

"So he is naturally, no better. Why," added my confidential friend, "he 's an offshoot of one of the best families in Ireland. He 's the image of the old Marquis."

"Ah! that accounts for it."

"Yes, sir; he calls his country-seat after the old place in Ireland. Ah! there are plenty of such offshoots here; many of them in humble calling, but bearing the name, and, my word, you can't mistake them; it 's the blood plain all over. Did you mark, the other day, that tall elegant girl who waited on you at the Captain's?

She's a L——, dresses in stuffs and prints, while her first cousins, the very image of her, are maids of honour to the Queen. But that's just the difference between the right and wrong side of the hedge, you know, and it 's here we have only the one."

" And is our friend an exception with regard to his luck in business or play, whichever it is?"

" Not at all; why, when you 've been here a little while, you 'll see men staggering home at night, half slewed with rum, dressed in coarse homespun you would not give to an ostler, who are worth seventy or eighty thousand, and yet couldn't sign one of them his name. Those were fortunes made in the good old times. Ah! those times are gone now!"

They were good old times of play at any rate, and of drinking too. These lusts in a new generation have sobered down, while we hold in common with the departed the third deep absorbing passion of our race. Had Colenso and Hugh Miller, while denying the possibility of an universal deluge, admitted its force as applied to the human heart by the passions of love, hate, and jealousy, they would probably have been doubly right in their conclusions.

It needs be so in our present story; for it was known at that time that in a cottage at the foot of the hill, beyond the little bridge which spans the stream just before it joins the blue expanse of Quiddi Viddi, there peeped ever and anon at passers by from behind the crimson blinds the face of a gentle girl, for the love of whom the acquaintance of two men, which should have been almost that of brothers, grew into fierce jealousy, and on one side at last rottened into maddening hate.

For it takes little enough for hate, once heated in the breast, to burst into the flame of destruction. So it happened that on a bright spring night, more than a generation back, a party of officers assembled in the messroom of the old Newfoundland Companies in Fort Townsend. There really was in those days something like a fort, with parapets well ditched, and a glacis stretching around, steep towards the town, and sloping gently on to the barrens beyond. The great cathedral, with the twin towers, which, like two fingers pointing towards heaven, can be seen for many miles around, was not then built: but the wooden barracks within the fort were just the same as now, the yellow wash not stratified quite so thickly on the walls, or the cracks and crevices admitting so much wind and snow. Among the group assembled to pass the evening in the usual way were a Captain Rodman and a Lieutenant Potter, the principals of this sad tale. Their names are slightly altered to avoid unnecessary pain to any surviving relatives even at this distance of time, and the outline of the story will be told much in the very words in which I have heard it narrated by men who were living witnesses of its principal details.

The snow still lay thickly on the ground in gloomy corners where the sun's rays could not touch the surface, and the westerly wind of the chill April night whistling through the old Government buildings made the cheerful blaze of the crackling logs doubly agreeable to the knot of officers and their friends there assembled. In front of the fire was drawn out a barrack-table covered with an old red cloth, on which lay scattered, much in the form of a flight of wild geese in the evening sky, a greasy pack of cards, veterans in the service for which they were made. On one side, on another table, were all the "materials" for brewing whisky-punch, barring the lemon; while several bottles of port, at eighteen shillings a-dozen in those days (now at fifty, and not so good), graced the tray as well. The kettle was put on to tune itself up, chairs were gathered round the red cloth, sixpences like silver gauntlets were flung into the centre, and the party set vigorously to work at a game of the real old Irish loo, first knave for dealer—the which game, provided it be played by gentlemen, has the merit of being the safest, liveliest, and most sociable in existence. A prudent player has control over his ventures and finances, so that it may be played without hazarding a penny on mere luck, and strictly without gambling. For a long time all went pleasantly and well, until, whether from the effects of the toddy, or a run of foolish ventures, combined with a naturally awkward temper, Lieutenant Potter grew gradually quarrelsome and unpleasant. He took up his three cards at a moment when the pool was large, and, replying to the dealer's question "Will you play?" with a loud "I will," dashed them back upon the table, with a chuckle clearly indicative of their value. This conduct, strictly contrary to the spirit of the game, induced the players to hold back, and to decline playing until Captain Rodman, the dealer, alone was left to declare. He looked at his cards; they were bad; and he hesitated to decide whether he would play, to risk forfeiting an equal sum to that in the pool, or give up the pool without a struggle.

"Will you play, I say?" cried Potter fiercely.

Rodman looked again at his cards, and then at the pool, in which there was quite a heap of shining silver, the accumulation of many undivided deals. For modest players the risk of putting in a similar sum was a consideration.

"Will you play?" cried Potter, with an oath, turning to the other players. "This is not fair, I'm d—— if it is."

"Come, old fellow," cried one, "be plucky, and defend the pool, for the sake of the table, you know."

"Gammon, Rodman!" said another, "don't do anything of the sort; better give the pool up."

"Last player always defends the pool," shouted a third; when, amid a chorus of voices, who cried yea or nay to this last assertion—

"I'll play," said Rodman, at last, drawing rather a heavy breath, as he laid his cards quietly on the table, and said to Potter—

"How many cards will you take?"

"One." He threw away the king of diamonds, and took in the ace of clubs. The ace of spades had turned up for the trump-card. Rodman rejected two of his cards, and took the two upper ones of the pack instead;

when instantly, amid impatient cries from the table,—"Now play away," "Two trumps lead one," "Loo him, Potter," "Play bold,"—Potter, looking triumphantly at his adversary, dashed the queen of trumps on the table. Rodman, who had taken in one good trump, capped it with the king; led the nine of trumps, drawing the four from Potter; then led the eight of diamonds, drawing the ace of clubs—and won the pool.

"You 're looed," "You 're looed, Potter," cried the players, excitedly. "In with the pool." "Reckon it up." "Forty-eight shillings and sixpence." "You 're looed; who 'd a thought it? deal away."

"I 'm not looed. "I 'm d—— if I am; he cheated," cried Potter, in a loud voice, clapping his hand on the pool.

There was an universal burst of surprise. "Come, come, Potter! don't be a fool, and spoil the fun." "Retract what you said." "You 're looed quite fair."

"I 'm d—— if I retract," cried he, violently, sweeping the pool towards his corner. "He did cheat. I 'll swear to it. He drew the king from the pack. It was the bottom card. I saw it."

A start of surprise thrilled plainly round the table.

"You saw it, sir!" said Captain Rodman, quietly; "you said you saw it, and said nothing about it, yet now pretend that *I* have cheated!"

"Gammon!" cried the player next to Potter. "You are wrong, I tell you—wrong altogether; and making bad a confounded times worse. I saw the bottom card while he dealt; it was the knave, not the king. Turn up the pack and look."

As the speaker said, the bottom card was the knave of spades, which Potter had evidently mistaken for the king; thus making his queen (as he thought) with the ace turned up the best card. It looked now very bad for Potter. Not only had he wrongly accused a player of cheating, but, by his own confession, had seriously compromised himself in the same light. With another man he might have retreated coarsely and foolishly enough out of the scrape; but with Rodman his present feelings were intermingled with a far deeper sore, and blindly he determined to brave it out.

"It's a lie! a d—— lie! I saw the king. He's cheated; and d—— me if I give up the money."

"Do you really intend what you say, sir?" said Rodman, rising.

"Take that, and curse you into the bargain," shouted the excited idiot, dashing, as he spoke, the hot contents of his tumbler into the Captain's face.

There was a general start from the table and a shout of disgust, while Rodman wiped the scalding liquid from his face. Reaching down his hat, he turned to quit the room, while Potter, barely restrained by two of the company, rushed forward and made an effort to kick him as he passed the door. Of course the party broke up in confusion, but before it separated a message arrived from Captain Rodman requesting Captain Withers at once to go to his quarters. All knew what that meant, and Potter, naming his own second, snapped his fingers defiantly, and left for his own quarters.

In those days an apology was a rare thing either to offer or accept. A duel, if not exactly a common, was certainly not a very uncommon, occurrence; and was looked on by the community in general without that special abhorrence it now excites. This resulted partly from a less polished state of society, but more truly by the indifference caused by the general harmlessness of rencontres while flint-mounted weapons were in vogue. Detonators and revolvers at twelve paces have been the real pacificators or purifiers of society, at least on our side of the herring-pond. Still, among the better classes in Newfoundland, as elsewhere, at that time a strong feeling against such barbarities lay dormant, requiring only a stirring tragedy to call its life into action. It came to their expectations, as we shall see.

Rodman, who was writing when Captain Withers arrived to his summons, looked up, and said—

"There's an end to all cards for me, Withers. If men cannot play except as brutes and beasts I'll have nothing more to do with it."

"Always knew what a cussed temper that fellow had; but this is quite beyond all bounds."

"Ah! it's not the cards; there's something besides that at the bottom of his conduct, which makes me particularly anxious to avoid anything public. Perhaps the fool will come to his senses in the morning, and if he will write an apology, which can be read before the party, I'd better look it over. But——"

"Apology! Well, of course you can do as you please; but when it appears to me a man has been first grossly insulted, and then kicked, it's rather late for—eh?—apology, eh?"

"Kicked!" shouted Rodman, starting from his chair. "You mistake, sir; he never kicked me!"

"Very true; he just missed you with his foot because we held him back as you left the door. But, *ma foi*, it's the same thing, *mon cher. Que voulez-vous?*"

Poor Rodman sat down again, passing his hand heavily across his forehead. "You are right," he said at last, "it's the same thing; we must go out, that's clear; yet I would have avoided it if I could, but it's too much, too much. It will be better that you, Withers, being in the regiment, should not act. Ask Strachan to arrange it for me as early as you can to-morrow; and now, good-night. I have some affairs to settle."

Somewhere about a mile from the post-office of St John's, behind the high hill above the town on which the Catholic cathedral proudly stands, there winds a deep, sheltered ravine, through which, by dells and fields and gardens, a joyous, chattering streamlet pours its bright waters into the lake beyond,—now over rough rocks, which crest its course with mimic waterfalls and snowy flakes of foam,—now gliding swiftly into the little weir to turn the merry-humming mill-wheel,—now eddying over stone and pebble, until the air is musical with soothing sound,—past copse, and wild, and moor, and under many a little rickety bridge, where boys and trout play hide-and-seek for hours together on the warm spring days,—then sweeping boldly into the broad meadow, to puzzle the cows with its many curves and folds, until its throbbings, like the heart of the human life, to which it has so often been compared, cease, in mingling with the great unknown level beyond. It would almost seem as if the deep, hill-girdled cup of Quiddi-Viddi (Qui-Divida)—for so the early Spanish settlers, taking this as the boundary, named the bright-blue lakelet—was so fashioned expressly by the hand of Nature, to collect together for the city the delicious rills bounding off the mountain's side at every point; to save them from running to waste too quickly in the briny, unsympathising ocean, through the wild fissure cleft in the rocks on the shore, past which the overflowing of the water rushes. Winding serpent-like among the meadows, across the slope of the hill, down to one of the bridges, and winding again up the opposite bank, on which to this very day a few scattered wind-blown pines stand sentinel over the landscape, we come to a little hollow, smoothly turfed, and screened from observation by copse and stream on one side, by cliff and hill upon the other. It was just the place, of all others about the town, where the tender buds of the wild azaleas and calmias, protected from the biting north-easterly winds, peeped at first shyly, and then pleaded for life with the golden sun above. Just such a morning as this of which we write,—a morning fragrant with loving answer from the King above, glorious with resurrection, restoration, beauty, life, and health,—a morning for sick creatures to throw open casements long sealed by winter's frost, and expand their lungs to the full with the soft southerly breeze,—a morning for lovers to walk with linked arms through the shady fir-groves, carpeted with the dead leaves of a hundred summers; for children to run wild with joy about the sprouting meadows; for old folks to stand and dream lazily over the misty memories of many such bygone delights; but not a morning, of all mornings, for two men, brothers professionally as well, to stand opposite each other with deadly thoughts of blood and murder. Yet so it was that here, concealed from all but the eye of Heaven, stood quiet and calm Captain Rodman on one hand, placed with his back to the sun by his second, Dr Strachan; and, on the other, Lieutenant Potter, still highly excited, and with an eye gleaming bitter enmity on his opponent. Potter was attended by the commander of a small man-of-war yacht, and was placed right opposite the full blaze of the sun.

Very coolly and pleasantly did the less-interested functionaries perform their part of the proceedings. With an amicable nod Dr Strachan placed the pistols behind his back, and having handed to Captain Fisher the one selected, they proceeded to place the weapons in the hands of the principals.

"I tell you again, Rodman," cried the Doctor, in a hurried whisper, "you have but one chance for your life: fire quick. He is a dead shot, they say, and looks hell at you. If he miss you once, he may not a second time."

"I will not fire at him," said Rodman; "he is a widow's son. I desire only to satisfy my own honour."

"You are a madman, then."

"Are you ready, gentlemen?" sang out the clear tones of Captain Fisher; "very good. I will say one, two, three; and when I drop my handkerchief—fire."

Covering his man most carefully, at the instant the words were spoken, Potter fired and missed. His ball just grazed the collar of Captain Rodman's coat, when the latter raised his weapon and fired in the air.

"Load again, I say!—load again!" cried Potter, with the voice of a baffled demon. "I'll shoot——"

"No, no, sir! that is not for you to decide. Fisher, I think this matter ought now to be arranged."

"Certainly," said Captain Fisher; "I see no reason why it should not be. My principal will leave——"

"I insist upon having another shot! I will not settle it!" shouted Potter, with an oath. "He called me here; not I him. I say I have a right to as many shots as I please."

Dr Strachan approached Captain Rodman, and said—

"What shall I do? The man is beside himself. Are you satisfied on your part?"

"Yes, I am. I don't want to injure him. I was obliged to call him out, you can tell him, to vindicate my own honour, but I shall now be glad to drop it."

"He called me out, I repeat," shouted the angry man, lashing himself into fury at the hesitation; "and I have a right to my turn. Why the h—— don't you load the pistols."

The seconds consulted again. "I fear," said Captain Fisher, "we must give in to his argument, eh?"

"Is it of no use? My principal was obliged to call him out, and has fired in the air. Surely that ought to satisfy him."

"You see the state he is in. We cannot deny his argument. I fear we must load."

So the fatal weapons were placed again in the hands of the combatants with the same precautionary notice, while Strachan whispered hurriedly to Rodman, "I tell you, unless you wing him first, you are a dead man." In less than a quarter of a minute the signal was given, and at that instant Potter sprang at least his own height into the air, discharging his own pistol wildly as he rose. Shot right through the heart, he fell back upon the young spring turf without a word or gasp—dead—dead.

"He would have it," said Fisher. "God help him, poor fellow! Is he really gone, Doctor?"

"Gone!" said Strachan. "Gone! not a doubt of it. Heart shot right through, I suppose. How terrible! I acquit you Rodman; I do, from my soul. You fired this time to save your own life. We must think o ourselves now. Heavens!" he sighed, while wiping the frothy lips of the dead man, and looking upward at the soft blue sky, "What a morning for such work as this!"

"Cover him with your cloak, Strachan," said Captain Fisher, "and let us gain time to conceal ourselves. I will let them know at Fort Townsend that there has been an accident, and they will send out a party, no doubt. How ghastly it looks! they will soon see that dark blotch on the grass. Now, begone. You know where to."

Strachan nodded, and passing his arm through that of Captain Rodman, hurried off the ground. Honour or no honour, now, when too late, what would he not have given to have undone the work of the last hour?

In less than an hour a party of soldiers might have been seen swarming over the wooden bridge at the head of the valley, and scattering in all directions over the grassy meadow which leads towards the sentinel pines on the crest of the opposite hill. In a few minutes a loud shout proclaimed their search successful, and they were soon seen carrying gently along the body of the miserable man who had just paid so terrible a penalty for passion and folly. As they passed up the slope towards the fort, numbers of people swelled the procession, and curses were loudly heaped on Rodman's head, the more when it was known that he had been the challenger. Most likely had he merely winged the dead man, or had the duel resulted harmlessly, there would scarcely have been a talk about it. But because the bullet had gone an inch or two out of the ordinary line, and struck a vital part (as if such a contingency in duelling had been quite lost sight of), the popular feeling in favour of the victim bubbled up and boiled over. It was on this account well that, for the first day or two, Captain Rodman remained *caché;* but it was known before the end of the week, that, partly miserable with his own thoughts in solitude, and partly on account of hearing that Dr Strachan had been arrested, he had surrendered himself voluntarily into the hands of justice.

There was yet another spectacle, the most solemn of all, to be beheld before the tide of feeling turned, and the truth began to be better understood. Three days after the duel, a vast crowd had assembled before the gates of Fort Townsend, between which, heralded by the muffled drums and the reverberations of the dead march, were seen issuing the remains of the young officer prematurely dead. As the slow procession filed down the steep slope of Garrison Hill, it was joined at each corner of the streets by many hundreds of all classes; until, in the old churchyard in front of the rectory, where now stands the English Cathedral, were collected a great part of the population of St John's, to witness the ceremony which deposited the dust, of what was hearty life and health among them three days before, to mingle with its kindred dust. The poor fellow whose remains were there laid in earth had friends, of course, among this motley crowd; but it was mainly the universal horror which had arisen in all hearts, aided by the reverberating volleys of musketry, re-echoing on the spot into each palpitating heart the cause of death—sudden uncompromising death—which filled each living listener with dread, and did much to put a veto on all such future deeds in this colony. The early grave was filled in, the last covering sod placed over, the last toll of the melancholy knell struck on the wounded ear; the crowd duly scattered, each to his tent, with words of grief and pity; and then, as usual, the other side of the story began to circulate, and a feeling of sympathy and pity to react in favour of the survivor of the wretched drama.

But though the good folk of Fish-and-fog-land soon began to reason fairly enough, yet the causes which influenced the ebbing tide of popular opinion to run swift as a mill-course in favour of the prisoners, were due to the extraordinary indiscretion of one of the great authorities of the community. Captain Rodman and his seconds were duly committed to take their trials for the crime of wilful murder, and although nothing could be fairer than this trial so far as the prosecution under the crown was concerned, luckily, as it resulted for the prisoners, though very much the reverse for the dignity of justice, the presiding judge threw the enormous weight of his own personal feeling and bias into the scale against them. The sifted detail of the circumstances which led to the violent sudden death of the young officer, left a favourable impression on the minds of the listeners towards the prisoners at the bar; yet, to the great surprise of the public, the judge summed up with extreme virulence against them; and after charging the jury and bidding them retire to consider their verdict, he was observed, even by them, conspicuously to turn down the pages of the great book which recorded the last read sentence of the law, and to index the place, ready to pronounce from it the awful form as there prescribed. It need hardly be said that the court-house of St John's was crammed to suffocation, while its doors and walls outside were besieged by hundreds unable to enter. The serious nature of the crime, the possible consequences which might result, the well-known bitterness of the judge, and the rank of the accused, raised an unaccustomed interest within those walls, where bright echo itself, for weary years, had grown dull in catching monotonous pleadings to prove that salmon and herring are not "fish" in the eye of the law, on a wrangle over a broken head, a violated contract, or the robbery of a cabbage-garden. Still the glad spring sun, dyeing the long windows with his golden flood, sunk lower and lower in the west, while the door of the jury-room yet remained closed and guarded. But for the charging of the judge after the evidence, no doubt existed as to what the verdict would have been, for until that moment the jurymen, honest, plain, unsophisticated planters, wore their opinions plainly in their faces; but their continued absence proved the counter influence sprung up, and who could foresee the result? At length—ah! what a thrill it sent through the beating hearts of the spectators, and made the hot faces of the prisoners in the dock blanch with sudden dread—the tinkle of a little bell is heard, and then one by one the jurymen filed into court. Solemnly rose the clerk, and cried with a loud voice—no need for that, for the chirp of a canary would have sounded like an organ—

"Gentlemen of the jury, are you agreed as to your verdict?"

"We are."

"How say you then? Are the prisoners at the bar guilty or not guilty?"

"Guilty—but without malice."

Down came the large, bony hand of the judge upon the desk, making its very framework quiver under the blow, while his stiff wig trembled with the agitation bubbling beneath, as his long form dilated up and up.

"What verdict is that?" cried he, stedfastly eyeing the abashed foreman; "what verdict is that, I say, sir, you ask me to record? Who desired you to give an opinion other than guilty or not guilty? Did you listen to my charge, wherein I clearly laid down what shooting a man in cold blood was? Go back to your room, and find a verdict in accordance with the law which you have heard expounded, or I 'll keep you there until you do." And the book with the fatal mark, which had been opened for business, was again closed, still duly indexed.

Then rose the counsel for the prisoners, a long-headed, clever man—(what a thing that is to have on watch at such a crisis of life or death)!—and looking at the angry judge, while the jury paused, half angrily, half doubtfully, and all ears were strained to catch his words, said—

"My Lord, I beg your Lordship's pardon, but I must ask ——"

"Well, sir—what—what is it?"

"I must ask, my Lord, that you will be pleased to record the verdict just given by the jury."

" Record it, sir! Certainly not. It is no verdict at all. I have refused it."

" I beg your Lordship's pardon, but I must maintain that it is a verdict; and that a verdict of guilty without malice is a verdict of not guilty of murder, which needs malice or aforethought. It is not possible for the jury to bring in a verdict of guilty now."

" To your room instantly, gentlemen," cried again the enraged judge, turning round to the jurymen lingering on the threshold. " Retire instantly, and reconsider your verdict according to the law I have laid down."

" Very well, my Lord; but I must respectfully enter my protest against your Lordship's decision for future argument."

It was never needed that future discussion. Happily the lingering jury had caught the argument of the counsel, and in less than ten minutes the tinkle of the bell was again heard.

" Are you now agreed, gentlemen," solemnly spoke the clerk.

" We are," replied the foreman, boldly and loudly.

" How say you now? Are the prisoners at the bar guilty or not guilty?"

" Not guilty." The words were scarce out of his mouth when a burst of applause, like the rush of a sliding avalanche, rent the court-house, and the vibrating waves of stormy sound ruffled the very wig of the judge as they tore confusedly along. Heavily came down the hand once more on the desk, as with a voice of thunder he roared—

"I'll commit the first—clerk of the court—silence—disgraceful—insult to justice—commit——"

He might as well have roared to the winds of heaven. Leaping over the barriers, throwing open the doors, pushing aside the keepers and constables, the multitude rushed pell-mell into the dock, and lifting Rodman and the other prisoners on their shoulders, bore them triumphantly along to receive an ovation from the crowd outside. Then arose a yell of ringing acclamations, seldom heard save from lusty British throats, the roar of which might almost have caused the bones of the dead man, lying not far off, to rustle and shiver in their bed. They carried Rodman up Garrison Hill, back to his barracks in Fort Townsend, in triumphant procession; and that night St John's celebrated the stirring events of the trial and the escape of the prisoners in full libations of rum-punch or whisky-toddy. Alack! for the applause, for the discernment of mobs, for the certainty of human discretion or wisdom! Had the judge been a temperate, or even a cunning man, the prisoners, at the moment the people were toasting them to the skies, might have been under sentence of death in prison, or, at least, condemned to heavy bonds and miserable servitude for many years of life.

Better as it was, for the punishment (if any were needed) of the soul was harder yet to bear, and followed quickly enough. The doctor died of consumption within a year, the disease probably accelerated by the sharp ordeal he had undergone. Rodman became a drooping spirit, and soon after left the Old Royal Companies. All that is really known of him is the fact, that his first act on reaching England was to seek out the mother of his unfortunate adversary, and make a provision for her necessities from his own slender income. It is not difficult to imagine what must have been the tender and acute feelings of a man who could act in this way, in reflecting upon that miserable passage of a half-wasted life.

This is the pith of a sad tale of Newfoundland; one of its few traditionary stories, well-nigh forgotten, save by a few of the older residents of St John's. For many years after it occurred the road running across the stream was avoided after nightfall. For, at a point close to the wooden bridge, where a latticed cottage once stood, and where it was said Rodman's horse shied three times on his way to the duel, and refused resolutely to go on, the restless ghost of the dead soldier was said to flit about, with one single blood-red spot upon his breast, which superstition said was shaped like the ace of hearts. But now the memory of that sepulchral tale has likewise vanished, and the latticed cottage, the abode of much love-begotten sorrow, is gone too. All down the road other pretty cottages here and there have started up, fronted by little gardens, in summer redolent of flowers, and bordered by meadows, where the mowers in the hot August days reap and turn the long bending grass. Yet ever and anon, as some ancient white-bearded resident of the place saunters slowly along the pleasant road with wife or grandchildren in a Sabbath evening stroll, he will point to the pines still standing guard on the hill top, and say, "Yes, do you remember, dear, that is the very spot where the young officer was shot." And the glad rivulet leaps along close by merrily as ever, tempting the children to run from the old man's side and dip their feet in its laughing waters; and raising, all the winding way between the heights of Three Pond Barrens and the blue lake near the sea, misty ghosts of its own for the fresh winds of ocean to chase away each morning. It says—oh! how plainly—to the saunterers on its banks, "For men may come, and men may go, but I——" Ah! plaintive little river! would indeed the "for ever" of the poet's boast were true even for thee. But surely, as the purity of thy sparkling waters were once blood-stained and dishonoured, so surely must the change, common to all things of earth, touch even thy rocky bed and flowering banks at last.

CHAPTER XI.

THE ANGLICAN BRANCH OF THE CATHOLIC CHURCH.

"WHO is that?" remarked the author of these humble sketches to his friend Nathaniel, as they strolled together through the by-streets of the city of St John's. Nathaniel, on passing by the entrance of a narrow dirty lane, had lifted his hat with much respect to a gentleman coming out of a poverty-stricken cottage. The stranger wore the look of a man of some sixty years, and was dressed with scrupulous care, in black greatcoat, gaiters, and broad-brimmed hat. He returned my friend's salute most courteously, and began picking his way across the muck and slush of an April thaw to another cottage opposite. Then, as we lost sight of him, my friend Nathaniel stretched out his honest broad hand, and cried—

"My, my! I protest! and you not to know! Well, well! Why, that's the Bishop!"

"The Bishop!" I muttered, aghast; for my thoughts reverted naturally to the proud towers on Cathedral Hill.

"Yes! THE Bishop—THE Bishop of Newfoundland—our Bishop. He arrived from Bermuda in the last packet. You 'll soon know him; and when you do, you 'll never have known a better man."

The Bishop! I saw it all now. There are Avons and Avons in England, and there are bishops and bishops in Fish-and-fog-land. Only a few evenings back Wolfe and I, returning from our evening stroll through Water Street, heard the broker's wife say, amid a gush of greetings, to the banker's: "Yes, my dear; William 's just seen his Lordship, and says he 's looking very well indeed." And again, that same evening, just as we reached Wolfe's house, from an opposite gate there rushed out upon us tumultuously a group of rosy-cheeked, cruciferous young ladies, who, flushed with some exciting news, all cried together—

"Oh, it 's so nice! Have you heard the Bishop 's come?"

No! stupid staid old fogies that we were, we actually had not heard the Bishop was come, and of course received the amount of contempt from the flashing eyes we merited.

But there were other sources from which the evidence of his Lordship's popularity among the fair rapidly accumulated. Presiding over the destinies of the pretty little farm on the bank of the lake close by, was a worthy woman named Joslyn—her real name; for, as all that has ever been known of her is honest, true, and good, I can see no reason for concealing her identity. Her husband, a sterling Devonshire yeoman, was there as well;

but, to all practical intents and purposes, was really nowhere. Mrs Joss was gray mare; and a better never-stepped. It was she who received her visitors, arranged the picnics, secured the band, sold the poultry and early vegetables (no such to be procured elsewhere), took the butter and clotted cream from house to house, scolded the maids, made the pies and pastry for the evening-parties, and kept the neighbourhood alive with the rapid yet cheery clapper of a marvellous power of tongue. It was always a treat to visit the farm-house at the end of our evening stroll—sure of finding, on entering the pretty hop-clustered porch, the cheerful housewife ready with a cup of tea, redolent of knotty cream, and a hearty welcome, which was even the better entertainment of two such good things. On such an occasion as this—one of many—we were sitting round her kitchen-table, while the goodwife was cutting into a home-made loaf, and offering slices of it spread with the freshest butter such as there was no refusing, when some one said: "Ah, Mrs Joslyn! no fresh butter for us this last month—not a pat! Now the Bishop's come, it all goes there, no doubt!"

"Oh, sir! Well, I'm sure! to think of that!—and the cows, poor things! fed on turnips and hay, will not give the milk; and how CAN I supply customers if I CAN'T get the milk? But the Bishop, sir!—no, sir; not a bit of fresh butter does his Lordship have of me, nor from no one else, I'm sure. He wouldn't afford it, sir, wouldn't his Lordship—to spend it on hisself, that is. There's Mrs J—— have a pat of fresh butter every

Wednesday, and she have his Lordship to tea reg'lar; and Mrs M——, she have his Lordship to tea of a Friday reg'lar, and reg'lar has a pat of fresh butter, too; and I'm particklar in seeing it is fresh, I do assure you, sir. And Joss, he likes a bit of fresh now and then, when I can spare it, he does. But the Bishop, sir!—he take fresh butter at such a price for his own self! Oh, no, sir; never—not now, sir! He's got a plenty of good uses for his money; and if all bishops was like him, sir——. And will you please take another cup o' tea, gentlemen? there's a plenty in the pot, and welcome."

Thus, as it flitted across my foggy thoughts that there must be something uncommon about a man who thus commanded the admiration and respect of sober folks, and impassioned girlhood alike, my friend Nathaniel, stopping before a long oblong stone edifice, said—

"How glad the Bishop must be to be again in his own church, for you know he built this cathedral!"

"He was not fortunate in the site, at any rate."

"No! Why? what? eh! I protest! what do you find fault with?"

"Simply that if you put a long building aligning the contour of a steep slope, it must look lopsided and ungainly. Then, you see, the front, which is good, does not face the harbour,—very unlike the plan adopted by the clever Romans, towering above us. Now, I am sure that any stranger entering the Narrows, and taking that long, blank, buttressed wall for a military storehouse, might be forgiven, eh?"

"My! my!" said my friend, every hair on his head

bristling with honest indignation. "I protest, if his Lordship heard you, I wouldn't be you. But come, there's the verger just unlocking the doors for evening-service; let us go inside and see what you say to that."

We entered the sacred portals, and as we passed down the long aisle towards the altar, the echo of our steps reverberated gently and solemnly through the empty house of worship. The sober fittings, the open pews with their plain dark oak carvings, the long and elegant lancelets of the west window, the soft dreamy light, chequered and filtered by tall stone columns on either side of the aisle; each in its own appropriateness redeemed in a great measure the error of the exterior site. But it was when we stood before the altar that my good friend's ire again rose high. There was no east window. The walls of the concave, holding the communion-table, were painted blue and bedabbled with golden stars; while uncouth texts, scrolled and garnished round the cornices, tormented the weary eyes with undecipherable scarlet letters.

As I spoke no word of admiration, Nathaniel laid his hand impressively on my shoulder, and whispered sepulchrally, as no doubt was becoming—

"Not yet finished, you see. The funds ran out, and the Bishop ——"

"Shut out the light and illuminated the place himself. Do you think he has succeeded?"

At which rebellious speech the good fellow cast his hand above his head, and crying, "Well now, I protest,

I will not hear another word," marched straight out of the cathedral.

I did not wonder at his vehemence, for I knew he loved his friend. In truth, it was not long before I found the good Bishop was either loved or respected by the whole community. Of love, what can one say? The thing is like the Chian wine of old, flavoured to him who drinks it. But for this, too, and all else besides, the secret simply lay in a conviction now rooted firmly, but long time struggling for growth in a rocky ungenial soil, that in striving after the glory of his Master and the good of his fellows, the man had forgotten his own self and his own pleasure. He had in as much as he could obeyed that Divine yet hard command, to forsake his own house, his own comforts, his own belongings, to follow, amid much opportunity for the dazzling things of earth, a self-denying pathway. That path men saw that he kept straight towards his end, doing the allotted work along its narrow sides nobly, honestly, to all; without fear or affection undue to any. It was said of him that he had engaged in the labour not willingly; but that, having accepted it, he took up the burden and heat of the day at once, calling on and expecting others in his vineyard to do likewise; and though men often complained that he was a hard uncompromising ruler, yet no one ever cried that he was unjust. It was, in truth, not difficult to imagine that he was stern in business matters; nor to understand, on looking at those clear deep-set eyes, at the small compressed lips, and at the firm expression reflective of the cast of the inner man, how that a resolution once formed was rarely set aside. "He's a man of cast iron; you might as well try to bend a crowbar," his clergy cried in the streets of him in former days. True enough, when he felt himself in the right, though they thought not: and yet the time came to him and to them, when they at length knew this iron man had a heart, in which the seeds of love, and peace, and goodwill to men, daily brought forth the fruits of a true and holy life.

For long before the Bishop came to Fish-and-fog-land, he in the great battle of life had, greatly rejoicing, cast his lot in a pleasant place. It is possible that no two people on earth, if suddenly asked to choose the happiest position which man could occupy in this vale of tears, could agree together. It is not easy to fix exactly the point where, safely removed from biting poverty, the cares of riches cease to clog, and cause it to be said that it may be *hard* for such and such a man to enter the kingdom. Some would place their faith in chariots and horses, some in the contentment of the little cottage beneath the hill. The range of choice, with thousands of intervening desires and opportunities, may be vast indeed. Yet, if it were suggested to many a puzzled thinker, that the happy medium might lie in the life of a country rector in the heart of merrie England; that the smoke of that English parsonage might be seen for miles in such a vale as where the soft Wye winds in crimson reaches toward the western Severn, where Pope called on his honest muse to rise and sing the "Man of Ross;" there to serve God in making others love His Name; there to live apart from the jars, the dirt, the tumult of cities;—many, indeed, might cry, "Yes, there; there it is; thus and thus we would choose to live." Even so, men said, had it been with our Bishop; nor did they wonder, when first it was proposed to him to give up that happy pathway, to quit for ever his apple-blossomed river, to root up all his tender plants, to go and dwell in Fish-and-fog-land, even as "Lord Bishop," yet amid the dreary barrenness of some earthly, and nearly all spiritual things, he should have gently, yet truly, pleaded the *nolo Episcopari.* But, happily for the snow-land across the Atlantic, the matter was pressed on him by those who knew the worth of the man, until perhaps he may have looked at it as a call to go and do His work; or, in the noble language of Archbishop Trench, when writing to a friend entering the ministry—

"Oh! let us not this thought allow—
The heat, the dust upon our brow,
Signs of the contest, we may wear;
But *thus* we shall appear more fair
To our Almighty Master's eye,
Than if in fear to lose the bloom,
Or ruffle the soul's lightest plume,
We from the strife should fly."

Thus it came to pass that a quarter of a century ago there landed on these shores a man destined to exercise a vast future influence in the spread of Christianity among the flocks who, scattered widely in bays, villages, settlements, and coves, for hundreds of miles round the coast, found henceforth a central pivot in his ceaseless labours at the capital. Yet, for all that, the new Bishop's commencement with his people was not auspicious. Long before his arrival rumour had bespoken his worth and zeal; and the Protestant body, at the annual meeting of the Bible Society, voted that the vacant place of President should be reserved for him. Soon after landing, he was, of course, duly made acquainted with the proposed compliment, if that, indeed, be the proper term; but, to the great mortification and surprise of the Protestant community, he, after reflection, declined it. Of course it is well known that the Bible Society is not exclusively the organ of the Church of England, but embraces in its fold all Protestant sects, who here meet annually on common ground, and cast aside their minor prejudices in the general acknowledgment and absorption of the one great truth. But the Bishop declined its leadership, and it fell like an unexpected knell on the hearts of a community who had already a desperate outward struggle for the mastery with the vast majority of their Papist fellow-townsmen. Men lamented loudly that the new Bishop, even if consistent to his own views, had made here a terrible mistake; for they cried for unity as regards religion, the more so indeed as unhappily, by party strife, their religious and political positions could not be separated. With unity, and a conciliation of their dissenting brethren, amounting only to a meeting of Christian men once a year on the same platform for the support of their common standard, much might have been done; great, they said, might have been the influence of a man of the stamp and character of the Bishop among the pastors of the closely allied flocks. It is not for us to judge the motives of such a man, even though we regret that decision; and regret the more from noticing that from that moment his path of duty, always difficult enough, became vastly more thorny from the suspicions excited among the Low Church section of his own flock. In truth, the battle-flag of revolt was raised soon after; and there was but little the Bishop said or did but what was scanned and criticised, often unfairly enough. That battle, long contested, is happily now over; the victory remains with the Bishop, but the wounds in some spots can never entirely close. For many years he was distrusted by a large section of Protestants; but as they rolled on he won, by his uprightness, modesty, and piety, at least the esteem of all classes; for against such things men found that there was no law, no cavilling. Yet that the controversy ran high, and waxed sore, may be remembered from the fact that on one occasion it unshipped a Governor who unwisely, in all senses of the word, measured his official strength with the Church; and that, as was said before, it left scars deep and scarcely to be healed, may be understood by reading the following lines from the pen of one of the highest officials of the Government, a gentleman now holding a high appointment elsewhere, and who perhaps deeply regrets the day when he ordered his publisher to disseminate through Fish-and-fog-land the pink pamphlet full of language of which one specimen will suffice us.

"But I had almost forgotten that your Lordship, with a degree of affectionate bitterness (for which, if I seem feebly to reciprocate it, I trust your Lordship will grant me absolution), has invited me 'kindly to suggest a rule' for 'your guidance,' which 'less savours of party,' and 'you will consider it.' I know I ought not in common courtesy to decline the invitation; and I could suggest a rule which, had your Lordship adopted and acted on heretofore, would eminently have tended to the prevention of party and division among us. But as I fear it is hopeless to expect your Lordship ever to restrain your feelings, or distrust your judgment, when under the influence of a temptation which so frequently assails your Lordship, I forbear."

Now, when it is stated that this letter was circulated because a sermon in one of the churches was preached in a white instead of in a black gown, and that, moreover, the Bishop had written to the heated official, protesting "that the surplice had not been used, and ought not to be regarded as the badge of any party in this diocese, and that he desired to set his own conduct above the suspicion of any party views or purpose," it will be admitted that the Episcopal lines had not fallen in pleasant places; and that he fairly might (had he been of that stuff) have looked back with regret to the sunny banks of Avon, after putting his hand to the plough on this ungrateful soil. Miserable as has been the strife between the two great sections of the English

Church during the last twenty years, our present question is, How does her mission succeed here? What fruit does the little colonial offshoot of the great parent vine produce? We look for grapes; but, alas! we shall find little but wild grapes, yet these in a garden which certainly yields to no place on earth for the heat and fervour of its religious zeal. There is a test, however, by which we may judge of the result of the Church's influence fairly enough,—the state of the funds of the Church Society of the community. This body was promoted by the Bishop mainly for the purpose of receiving the collected subscriptions of the flock all through Fish-and-fog-land, in order that from these funds, independently of building churches and schools throughout the diocese, the stipends of the clergy might be regularly met. Anterior to the formation of the society each clergyman collected among his flock what he could for himself; being, therefore, entirely dependent on their goodwill (in addition to the little assistance yielded by the S. P. G.); a fact productive of evil and inconvenience where God's Word required the whole truth to be fearlessly spoken. If influence, personal and affectionate, could have worked success for the society; if example of piety and self-denial had their due use and effect; if a light which could not but be set on a hill could have illumined the darkness of men's charities, then the whole tenor of the good Bishop's life should have filled the coffers of the society to overflowing. Yet year by year the Bishop has to go down to the annual meeting, and sorrowfully announce the amount of the subscriptions, in a place where the exports and imports of commerce amount to more than three millions (the greater part of which is in the hands of Protestants), to be something over or under £800! dividing some £40 or £50 a-year among a number of half-starved clergymen, God save the mark! and leaving a pitiful balance in his hands for churches and parsonages. It is a dreadful contrast to the princely revenues of the other great Bishop on the hill, computed at about £20,000 a-year. Yet it is not that the men of Newfoundland are misers; far from it. It arises, independently in a certain degree from the bad fisheries, from the fact that the services of the Church of England, unsuited to the wants of this generation in a large measure, and especially to the case of the poor, have no longer that hold on the people as to impress them with the necessity for, or value of her ministrations. This is not the place to discuss the reasons why; but the fact remains, that miserable are the pittances which the rectors and curates of the parishes of Newfoundland, chiefly lying along the extended coast line, enjoy. The word is not used ironically—heaven forbid! Enough to keep body and soul together, on the coarsest food and with the humblest raiment, is in most cases their lot in this world. Yet, in the faces of all the men I saw engaged in this work, contentment and peace were unmistakably stamped. Nor is it alone to poor living, mere absence of comfort, their hard lot extends. This might be borne amid humble domestic joys, and a circle of duty close at hand; but that circle extends for decades upon decades of weary inhospitable miles, from fishing-cove to fishing-cove, where the Sunday services come round to each once in so many weeks or months. Upon the instant must the parson rouse and trudge through snow and ice, no matter the weather, no matter the distance, on a summons from a parishioner; for though his task be one of hearty love and goodwill, he knows any want of alacrity would speedily bring the priest, ever on the watch, to the sick person's bedside. With wallet on back, amid the dreary winter, he turns away from his modest roof, and departs, it may be for a month or more, on a tour through his wide district (parish is a ridiculous term), obtaining a lift here or there, or the chance of a ferry across a lake; sleeping in the fishermen's huts, amid fry of all sorts, where cleanliness and comfort may be things almost unknown. Yet the welcome they have to offer, with little more than a cup of tea and bit of salt cod, is given heartily. The good old minister of St Thomas, our garrison chaplain, for many years missionary in the roughest and wildest parts of the colony, used to say that never but on one occasion had he been received churlishly, or indeed without pleasure, when seeking shelter either from Roman Catholics or Protestants.

Yes, we may say of both persuasions, such men are truly missionaries, from the Bishop to his youngest curate. Nor is the title written without a little reserve, inasmuch as it is one but little honoured among a large number of thinking men at home. It is well known that there have been seen in our colonies men, so called indeed, yet often little worthy of the apostolic standard; illiterate, greedy of gain, coarse, essentially worldly in their pursuits and acts; if not much despised, at least little honoured. We speak of them simply as a contrast to their worthier brethren here. Here, indeed, we find men who, not hiding their laziness behind stone walls under a pretence of religion, give up all to God save reproach or poverty, and fight in pure faith the great battle amid all its temptations, with all its sweat-producing trials. They seek to be of the band with "Him who overcometh." In the simple belief that they shall reign with the King hereafter in a better world, they cast the joys of this one at His feet now, and use their substance and strength in His service, trying to walk even as He walked on earth in doing good to suffering sinful men.

The influence of good as of evil is contagious, and the chief missionary who gave up his delights on the fairest vale of earth, has not wanted followers even in this sacrifice. One summer day, when Italy might have claimed the blue canopy overhead, we, a party of friends, drove to celebrate a birthday in a distant outport. Mile after mile of a gradual ascent upon the slope of a broad hill, along which were scattered little farms, cut out like oases in the desert of bog or barren, were passed, ere we turned the crest to plunge quickly down the opposite slope, where, at each angle of the road, the broad waters of Conception Bay flashed back the dazzling sunbeams. Leaping between the clefts of rock some hundred feet below us with many a little foaming fall, from level to level, a little babbling burn ran, a glad herald before us to the sandy beach. There a few straggling houses at the foot of the hills led, of course, to a larger fishing village, whose whole population of women, children, and cripples, were at that moment on the flat flakes which fringe the beach, to spread the half-dried fish before the welcome sunbeams. Beneath a clump of spruce, upon a bit of velvet sward, our merry dinner is discussed; then, while the younger fry seize the golden moments for a more active process of digestion, we elders strolled into the village to observe, and in so observing laugh or learn. Suddenly, from behind a fir-grove, was heard the tinkling, tinkling, tinkling of a vesper-bell, gently bidding all good folk and wayfarers to come and join its modest worship. Except from a Roman source it was almost the last thing one might have expected to hear in such a place, and yet we soon found that this invitation came from an orthodox offshoot of "the Anglican branch of the Catholic faith," as some folk here so love to style it. Just as we entered the portals of the neat wooden edifice, a thin elderly man, who had been tolling his own summons, ascended the lectern, and began to read the daily evening-service of the Church. None but ourselves, chance visitors, were there; and we, who came not to scoff, remained with that simply trusting man to pray. After the service, my friend Nathaniel whispered that this was another blessing to the Church brought by the influence of the

Bishop. They were personal friends and first-class men at Oxford; and, like the Bishop, this man (besides being the possessor of ample private means) gave up his living in England to come out and work under his old college friend in this remote fishing-village on the edge of the wild Atlantic, where his intercourse with the great civilised world beyond was but scant indeed. While he told us this simple tale of loving faith, its hero joined us close outside his cottage-presbytery, which he asked us to enter. What a strange interior it was! Boxes, trunks, deal chests by dozens, lying about in every direction; tables and chairs, littered with pamphlets and letters, scattered broadcast around. It was a literary chaos, through which one could barely move: a true picture of a man without a helpmeet, of a house which was not a home. The uncarpeted room served both for parlour and kitchen, and the parson's humble fare—tea, bread, two eggs boiled with his own hands, and a large basin full of butter cut with a spoon—soon appeared on the table. Thus the hermit lived, keeping no servant, but depending for a scrub to his house, for the making of his bed, and, indeed, almost for the simple necessaries of daily food, on his friends in the village below. If they came to his need, well and good; if not, he rubbed on, without thinking much of or heeding his necessities, so that he might have health and strength to ring his little bell for matins and evens, and watch over the sick-beds of all who wanted him. He preferred to spend his own means with those who wanted, to seeking the comforts of the outer world. This is to be a missionary, to be a man of God in many senses of the word, even though it contain an example which few men could strictly or even should follow.

This is no solitary case—stranger can be put on record. Yet not all can put their hands to such work without looking back. I remember a young clergyman, full of zeal, who, with a bride, went off for the solitary wilds of Labrador; but he came back after the first year, and said, very meekly, "that he could not stand it." The maid would not stay with the young wife, who was sometimes left in the cottage *alone* for six weeks at a stretch, with nothing but a barrel of salt pork to which she could appeal for nourishment. It was a wonder she survived the hideous solitude; and it would have been simply insensible murder to persist. And there was another man who fought the fearful battle for many long, weary years on that iron northern coast, where the snow lies upon the withered ground nine months out of twelve, and intercourse with scattered neighbours is interdicted by the season at a stretch. He, too, was a man possessed of ample means of this world's goods, yet, at the call of his friend, came out from England to take up his dwelling in the benighted fishing-village, intent for the future on one great object—the proclamation of the glad tidings to all who would hear them. It was wondrous how he could have borne the strain upon his nerves so long. In such a man, to live amid the eternal blank of snow, without a creature of one's own kith or class—depending on a barrel of pork and hard biscuit—forced to go from harbour to harbour, with vast intervening distances, often unable to find the place, deep-buried amid the equalising snows—without books, news, friends—eight months at a time without intelligence from the great outer world;—this for a season might be terrible, but for life it is nothing but slow martyrdom. How glad we were when the Bishop sent for the faithful missionary, to recruit his health among us. He was a child again amid gardens, flowers, and fruit. Books, old to us, were worlds of delight to him—photographic-albums and telegraphic-messages, awful as the oracles of Delphi to the ancients. At first he walked about the busy world as a man long confined in darkness and still half-blind. By degrees his strength returned, and with it, alack! the desire to return to his scene of labour, and conflict again with all that flesh holds dear. Earnestly his friends besought him not to go, to sacrifice everything, perhaps reason itself; but all in vain. Can any cloistered monk, throughout the wide realms of indolence, superstition, or fanaticism, show labour and sacrifice equal to this? Yet a greater proof of his resolution, a harder trial of his unflinching faith, awaited him. During this furlough, like foolish and wise men alike, he fell under the soft redeeming influence of our fallen nature. She (God bless her for a trusting woman!) would have gone with him to—where shall I say?—farther than any word that can be written, or thought can invent. But her parents wisely said "nay:" and an old clergyman, himself a zealous missionary in its real sense in these wilds, on being appealed to by them, counselled our good friend not again to tempt the fearful shores of Greenland, but now to fulfil for the rest of his life his social duties, in conjunction with his zeal to God, in a more genial land. He received no reply but a sad and gentle shake of the head: and when the old prophet added, that he might surely now resign such hardships to a younger man, sternly the gentle martyr raised his voice, and cried—"Get thee behind me, Satan—I say, get thee behind."

So the vision of sweet love and of a new home melted away, and soon after he departed again for those frozen shores. We will not say he was right; or of the old prophet, in his entreaties, "Alas! my brother!" We cannot judge of the terrible conflict between the Maker and His servant; but we may ask once more, Can any cloistered monk throughout the world show zeal or self-denial such as this man—bound by no vows, confined by no walls, fettered by no will, save that of his conscience in treaty with his God?

And yet, I protest, one more instance of a self-denying zeal must not be unrecorded. There was, not many miles from our fish-capital, a poor clergyman, with a young family, who, in the midst of the poorest district of the place, struggled for bare existence for many long years, his shoulder ever gored against the collar, and yet sharing with the wretched poverty around him his unbuttered crust, when he had nothing better (and it was rarely he had) to offer. At last it so happened that a neighbouring bishop, having heard of the man and of his worth, sent to him an offer of a far better living than the one he held. Great was the rejoicing under that humble roof when the news arrived; but, by the following mail, a letter told him of the bitter disappointment this offer had occasioned to a curate who had been there several years, and who was, if possible, a still poorer man than himself. He actually sat down and wrote a second letter to the Bishop recalling his first acceptance, and expressing a respectful hope that the claim of the curate might not be forgotten! Ah, ah! how often, in our long journeys through life, with our vast opportunities, do we imitate this grand unselfishness!

Yet, with such godly men as these, for example—with such a Bishop as leader—the "Anglican branch of the Catholic Church" languishes in the heart of her people. Adapted for generations born some centuries back, her rulers hesitate, in a world ever changing, to suit the services of the worship of their Creator to the requirements and wants of the living. Her doctrines may stand on a foundation of rock, but her manner of setting them forth to the simple rests on a bed of sand. With a lax or indifferent bishop the Anglicans of Newfoundland might long ago have been shunted into the many by-ways of Dissent—leading in all directions from the king's State highway, while not a few, here and there, run almost parallel to it. The piety, earnestness, simplicity of life of the bishop, combined with the high tone of an English gentleman, have influenced many of this generation to linger in the old paths yet. Alas! stronger testimony to the worth of the man, and to the suicidal weakness of the Church over which he presides, and so dearly loves, could not be recorded.

CHAPTER XII.

SPRING—THE ARGONAUTS OF THE NORTH.

DESPERATE, as pitiable, is the state of destitution in which the lower classes of the capital are plunged during the inactivity of winter. Large wages are usually earned all through the summer, but saving in harvest-time is a thing unknown here; and although the merchants are bled for supplies to the uttermost farthing, yet by the beginning of February things look pretty bad in the slums of the town and the villages near about. But after Valentine's day they take a sudden turn. The busy sound of axes and hammers reverberate hummingly from the hillsides around the snug harbour; and not a rotten old schooner, brig, or lugger which can swim, or swimming can be insured, but is trimmed up and provisioned to join the great spring seal-fishery. From that day to the end of the month the excitement as to the men who are to sail on this momentous expedition increases rapidly, and the grog-shops of Water Street reap a rich harvest, the greater part of the score being reserved to be wiped off at the end of the voyage.

For many years past this great fishery, or hunting excursion on the ocean fields of ice, as it should be more properly named, had brought hundreds of thousands of pounds sterling among the community yearly; and lucky was the man esteemed who had secured his berth in a ship to be sailed and commanded by some smart and experienced hand.

Long ere the first days of March had stolen on us, the fleet had gathered one by one in battle order, as it were, beneath the dark shades of the south side hills. It was at this time, when the preparatory excitement was at its highest, that, walking with Wolfe up at the west end of the town, near the head of the harbour, we came upon the loud sound of angry voices proceeding from a crowd gathered round the closed doors of a merchant's office. Some of the men were knocking at the knotty door, some beating with the flat of their hands against the clattering shutters; while, amid the tumultuous clamour, we could distinguish the sounds of "Larry! be all the saints, and be the Holy Mother!"—"Larry, not a man will be going for ye!"—"Larry!" this, and "Larry!" that. It was evident something very exciting to those weather-beaten, unsavoury looking customers was going on.

"It's the berth-money, yer honner," said one of them, dressed in a tight suit of yellow canvas, steeped in oil and smelling horribly. "It's the berth-money the boys is disputing; and Larry, the old villin, won't put down a man of us at the same rate as last year. He's riz ten shillings, and faix he's too hard altogether."

The berth-money was the fee each man paid for the ticket for his chance of the voyage, including provisions put on board by the merchants. If he was keen in his bargain, all that can be said is that the old coon knew his customers; for while we talked to the would-be-sealers, there was a split among them, begun by observing one or two slipping round to the rear of the wharf, and entering their names in the ship's books, leaving the others either in the lurch or at once to follow their example. A few days after this not a vessel was to be seen in the harbour. Taking advantage of a southerly wind, they had slipped out at break of day in the pursuit of their hard exciting voyage to the northward.

Then, for the next three weeks to a month, the hearts of all classes in the great fish-colony palpitate between hope and dread incessantly. The first thing on waking, the làst before sleeping (if, indeed, some slept at all), the only observation hazarded in the streets, was the state of wind and weather bearing on this momentous voyage. All had a stake in it. The merchant in his ships, stores, and winter credits to the fishermen; the fishermen to pay these debts, in order (and in order solely) to obtain more credit for the summer cod-fishery. The grocers, haberdashers, lawyers, publicans, barbers, butchers, bakers, coopers, tailors, planters, insurance companies, priests, ministers, gentlemen, and shoeblacks, all depend, practically, for very existence upon this great venture. About the time when news may possibly be expected, the excitement rapidly increases towards fever-point; the grog-shops drive if possible a still more roaring business, straining credit to the verge of credulity; and all manner of wagers are laid upon the first ship making her voyage home, and the number of seals in her hold. The pretty girls may be seen gloating at the shop windows on the finery they hope to wear soon on Sunday, when their sweethearts return; and the little razéed old men, who have lost their legs at the knee-joint, frozen off in former memorable voyages, and who for eleven months in the year stump about quite unnoticed, are now hauled into the tap-rooms, and with unlimited treats cross-examined on their former experiences. Those great captains of history, Cuttle and Burnsby, could not acquit themselves better in enlightening everybody without compromising themselves. Poor fellows! they have a glorious time of it for a week or so, but it is indeed a hard-earned joy.

Yet day by day may pass away without a sign fluttering from the cross-yards of the post on Signal Hill, though, as the merchants and other good folk peep anxiously upwards, the signal-man like a speck against the blue sky may ever be seen with his glass towards the north. It is almost pitiable to watch the anxious faces straining their eyes upon that flag-post, while every now and then some two or three, buttoning their coats up to their chins, start off to breast that heart-breaking hill, and take a look for themselves. It is pitiable to watch their downcast looks as they descend, and to listen to their sad good-night at the corner of the street. But, at length, the sun rises on a bright breezy morn, with the wind nor'-west, and a flutter runs through the city, the presage of something coming. Men meet and wag their heads as they pass, saying, "This is the wind, my boy! we shall hear of something before to-night." Ah! how they do strain their eyes upon that signal-staff, until at last—yes, no, yes—it cannot be—the man drops the glass, looks again, seizes a halyard, and runs up a ball to the northward, and soon after a pennant from the truck is proclaiming, "A schooner to the nor'-east." Heavens! is the town gone mad? They are running up the hill by hundreds, out-racing each other, and storming the look-out in a phalanx. Hilloa! there is another ball, another pennant! "A number of vessels to the northward?" All the women are at the doors and windows, and business is suspended except at the grog-shops. The fleet is evidently coming in, and "Have they made a voyage?" is the awful question on every tongue. "Will they be up before night?" "The wind is shifting round." "How leaden the clouds are gathering up." "We shall have snow." And so night creeps on apace, and covers the slushy streets once more with its cold white blanket, which it were better could it but chill down the feverish pulses which chase away all rest and sleep from the homes of both rich and poor. Far out on the horizon, beating against the southerly gale, how does it fare with the weary mariners? Across the broad light which gleams at the entrance of the Narrows, what a vast network of thought is interweaving between the sailors and their homes on land. It is a theme which some one (I know not who) has tenderly touched in graphic lines, which deserve a better place for immortality than these humble pages can hope to secure for them.

MAKING THE HARBOUR-LIGHT.

The snow falls thick, so you may not see
  The foresail gleam from the break o' the poop—
The long-boat looms like a rock on the lee,
  And the drift lies a foot on hatch and coop.

Long glimmering lines of dark and light
  Mingle in wavy dance up aloft—
And the topmast-head goes into the night,
  Capp'd with a head-dress white and soft.

Phantom-like figures grow in the tops,
  And the bunts of the furled-up sails are piled
With a heavy freight that sullenly drops
  When the good ship bends to a gust more wild.

And the clues o' the courses, stiff as a board,
  Catch up the flakes into bossy heaps,
Till, a flap, and off whirrs the sparkling hoard,
  Startling the tars in their standing sleeps.

Still, stoutly onwards we hold our course,
  Hugging the wind with a bear-like grip—
Holding each inch we gain, with a force,
  And passing the credit to our good ship.

The helmsman's eye, from under the rim
  Of his slouch'd sou'-wester, beams a-glow—
No matter how braggart the wind to him,
  And little matter the fall o' the snow.

Hand, eye, and ear are serving his soul—
  He "feels" the flap o' the topsail leach,
And steadily over, watching the roll,
  Whirls the wheel to an arm-long reach.

Grasping the weathermost mizen-shrouds
  As grimly as if were gript in his hands

Our fifteen lives, and swathed in a cloud
Of sleet-stuff and snow, the master stands.

Into the darkness and whirling flakes,
Into the heart of the brooding bank,
A long, dim alley his calm eye makes,
And the world outside is all a blank.

Empires and kingdoms may foundering be,
And bloodiest wars afoot on the land ;
But his the duty to conquer the sea,
And keep his soul and ours in command.

Not for him to peer at the compass-card,
And blur or dazzle the steady eye ;
But, sternly staring, he mutters hard—
"Keep her close at it," or "Full and by !"

No voice, save his, on the midnight stirs,
No sounds save the plash, and swish, and swirl,
As, under her bows, one ceaselessly hears
The slush-covered water part and curl,

And gurgle along the sloppy sides,
Clutching the snow out the chains at a jump,
Then slipping away with the murmuring tides,
Or striking the quarters a sluggish bump.

With the quiet flakes on his stiffen'd feet,
Searching his neck, and nipping his eyes,
On the rounded coils of the spanker-sheet,
A youngster, half-dreaming, shapeless lies.

He knows that, true to his will, his hand
Would promptly obey the master's shout ;
But his thoughts are far away on the land,
Nor heeds he for any perils without.

He dreams of a valley, spread broad and fair,
With grand old mountains upon each side ;
He dreams of a red lamp's cheerful glare,
Welcoming ships to the old wharf side,

Of a little room, with its walls a-blaze,
  On happy faces, all bright with joy!
And he hears the voices of olden days,
  Before he went as a sailor-boy.

Dear, kind, brown eyes, seem his to greet—
  "God bless and guard her!" he prays, "'tis she!"
When a cry "*Ease off that spanker-sheet!*
  Hard up the helm, and keep her free!"

One glare, one flare of a flashing light,
  And the visions die with its sudden ray;
The lee-braces fly with a circling bight,
  And the sheets spin out with a wild hurra!

The water seethes at the bluff o' the bow,
  And the helm churns it to hissing wrath—
And the strain on the ship and the master's brow
  Relax to welcome the well-known path.

With a surge and a bound the yards swing square,
  And the night's alive with our cheery cries,
As before the snow-storm, free and fair,
  Merrily homewards our good ship flies.

Scarcely daybreak out on the hill-tops, yet the merchants, wrestling for glasses and watching the fleet some miles off (chary of the iron-bound coast), lay heavily on the first ship past Fort Amherst, the number of her catch of seals, and the house she may belong to. There is one vessel at least two miles nearer in than her consorts, her number is flying from the peak, but they cannot quite make it out. Ah! what palpitation! what tantalisation! The top flag is a 2; the lowest a 7; no, it is a 9,—which is it, Bowring or M'Bride? for it is clear it is one of the lucky twain. The schooner yaws for a second, but that's enough;

the numbers stand out bravely in the breeze; and John Bowring, jumping up, shouts to the signal-man to hoist the number of his house. Look over the Queen's Battery, across the harbour among the still hazy wharves and ships; almost in less time than it can be written looms out a puff of white smoke, and to the faint boom of a gun the signal-flag of the house on their own wharf is run up in acknowledgment of the joyful news. In ten minutes more they know that 7000 seals are in the schooner's hold, and honest John, with a crushed hat, flushed cheeks, and well-bespattered clothes, comes tearing down the hill, heeding nothing as he rushes past to his counting-house. He knows he has driven that last hour many a nail into his future villa on the banks of Mersey. Good honest fellow! no one is jealous of his luck; and yet few would like to take him for a partner at our whist-club that evening; his revokes would probably be something awful!

One by one, all through that great day of all others in the year, they come gliding through the Narrows, until, just as the sun tips the crest of Signal Hill with a farewell crimson kiss, the last laggard of the fleet anchors in the channel, to wait until the little, busy, bewildered tug shall have leisure to haul them inside. But in truth it matters but little whether the ships anchor or not, for surely as the sun sinks, out go the boats, and leaving the captain to take care of the ship as best he can, in a few minutes the greasy hunters jump on shore, and are hauled off by friends and women as mad with joy as they are. In streets, in lanes, in cottages of the poor, as well as in mansions of the rich, the night is prolonged in one great universal orgie. It was on one of these occasions that an officer of rank, sent up to Fish-and-fog-land from Halifax on an official commission, said, in answer to a question as to what sort of a place it was, "Well, sir, I was only there three days, and they appeared to me to be all drunk."

Alas! it was not destined to be my good fortune to witness so pleasant a prosperity during my three years sojourn in the great fish-colony. The grand harvest of the Arctic Sea was not gathered in. Our worthy merchants came down, in those sad years, from Signal Hill more slowly than they ascended; and, though it is very probable the amount of liquor consumed in the slums and groggeries was much the same, yet, on these occasions, it was drunk not to celebrate a rejoicing, but to drown sorrow for bad luck, as well as, perhaps, to honour the health of those accommodating patrons who had been feeding their families all the winter, and were about to do the same for the summer, without a halfpenny returned. If they drank for luck the first year of failure, it brought no good fortune to the next year's venture; and then gaunt women and children, often barefooted, all through that terrible winter, through ice and snow, were seen in numbers running from door to door begging charity sorely needed. Yes, in the wintry months of 1863 poor Fish-and-fog-land was, indeed, hardly pressed; but the elastic Irish heart woke up with the strengthening sun in spring, and the ships were once more rigged out for the old venture almost as gaily and gladly as before: Four—five—six—long weeks passed by, and not a vestige of news reached the trembling city from the north. It was sickening to behold the anxious, long-drawn faces at the doors watching the staff on the Signal Hill, from which, sad to relate, the pennants for the returning fleet were never to fly. But the ill-tidings came at last. The ships had never struck the seals at all; but, caught by easterly gales between the ice and a lee-shore, had been jammed until they had been crushed like walnuts in that iron grasp. The men, poor wretches! had escaped on shore; and the news came that they were starving in the out-harbours to the northward, from which the miserable, broken-looking wretches came down by driblets, and slank away to their equally miserable lairs. Down tumbled insurance companies, never to raise their heads again; and old-established houses, of undoubted strength and reputation, shook and trembled under such terrific blows. Bad enough for these, but worse for the fishermen to endure. What a sad, sad picture it must have been, to witness the return of the disappointed, starving man to his cottage, with starving faces before him, to whom he brings no help, and his own strength for work all but exhausted! That night they anxiously debate the prospect of seeking a little more credit—of feeling whether there may not be just one ticket left in the great lottery-bag, as an escape for themselves and little ones from death. In very many cases this is no exaggerated picture of unfortunate Fish-and-fog-land in the disastrous spring of 1864.

There is one curious consideration connected with the seal-fishery for which I never could obtain a satisfactory solution. It is the very short time—a bare three weeks—which this usually rich harvest lasts. The hunters strike their prey on the great pans of ice floating down from the Arctic seas; but, after the vessels are once filled—or rather, whether lucky or not, after this stereotyped portion of time has passed—no attempt to follow the seals to the southward is ever made; nor could any one ever explain what became of the great shoals of these animals after passing Newfoundland. Perhaps this is just as well; for, if it be true that the female seal only produces one young one yearly, they certainly would, unless they escaped some years, have long ago been exterminated. It is probable that, after running down with the Arctic current as far as the great Banks, following the vast and various shoals of fish which are seeking the shallow waters round the coast, in which to deposit their spawn, the seals turn to the westward up the Gulf of St Lawrence, and make terrible havoc among the salmon and sea-trout at the mouths of the numberless streams which flow into the mighty father of northern waters. Moreover, it is certain that, in some of these tributaries, little known or frequented, save by the Indians, or by the amateur fly-fisher who rents the water for the season from the Canadian Government, they are often seen in untold numbers. I remember hearing that, in 1865, an officer of the Montreal staff, with his wife, pitched their tent, during one of these excursions, far up on the wild unknown banks of the St John, for the combined objects of fishing, photography, and the pleasant, unshackled life of the wigwam. One sunny afternoon, in July, they were out in a canoe in one of the reaches of the stream, when, on a large bare flat rock, projecting into the river about four hundred yards ahead, they suddenly saw a vast number of moving creatures. What these were they could not imagine, unless they were bears or wolves driven inwards by a concentrated backwood fire. At length, after a steady survey with the glass, to the lady's great relief, the astonished officer pronounced them to be seals in countless numbers. He made a stealthy approach to within a hundred yards, the canoe was stopped, and the contents of a double-barrelled rifle poured in. Almost by the time the piece was lowered from his shoulder the whole area of the rock was cleared, while the river beneath literally boiled and foamed like a cauldron. They climbed the rock and looked down upon the hundreds upon hundreds of seals, whose myriad eyes watched them from below. Conceive the havoc these hungry brutes must make with the salmon; and conceive, again, if that be possible, the prodigious quantity of salmon there must be in the river to supply their ravenous appetites, and yet allow a good angler to play and kill his twenty-five or thirty fish a-day. As an Irishman said, of the stake-nets in the Shannon, before the Commissioners—"Bedad, gintilmen, if it warn't for them there wouldn't be wather enough to float the sammin."

This, however, by no means settles the disputed point, as to what becomes of the seals when the ice deserts them, on striking the shoulder of the Gulf Stream below Newfoundland: and, pursuing our inquiry, it is not a little curious to find a fish, which breeds both in the Arctic and Antarctic regions, plentiful in the tepid waters of the Caribbean Sea. From the lighthouse on the palisades of Port-Royal, at the entrance of the harbour of Kingston, in Jamaica, for many miles westward along that coast, a line encloses a system of low coral islands, reefs, banks, and shoals, colonized by innumerable birds and fishes. Each kind has its own locality, and keys and islands never interchange inhabitants. The bank that gives the king-fish gives neither the snapper nor the grouper. Southward from the extremity of this long bank, at a distance of some few leagues, the great Pedro bank is reached, stretching another hundred miles, the keys of which attract yearly vast numbers of fishing-boats from the main, for the great egg-harvest. Some three miles out, to leeward of the South-west Key, lies Seal Key. It is about three acres in extent, and some twenty feet in height. There is no approach to this islet but in very fine weather, on account of the sunken reefs, on which the surf plays with fury. At the best of times landing is not effected without great peril, as a continual sea rushes up the shore. There is not a particle of vegetation on this key: the booby-birds repair to it, but do not breed there. It is the congregating place of seals alone. There they seem, in vast numbers, to delight in basking in the hot sun, and to huddle together and grunt out their pleasure in each other's company. In truth, save from the shot of a rifle, they live here in safety; though, as these reefs are visited only once a-year, for a few weeks each spring, it is not known whether they remain for the whole year round, or are merely there in their passage north or south. I remember hearing of a party who did succeed in landing, and in heading an old bull-seal before he could gain the beach. They killed him after a hard battle. He proved to be an aged patriarch, with teeth worn down to the stumps, and a hide gashed and seared with scars got in many a fierce fight. Who can tell us more of his history, and whether he ever crossed and recrossed the great river of the ocean between far-off Greenland and the hot, barren rocks in the centre of the blue Antilles?

Yet, notwithstanding the havoc made by the seals upon the salmon, we were not without that luxury in its due season in Fish-and-fog-land, though it was rarely until the beginning of July that the first specimen of this glorious fish was brought in from Portugal Cove. The great object which amateur gardeners had in view was to raise a cucumber to match this noble dish,—a feat which, late as the season was, has never been to my knowledge accomplished in St John's. For want of experience, combined with an undue fear of frosty nights, while the snow still lay thick upon the ground, our hot-beds were always begun too late. True, we had surer work to go by, but for all that we never managed to eat our salmon and cucumber together: the more's the pity, for such salmon as these are unknown elsewhere. Our fish were caught ere they left the sea, the numberless mountain streams round St John's being too small for their ascent. Every day that a salmon out of the salt ascends the fresh water, he loses in firmness and sweetness; so it was doubly hard lines that, first in season we had the lobsters, next the salmon, then the salad, and last of all the cucumber; but never in the great fish-colony could these luxuries be procured *ensemble* for love or money, and no doubt for want of skill.

In truth, spite of the good results, and the pleasure afforded by the occupation, horticulture in Newfoundland was a terribly uphill game. No sooner did the brown head of Signal Hill peep from beneath its winter blanket, and long before the weary stall-penned cattle were suffered to roam the fields again, usually about the beginning of April, than spade and shovel began tickling the ribs of our common mother, in the hope of seeing the smile of a bountiful promise spread quickly over her face. The sun, which (in the latitude of Paris) is now powerfully felt, soon turns this promise into reality, and the trim little gardens began to be gay with hardy flowers; while between the rows of blooming gooseberry and currant bushes, peas, beans, lettuces, and many other kinds of the good old sorts, look day by day more boldly at the bright king above. By the end of the month, or beginning of May, there is just a patch or two of dirty snow left in the corners of the streets; the musk rats are swimming gaily in the lakes and rivulets, the snipe is drumming joyously overhead, and the old man's beard, a frozen torrent on the south side hills (always the last relic of winter to be seen), has dwindled, as it were, into a few long hoary hairs. Frost! the idea is simply absurd; or even if it should come, it can be but a gentle touch which can do no great harm. But one afternoon, somehow, there is a queer, chilly feel in the air, and the olive-tinted hills look gray with dark-blue cavities; the sun sets blood red, and the cloudless sky at night flashes as a vast steel-embossed canopy overhead. It was cold; but I little suspected, when the doors were closed for the night, the havoc which morning's light would display. The little garden was not; the black earth was there, but the flowers and tender plants were gone. Repining was of little use; there was yet time, and cheerfully we set to work to sow and plant again, until in three weeks more the garden began to smile again, and the old trial was almost forgotten. Then it happened that, one evening returning home after our usual stroll, as the peep of the vast Atlantic opened through the Narrows, lo! the entrance of the harbour was almost blockaded by a huge white iceberg, and the Arctic ice, detached from its great parent depôt, was running with the current down our coast, charged with cold chills for the earth, and heavy fogs hereafter in its battle with the warm Gulf Stream to the southward. Thus it went on running past us week after week, while every now and then a stronger south-easterly wind than usual would completely block up the Narrows or harbour with the hideous alabaster-looking lumps. We, poor frozen-out gardeners, stood and looked in utter disgust at the prospect; as well we might. The young plants did not die, but they refused to grow. It mattered not a whit to the young ducks that the peas to match them stood still; but like the story of the salmon and cucumber aforesaid, it happened that young ducks and young peas could never get together. April past, May past, June almost gone; weary, weary, weary. But at last the heavy fogs came rolling up over the south side hills, showing that the great annual conflict between north and south had begun, and the white-clad armies of the north melted daily away. (*Would that it had always been so elsewhere.*) Then came our reward at last with bright sunny days, so doubly enjoyable in a place where the heat of the glad sun is a thing not to be dreaded but enjoyed. Beneath his witching looks the dull brown livery of earth's sad surface changed to a living emerald. Beneath our very gaze the eager tendrils of the hop, convolvulus, and scarlet-runner seize the strong arms ready to raise them from the ground; while birds in troops from warmer climes fly past to the great inland woods and swamps, there to coo, and build, and raise their young, undisturbed by the murderous hand of man. Country, gardens, fields, cliffs, mountains, all is delightful now as the bower of roses by Bendemeer's stream or fairyland itself. But, ah! how short it sometimes is. This very year of which we write, cut off by frost once, twice, and the harbour full of ice on the 3d of July! Yet we followed the command of the Preacher to sow in the morning and withhold not the hand in the evening, though much of the seed cast into the earth this year never came back after many days to bless the sower. Rising one morning very early on the 2d of September, to start on a shooting expedition, terrible was the sight the hitherto beautiful little garden presented. It was just as if the breath of a furnace had passed through it, and blasted the beauty of earth for ever. Stalk, flower, leaf, fruit, were all alike the prey of that cruel herald of far-off winter. Nearly all the joy, all the labour for that year, was for the third time gone, and so the Preacher was right when he preached of vanity, and that there was no profit to a man under the sun. Happily all years are not like this: and the destroyer seldom comes before the harvest of field and garden is safely gathered in. We have no peaches or plums, and but few apples. But our small fruits ripen well, and our vegetables might have been shown in Covent Garden without discredit.

Yet for many years after the colony became civilised, vegetables and fruits were practically unknown; for no one believed they could be grown. The ground was apparently half-rock, half-swamp. Certainly, were a stranger to walk over Signal Hill or the steep South Side slopes, he might be pardoned if he were a little incredulous on the subject of cultivation. Yet the slope on which the city stands was just the same but a few years back, and now fifty gardens bear produce fit for an emperor's table. A few humble potatoes led the van, until, finally, the triumphs of hotbeds with cucumbers and melons was attained; and the day is not far distant when orchard-houses and conservatories will lend their charms to adorn the tables of the luxurious, and the sick-rooms of the poor as well. How the rich in those days existed without them so long would be incomprehensible, did we not learn the secret lay in the rapid fortunes acquired formerly in the successful fisheries, and the consequent "vamosing" of the lucky speculators, leaving not a wreck behind them. And yet so strangely does the silent finger of God work, that, in spite of present suffering and loss, there can be little doubt of the failure of the fisheries for three successive years proving a blessing in the end. The merchants finding the days of quick fortune-making passed away, moreover beginning to understand that the prime of their days, at any rate, must be spent in this country, are wisely settling themselves more comfortably, more luxuriantly. They begin to build themselves villas on the banks and borders of the dark-green lochs, with ornamental additions of little infant conservatories and flower-gardens. Better kinds of fruit-trees and choice vegetables were being imported from England or Boston, and gardeners will be soon wanted to take care of them. Art in a thousand forms to administer to these luxuries will be called into rapid requisition, and the higher skill of labour will bring a higher grade of civilisation and refinement in its train. Superior schools will be opened for the young; and actually a people's park and garden was about to be laid out. Government, to employ the starving poor, are compelled to open new roads; so that one of the chief wants in all civilised communities receives a little of that attention long and loudly called for. The fisherman, amid the shocking trials of starvation, is beginning to trust a little less to the lottery of the sea, and large patches of unpromising-looking ground are cleared and drained yearly. The cultivation of flax, for which the country seems eminently adapted, is beginning to attract attention. Should this succeed, enormous benefits would at once accrue to the poorer classes, as they would find employment in cleaning and scutching the fibre during the long winters. With every possible acre round the city reclaimed, and the day may not be far distant but that this may be, property will rise in value. Thus, amid tribulation and chaos, the unerring mysterious finger of order is crystallising and arranging all these changes, sternly teaching of untold gifts blindly spurned in generations past; though more than one good ruler (among whom, for this foresight and encouragement, Sir Gaspard Le Marchant should especially be remembered) earnestly sought to remedy these evils. It shall yet be told, as a strange story of these times, how the brave old Governor Sir Alexander Bannerman went down to the House year by year to lament in his opening speech the evil times which were come upon his people on account of the failure of the fisheries, hitherto their only stay; and how, thereupon, the members on both sides of the House, with much lamentation, voted an address in sympathising reply to his speech, and then folded their hands in utter helplessness and dismay. And they, in those after days, will think how the angels must have smiled to have heard the pitiful conclusions and forecasts of man's guesses on the Wisdom overruling his destinies, or wept to see how that he can only be taught by the bitter experience of famine, misery, and death, to gather up some of the numberless riches and blessings always within his grasp, if sought for by the sure labours wherein we are permitted to imitate the slow and silent progress by which, under the Creator's hands, all things approach perfection.

CHAPTER XIII.

THE HARVESTS OF THE OCEAN.

F, as has been already mournfully chronicled in these pages, the hopes of the great seal-fishery set year by year (in these days) in sorrow and disaster; if, as the snows melted, then fell, and melted again, our trials in horticulture were manifold and severe, as even Habakkuk might have nobly faced with unswerving trust; the sweet breath of summer, direct from southern seas, late in coming, but all the more welcome for that, lulled in renewed hopes all our troubles of the past. A modern writer has beautifully written, "There is always one day in the year when nature seems to me truly to awake. The snow has been gone for weeks, the sun has been shining briskly, the fruit trees are white with blossom, yet the sky remains hard and stern, and the earth is black and inhospitable, as if the remembrance of winter had chilled its heart. But one morning you wake unwarned, and you have barely drawn aside the curtains ere you are aware that the bonds of death are loosed; that a new life has been born into the year, and that, like the eyes of a girl who has begun to love, the blue sky and the fleecy clouds have strangely softened since nightfall. Summer is abroad upon the mountains, and her maiden whisper thrills your pulse." It is a short yet most delicious season here. We live in the latitude of Paris with the temperature of Balmoral, and for this brief time all nature, both animate and inanimate, worships eagerly at the golden shrine of the God of Light. Almost until midnight we linger now in the garden beneath the shelter of the balsam-poplars, breathing in the incense of the mignonette and roses, or watching the vapours on the dark basin of the harbour lift and mingle with the shadows on the south side slopes, as the white moon walks gently up and peeps over the shoulder of the opposite Signal Hill. Ah! the poets may sing as they please, but we are very certain that no houri basking in perpetual sunshine, no Paxton in his enchanted palaces, ever revelled in summer's gladness as we do now. To understand our delight, they must first stand our weary baptism in snow and ice, cabined up in double windowed cells for five months at a stretch, without freedom and exercise such as an Englishman must have to live in health. Hark! that glad laugh born of light and heat, yet never heard abroad in winter. A young girl crowned with golden ringlets of laburnum is running down the hill chased by a dozen companions jealous of her lovely prize. Stand on the rise above the lake, as the sun bends towards its western edge, and watch the parties of idlers sauntering round the clear margin of the water, or stopping ever and anon to shout to the fishermen who have been patiently beating the dark pools for hours past on the jutting points of Bennett's Wood. Deeper and deeper grow the shadows, until a white mist hangs like a rolled-up curtain over the sleeping waters; yet still by keen ears the whispers of some loving voices might be caught far into the small hours of night. Ah! such delicious air to drink into the heaving breast as dwellers in cities or dry arid plains, where rushing waters are not, never know. Birds from the torrid southern steppes, in teeming flocks, are hourly passing onward to coo, mate, and build their little homes. Cattle, released from the close steaming stalls of winter, bound over the meadows, mad with the joy of liberty again, or stand half mesmerised by the soft air in the rippling shadows of the lake. Here, on its margin, the echo of the thousand sounds of awakened labour is gently borne onward by the western breeze. Ah! now we say, Would it were always thus; yet forgetful, so soon forgetful, of the dreary past, or that our joy in the present is multiplied by the infinite contrast with the white misery so long and patiently endured.

Wolfe is outside the garden-gate whistling to his dogs. "Let us go," said he, looking over the paling, "up on Signal Hill and see the cod-boats come in." We pass through a dirty suburb answering to the un-euphonious title of "Maggotty Cove"—not altogether misnamed for all that,—and commence at once the rough steep ascent of the hill, the scenery as we climb becoming wilder and more rugged. High above on our right a ruined monolith, on a mountain peak, marks the site of an old battery, while to the left, sunk in a hollow, a black bog lies sheltered amid the bare bones of mother earth, here mainly composed of dark red sandstones and conglomerates, passing down by regular gradations to the slate below. A sudden turn of the road reveals a deep solitary tarn, some three hundred and fifty feet above the sea, in which the guardian rocks reflect their purple faces, and where the ripple of the musk rat, hurrying across, alone disturbs the placid surface. We pass a hideous-looking barrack, and crossing the soft velvety sward on the crest, reach a little battery, from the parapets of which we look down, down, almost five hundred feet perpendicularly, right into "the Narrows," the straight or creek between the hills connecting the broad Atlantic with the oval harbour within. The great south side hills, covered with luxuriant wild vegetation, and skeined with twisting torrents, looms across the strait so close that one might fancy it possible a stone could fly from the hand to the opposite shore. On our left the vast ocean, with nothing, not a rock, between us and Galway. On our right, at the other end of the narrow neck of water directly beneath, the inner basin, expanding towards the smoke-hung city, with the background of blue hills as a setting to the picture, broken only in their continuous outline by the twin-towers of the Catholic Cathedral, ever thus, from all points, performing their mission of conspicuity. Right below us, four hundred feet perpendicular, we lean over the grass parapet and look carefully down into the little battery guarding the narrowest part of the entering strait, where, in the old wars, heavy chains stretched from shore to shore. We see a woman, not much bigger than Ham's wife in a child's ark, the wife of the gunner in charge, hanging out linen to dry; and if a pebble stirred from the bank on which we sit, it would light unpleasantly near to her. We shout, and the opposite cliff hurls back the challenge, while five hundred eyes glance upward to our eyrie seat. The Narrows are full of fishing-boats returning with the silver spoils of the day glistening in the holds of the smacks, which, to the number of forty or fifty at a time, tack and fill like a fleet of white swans against the western evening breeze. Even as we look down upon the decks, they come, and still they come, round the bluff point of Fort Amherst from the bay outside. Standing on the flat flakes echelloned on every cranny of the rocks are the women and children, ready to catch the fish as they are pitchforked up out of the boats, and place them ready for the splitter. Alack, the evil time! they have not long to wait; for like the disciples of old, many of them have toiled all day and caught nothing. In former years, when there were fewer fishermen, fewer planters, fewer murderous dodges against the fish, these flakes of an evening could scarcely bear the tremendous weight of the great ocean harvest. Now happy is the planter who sees his flakes occasionally covered with fish. Yet there cannot be an effect without a cause, and why the poor fishermen's families starve in winter, and why the merchant has to wait so many more years before he can hope to build that house in Greenock or Liverpool, must now needs be told or guessed at.

In the first place, there are now many more merchants, many more planters or middlemen, many more fishermen to divide a catch which has averaged pretty much of a muchness for many years past. In the second, the new styles of fishing, introduced on the principle of quick returns and devil take the hindmost, have done vast injury to the fisheries. In the good old times—really good in this wise—the proper sized fish only were taken with hook and line, at no injury to other fish in the waters. But, to carve a short road out to riches, first of all was brought in the cod-seine, which utterly destroys the chances of the legitimate hook and-liners, if used anywhere near their ground; and by it, moreover, tons of young small fish, useless for commerce, are cast out and thrown aside. Next came in the bultow, which swept into its maw numbers of heavy mother-fish, at a consequence to the future which needs no further explanation. And lastly was introduced the infernal jigger, which, barbing and tearing among a shoal of fish, like a Malay running a-muck in a crowd, for every fish taken by it, possibly injures half a dozen others cruelly, and finally drives the whole lot, thoroughly frightened, from the bank. Verily, the goose with the eggs of gold is killed and cooked to perfection.

Thus, it is not difficult to perceive that, in the cod-fishery—the great harvest and business of the country—it is, from first to last, a sort of pull-devil, pull-baker sort of system, the evils of which, accumulating for years, have now begun to be seriously felt. The fisherman, with his family, eats his bread long before it is earned, and then struggles against nature to win a hopeless victory. Just as in the gambler's game of *rouge et noir*, every now and then great coups by a few individuals are made, exciting hundreds of others to try their luck; yet the chances, as a standing quantity, being ever in favour of the "hell," the victims sooner or later are all cleaned out. So, under this sad system of undue credit and overwhelming charges, the very first hint of a falling house is the signal for the fisherman's revenge upon his creditor; and, like the rats in the sinking ship, he turns tail at once, and transfers his fish (already mortgaged) to another merchant, without scruple, for cash prices or a new credit, or sells it to the cute Yankee ever on the watch along the banks for such a chance.

Far out on the dark-blue waters, and even then almost too dazzling by the glory of its pure whiteness, floats an iceberg like the topsail of some fairy ship whose hull is hidden beneath the horizon. Looking northward from our pinnacle, here and there we see others gleaming in the rays of the setting sun, borne to the warmer south by the Arctic current, so fatal to our hopes of early summer; but yet fraught, by the All-wise hand who adjusts the compensating balance of good and evil, with rich blessings for the land we stand on. It is the cold waters of this ocean-river which attracts the cold-blooded fish from southern latitudes to seek their more congenial abode up here. Often was it said in my hearing—"Ah, what a country this would be could the Gulf Stream but break upon our shores! Why—why does it turn away so enviously, so cruelly, just as its glowing lip touches our longing, sterile banks? Look at the undulating land, the hills, the streams, the long reaches of pasture; and think what a beauty, what a glory might be here, if but the moist, warm breath of this great mother of life vivified creation into a higher state of activity!" But the great Adjuster had other uses for the land and for the men who were to dwell on it. True, the Gulf Stream would bring heat and corn, wine and cattle in abundance; it might make the land in time "a land flowing with milk and honey;" but the men could be no more fishers or gatherers-in of the great harvests of the sea, for there would be none to gather here. These would have passed to other shores with the colder streams, and the world would have been all the poorer. The great products of the ocean-beds must be collected somewhere, and it has been ordered that it shall be done here, as of the harvests of corn and wine in other countries. And see how wisely the circle of causes runs round, to keep, restore, and renew this balance of gifts for the use of man—ay, of all living creatures. The Arctic current, which now we are watching from the hill-top, turning aside the warm waters of the ocean-river, to bless and fecundate the coasts of Europe: that river, passing outward from the great cup of the Caribbean Sea filled to overflowing by the winds which press the surface of the Atlantic into a basin from which the guardian isthmus grants no escape: the winds, sucked hither to a focus from the colder north, to fill the vacant place ever left by the air, ascending from the surface of the two great divisions of the American continent, to rush toward the frozen poles: line upon line, curve upon curve, circle within circle of the wonderful machinery working harmoniously together upon the central pivot of the solar orb. See what a chain of links is here formed towards apparently one great end, yet connected with myriads of other chains encircling the universe, all apparently proceeding from the same source and working round the same pivot. Sun and ray, cold and heat, ever changing the specific gravity and condition of air and water,—causing vast currents in the elastic covering of the globe, and mighty ocean-rivers in opposite directions to pierce the waters which fill the great chasms between earth's continents. Little does the rude fisherman, now pitching out his spoils upon the flakes far beneath our feet, think what stupendous causes, acting through incomprehensible distances, have brought them to his lines. Yet is the same vsat machinery at work ever and ever; as ceaselessly and silently engaged in perfecting the life of the meanest blade of grass, as in providing for the luxury or welfare of the last and chief work of the Creator's hand; to teach us that nothing resolves, nothing changes, throughout the universe, except through fixed, unalterable laws, of whose mysterious and mutual relations we have as yet discovered but the merest rudiments.

Ably and straight to the point has a modern writer witnessed thus: *

"In an age of physical research like the present, all highly-cultivated minds and duly advanced intellects have imbibed more or less the lessons of inductive philosophy, and have, at least in some measure, learned to appreciate the grand foundation conception of universal law—to recognise the impossibility even of *any two material atoms* subsisting together without a determinate relation—of any action of the one or the other, whether of equilibrium or of motion, without reference to a physical cause—of any modification whatsoever in the existing conditions of material agents, unless through the invariable operation of a series of eternally-impressed consequences, following in some necessary chain of orderly connection, however imperfectly known to us.

"This operation of a series of eternally-impressed consequences could hardly be described more graphically or forcibly than in the following words of a great German philosopher: 'Let us imagine, for instance, this grain of sand lying some few feet farther inland than it actually does. Then must the storm-wind that drove it in from the seashore have been stronger than it actually was. Then must the preceding state of the atmosphere, by which the wind was occasioned and its degree of strength determined, have been different from what it actually was, and the previous changes which

* Quoted from Professor Mansel's Essay on Miracles in "Aids to Faith."

gave rise to this particular weather, and so on. We must suppose a different temperature from that which really existed, and a different constitution of the bodies which influenced this temperature. The fertility or barrenness of countries, the duration of the life of man, depend unquestionably, in a great degree, on temperature. How can you know—since it is not given us to penetrate the arcana of nature, and it is therefore allowable to speak of possibilities—how can you know that in such a state of the weather as we have been supposing, in order to carry this grain of sand a few yards farther, some ancestor of yours might not have perished from hunger, or cold, or heat, long before the birth of that son from whom you are descended; that thus you might never have been at all; and all that you have done, and all that you ever hope to do in this world, must have been hindered, in order that a grain of sand might lie in a different place.'"

Thus, then, it is (setting on one side the other great consideration in the power of the mind over matter), that just as the grain of sand by causes traced back and acting under fixed compensating laws, lies just where it has been directed by the force of those laws, so by the same balance of power the hand of Providence, which created these laws, is, by their operation, checking the ultimate ruin of this country, even by its apparent ruin at this moment. The fatal desire for rapid wealth, which hitherto has driven its merchants away from their social duties, must soon give place to a more healthy desire for promoting the good of the place in which the prime of their days is passed, even though it should come to pass by attending to their own business and comforts. So long as the fisheries brought enormous profits there was no hope for the country, for no one of the higher classes looked to it as a "*home*." "Lightly come lightly go, a jolly game all round," said a rubicund merchant in my hearing in the ante-room of the House of Assembly. "And," continued the worthy legislator, laughing and rubbing his hands together, "if my boats'-loads of fish don't come in, my son is pretty sure to pick up somebody else's at sea."

Even apart from all other consideration of eventual good, little pity on account of the failure of their trade do the merchants of Fish-and-fog-land deserve. For years and years they have drawn away their wealth and influence from the place, returning few tithes of gratitude to the Great Giver of their prosperity; doing little or nothing for the public good, and separating themselves as from a contaminated community as soon as possible. Thus while men of any education fly to happier lands, you may see here a good many with thousands upon thousands who cannot even write their own names; and the great masses of the fish gamblers, poverty-stricken from the first check, unable to rise in the great human scale generation after generation. The system strikes at the root of all that is right or elevating, and keeps the standard of public opinion, if indeed such a thing can be said to exist at all, at its very lowest mark.

This, then, was our discourse upon the apex of Signal

Hill, overlooking the harbour, while the last beams of the departed sun lingered over the western horizon; the beauty of the scene spread before us as on a map; the great harvests of the ocean proceeding by fixed yet incomprehensible laws for the food of man; and the means of defending this, the great fish granary, from invasion. Heavily the moisture from a cloudless sky condensed itself into drops of diamond dew upon the spearlike grasses, as we descended from the rocky heights, making the verdure of the garden and the sweetness of the mignionette for the moment by contrast a thousand times more grateful to the senses. Ice and snow and frost are at last forgotten things. We say we can never tire of walking round by the soft moonlight, amid all the blossoming fruits, and climbing blessings, almost unfolding visibly as we look upon their beauty. Now is the time for the country, we all agree; "let us go and see it," is passed by an unanimous vote, and a picnic party for the next day is formed upon the spot.

On either side of the city of St John's, stretching in a semi-circle along the rugged coast, at an average radius from the centre of seven or eight miles, a number of little fishing coves, or bays, attract, during the sweet and enjoyable summer, all persons who can command the use of a horse to revel in their beauties. Each little bay is but a slice of the high cliffs scooped out by the friction of the mighty pressure of the Atlantic waves; and leading down to its shingled beach, each boasts of a lovely green valley through which infallibly a tumbling, noisy trout burn pours back the waters evaporated from the parent surface. Many were the pleasant evening drives and picnics we enjoyed in those charming spots. By one o'clock the carriages were marshalled in front of Fort William, at Bakehouse corner, and the signal given for a start. The blue sleepy waters of the sweet lake, as we passed across the King's Bridge at Quiddi-Viddi, might alone have tempted us to stop with their all-sufficient gladness; but another mile up hill, and then another across the Ballyhaly bogs, covered with wild calmias, azaleas, Indian tea-plants, and a hundred others unknown by name at least to me, among which the young snipe were preparing for the sportsman's gun, brought us to the gates of Virginia Water, the former summer residence of the governors of Newfoundland. At the entrance of the dark avenue a rapid rivulet ran busily across the road, from the shades of a dense wood of firs, beeches, and birches, which quite concealed the lake from passers on the road. It is a sheet of deep water, about three miles in circumference, indented with little grass-edged bays, fringed and feathered to the limpid edge with dark dense woods. Often of a still summer evening, watching the musk-rats cut their lines along the glassy surface as they swam to the opposite groves, did I think what a site for a house might this be for a man with means at his command to do the thing well. His skating-rink in winter, his miniature Killarney in summer, the boat-house in the little sheltered bend, trout-fishing, pleasure-grounds and garden, wooded hills and autumn shooting, conservatory and orchard houses, all dependent on skill now well understood in its application; returning to the old country, say from February to May, while the seasons shifted and reformed themselves; and above all the revolutions and improvements among social things which he might create about him. What a pleasant field for a man of means, taste, and energy! How different a life from rotting idle in the suburbs of Liverpool or Greenock, on the gains of a land drained away from their natural outlets!

Thus the dark woods of Virginia on the left, and to the right the undrained flower-covered flats of Ballyhaly, are passed by, when, from a gentle rise we look back over both to catch the last glimpse of the dark hills round the harbour, crowned with the ever-to-be-seen towers of the Catholic Cathedral. Over the brow of this hill we turn sharply to the right, down a sheltered fir-lined avenue, where the long trailing branches of the cone-shaped spruces, intermingled with the graceful lady birches, might almost tempt a new-born Ovid to sing of fairy transformations, and weeping women awaiting a return to human shape and semblance. Here and there glints of golden buttercupped meadows break for an instant between the dark walls of green; and as the narrow road winds we catch a few inches of cobalt far beyond, of purple cliffs crowned, as they always are on a bright day such as this, with that mysterious indefinable haze of gladness which hovers over the union of earth and sea. Out of the dark avenue a zigzag path, leading of course to a noisy boulder-bewildered stream, descends in a gap of the great cliffs to the water; and when we crossed the rickety wooden bridge, near the shanties in the hollow, the sea in all its beauty at Logie Bay burst suddenly upon us. In the feeble shelter, afforded by the projection of the cliffs in a shallow arc, is one of the many little outlying fishing communities who supply the merchants with their produce. Here, in the summer only, live the fishers and their families, in huts and shanties of turf and boughs intermingled, erected on the sward on the edge of the smooth rocks close to the flakes, where they unceasingly watch the drying and curing of the fish. This, if not attended to, and covered in from a passing shower, would be utterly spoilt. Ah! it is delicious, in this hot summer noontide, to sit under the shade of a huge boulder, and watch the leap of the rivulet over the last ledge of rocks into the briny ocean. Beneath our feet, in the chasm, the spray of the little waterfall has charmed the fronds of the bright green ferns into larger life and beauty; and tiny feet risk tumbles and slips to pluck them from their niches in the rocks. Before us, in the vast expanse of soft hazy ocean blue, the white sails of the fishing smacks chequer the surface thickly; while here and there the spout of a whale makes the children cry with wonder at the seeming mystery of the upheaved waters. A long line of cork-jointed netting, undulating like a snake by the lift and fall of the sluggish wave, stretches along the arc of the bay from cliff to cliff; and before we leave, many a lovely specimen of the silver-guarded king of fish is offered for sale. Down in the boot of the carriage, tenderly covered with ferns and grasses, we stow away a noble salmon for to-morrow's breakfast, just as the signal is given by our leader for a fresh start to the other bays of the adjacent coast.

Over the hills at the back of the great cliffs, past field and homestead plucked from the wild fruit-bearing barrens, and down again by a winding road, garnished thickly with copse of birch and pine; until we meet the merry stream at the bottom of the vale, where the great cliffs again fell back to let the curious sea come and take a nearer view of earth's glory within. Here, between the sheltering sides of Middle Cove, the Atlantic waves tumble everlastingly on a pebbly beach; while (something like a huge monster with open mouth and gaping jaws) between the cliffs is stretched a web of flakes in intricate mazy confusion. Fish,—fish,—fish, is the only thought of the fishermen's brains in summer time, with here and there a glance after the pig, fed, alack! on the fish offal with which the pebbles under the flakes are thickly larded. We look around in vain for the trim gardens which should be here in a dell, bright as an emerald with nature's sweetest colours, inviting man in speaking living words to come and seek her gifts. In vain she cries; there is a possibly shorter road to wealth, or at least coarse food at their doors, and to that alone they turn.

Under the network of interlacing flakes, amid a crowd of hungry curs and pigs fighting for the fish-waste festering in heaps, we pushed for the pure bright air of the wide free beach, and there beheld a sight especial to these shores. The sea, locked between the arms of the cliffs and far out towards the curved horizon as eye could reach, was alive with fish, which had actually taken the very place of the waters. The harvest of the capling, a little fellow about six inches long something between a smelt and a silver eel, had set in, and stupendous was the multitude of fish. When the lift of the wave touched or receded from the pebbly beach, boys and girls gathered in the spoil as fast as they had strength; while farther up towards the flakes huge mounds of the wriggling glittering fish awaited carting inland. It was literally here the old story of the man who could open oysters faster than another could eat them. Here they actually caught fish before our eyes a hundred times faster than they could be carted away!

"Would yer honner buy a bucket-full?" cried an urchin in natural knickerbockers, who wielded an old butter-tub with a string, like David armed to meet Goliah. In went the would-be bucket among the surf as far as the string could reach, and was instantly hauled back full of quivering fish.

"Shall I take them up to yer honner's carriage for two coppers," pursued the urchin; while fifty others all along the stretch of beach cast in their tubs or buckets, and pitched the harvest in heaps above high water mark. The little beggars ran out into the surf, and stood up to their hips, not in water but in fish; ay, of the numbers of the multitudes, now for hundreds of miles round the coast of Fish-and-fog-land, no man could presume to guess within scores of scores of millions.

Where they come from, these awful shoals of animated creatures, to spread their eggs upon every shallow bit of water round these shores, or whither the vast numbers of survivors go, no one knows; few care. The poorest at this time are gorged with the delicate food; the whales, cod, and mackerel swallow huge quantities; and heaps upon heaps are spread broadcast over the fields for manure, a practice as stupid as it is short-sighted. Nature, careful of her gifts and riches, never intended the harvest of life to be used to so vile and wasteful a purpose, without first undergoing preparations by other necessary transitions. The farmer, by using the fish as a manure, enriches his pastures for a season, but impoverishes the ground rapidly; while, in revenge for the outrage, vast myriads of insects, grubs, and caterpillars, are developed from the putrid soil, suddenly over-enriched, and which soon spread havoc wholesale in fields and gardens on every side.

Not homeward yet; for when we strike again the turn down into Logie Bay, by which we have completed our gero, the carriages with one accord diverge into a gate and cross the rise of a field, until they pull up at the doors of a whitewashed cottage on the edge of a fir grove facing the distant city. Scattered all about the field, many of our party were already busy among the crannies of the rocks, searching out from their fairy haunts the wild strawberries, too easily revealed by their blushing beauty in the slanting rays of the setting sun. Under the deep shadows of the firs, a rough table groaned with tea, hot cake, and golden cream to match the fragrant fruit; around, the broad fronds of the tender ferns, intermingled with stars of Bethlehem and many other flowers, all in the tremble of a gentle symphony of happiness to the departing breeze of evening. It was a spot where, at such a moment, one might in very happiness cast off the cares and dust of busy life at the echo of the children's voices down in the deep of the woods, joyous with the prizes of the modest fruit. God only knows what secret cares and sins rankled in the hearts of those around that merry table: we ourselves only knew them cast away for those moments of our too quickly passing joy. Even in that Fish-and-fog-land, so far far away from the thoughts of the poet when he wrote the lines, we could sing with him of our summer evening thus :—

> "Oh! then the heart seems hushed, afraid to beat
> In the deep absence of all other sound;
> And home is sought with loath and lingering feet,
> As if that shining track of fairy ground,
> Once left and lost, should never more be found.
> And happy seems the life which gipsies lead,
> Who spread their tents where mossy nooks abound;
> In nooks where unplucked wild flowers shed their seed;
> A canvas-spreading tent the only roof they need."

Sic transit; even like all other things terrestial. The deep shades of the solemn firs blend earth, and flower, and tree, together in mingled gloom, whence, down in the far recesses, came back now and then the ringing laughter of the maids and children. Just as the horses were putting to, in they came, fern-crowned, with fragrant blossoms drooping from every hat. There was some little dispute among them as to the merits of the Atalanta of the group; when, amid the babel of friendly repartees, a young lady of some eighteen summers, pretending to stand on her dignity, exclaimed,

"Bah! if I get one minute's start, no one shall catch me before I return to the carriage."

"Done with you, Miss Kate," returned a smart young fellow, ready enough at such a chance; while the clapping of hands at the novelty of the race almost started the sober nags out of their propriety.

So out came the watches with minute hands ready to do their part, and at the word "start," off she flew, vanishing like a sprite into the gloom. Sixty seconds after, away sped the pursuer, and he too vanished out of sight. Five, ten minutes passed, the ladies chatted, the horses pawed the turf. Another quarter of an hour and then another. We grew impatient; the ladies fractious. Then we began to shout, until the woods rang with the dull echoes of our voices. Not a sign of response from the truants. Another half hour, and the cry was, "What was to be done?" It was a beautiful star-light night, but the woods were as dark as pitch. We lighted pine torches, and began shouting and exploring the paths, but all in vain; and when we returned to the carriages the ladies could stand it no longer.

"What a strange girl!" said one.

"So extremely inconsiderate," cried another.

"Can she possibly be drowned?" suggested a third.

"Impossible, ma'am; there is no pond about this place," said the farmer's wife.

"Perhaps she has struck her head against a tree, and is unable to rise."

"Then surely he would have returned for help."

It was very mysterious, very. But we could not stop there all night, so at half-past eleven, the women, full of sinister forebodings, beat a retreat, and not knowing exactly what to say to the friends of the lost girl, drove straight to her door: when, lo! to our amazement and consternation, there she stood, while round the back of the shrubberies, by another gate, there sneaked off a figure uncommonly like that of the gentleman-pursuer. With the most charming innocence she expressed surprise at our late return, and when asked to explain where she had been, naïvely said, "Oh! we had a long chase,—so long you can't think,—and you know he caught me just at the end of the wood; so we thought you had all gone, and that we had better walk home, you know; such a lovely night, we quite enjoyed it."

Not a doubt of it! poor stupid owls that we were, not to understand the dodge before this. But it didn't surprise me, some short time after, to hear a lady say to another, "Do you know, my dear, they say that Lizzie W—— is engaged to Mr H——! who'd a thought it?"

"Why, any one, ma'am, who had seen that fictitious

chase in the dark wood, and the summer moonlight walk across Virginia Wood afterwards; if that wasn't enough to settle a man's hash with a pretty girl, the deuce and all's in it, ma'am; and we were precious green not to see it all before."

Yes; this is summer in Newfoundland; when we taboo the fish and fogs very cheerily, and think the ferny dells, if not so grand, yet fresher with Atlantic dews than any other valleys of earth. If, with its brightness, there are drawbacks (for the sparks fly upwards everywhere), still, thank heaven, we know nothing of the suffocating siroccos, the stifling dust-storms, the hard, dry east winds, the blasting breath of the simoom, which desolate other and sunnier lands. And if the compensating balance of God's providence in good and evil was poised for this green Erin across the Atlantic, the scale of blessings would, in the judgment of considerate discerning men, preponderate against the cup of miseries, largely in favour of the dwellers in the often lost land of Fish-and-fog.

CHAPTER XIV.

AUTUMN—THE FIRST DAY OF THE SEASON.

"SURELY this is spring!" would exclaim a stranger from the old country, as he looked at the peas and scarlet-runners in full bloom. "Nay," might reply another, busy among the strawberry-beds, "it is surely summer!" Yet it is autumn all the same, with spring and summer so closely left behind that they are intermingled pleasantly yet confusedly together. It is the time for especial enjoyment to Wolfe and myself, and, alack the day! to too many others such as us. For the grouse are reported strong on the wing along the upland breezy barrens; and about the end of August we are very busy preparing to give them an early call.

It is at last come to the evening before the eventful day of the year, the 25th of August, on which the Legislature has directed that grouse-shooting should commence; the only precaution (unhappily) as yet taken for the protection of this noble game. The sun was descending behind the purple hills amid bands of gold and red, tinting all round with the gladness of a fair to-morrow; and the brown face of my friend Wolfe was bent deep in thought against the lintel of my little garden-wicket. The inner consultation was indeed momentous, being no less than concerning the route we should follow for the first day's shooting, a great number of considerations influencing the decision.

"I think," said he, looking up at last, "we'd better take the Cody's Well ground, and shoot down towards Tor Bay."

"Very good; but you know that Grant and Thompson are gone to encamp out there, and are sure to be before us."

"Umph! it's no use going to the Three-Pond Barrens, or the Deer's Marsh, or Petty Harbour. I know twenty parties going to each. What do you say to Broad Cove?"

"Splendid! but an awful road part of the way to get at it; better take something easier first of all, so as to be early on the ground,—that's the main point."

"Then let's try Flat Rock, and we can pick up Jem Strongback on the way; he knows every inch of the ground, and we could hardly do better than take the first day with him. I spoke to him about a month ago."

This settled, the burly form of my friend slowly vanished in the gloaming under the shadow of the balsam-poplars which lined the road towards his house. Less than six hours after, before the deep violet of the White Hills shaded into a distinctive hue of their own, we met again. He was standing in his porch with dog and gun, waiting for the phaeton. It was worth this rise before dawn to see the sparkle in Rover's eye, responsive to the heavy flap of his tail upon the ground,- as he waited the order to jump in and coil himself away beneath our feet. Five minutes to pack the trap snugly with ammunition and basket of prog; stow Green, my man, and the dog behind; and then away we go down across the King's Bridge, with a sniff of the dews and fogs brooding heavy over the lake, and four miles on over hilly ground, past the little farms all fast in sleep, till pulling up at Jem's, we saw his little gig ready, and his dogs all yelping for a start. Jem Strongback was a sort of mixture of farmer and publican, with a dash of the fisherman in his composition, and a capital shot into the bargain; the more 's the pity, as he was well known to be a sad destroyer of game out of season. He was an Englishman, and a hardworking, simple sort of fellow, about forty years of age, turning his hand at something or other to support an enormous string of olive-branches. All the summer he took in cattle by contract from the butchers of the city to fatten on the rich grasses of the wild barrens, at so much a head: so as these hundreds of beasts roamed where they pleased over the vast leas, moors, bogs, and woods; Jem knew every inch of the country, and in his continual wanderings after stray cattle (for which if lost he had to pay) found out the haunts of every brood and covey of grouse, and every snipe's nest in the peninsula. Not that Mister Jem always showed us the cream of these golden spots; but who could blame a man with his living dependant on this knowledge? Moreover, Jem was a liberal, honest fellow enough; and here he was at his doorway on the instant at the sound of the wheels, his broad face ruddy with the reflection of the great wood fire therein, over which, quite regardless, he had evidently been filling a powder-flask, still in his hand with the top unscrewed.

"Get down, gentlemen, get down. Jim, hold to the horse. Come in and take a cup of tea and an egg. I'm short of caps; that rascal of a boy, Jim, was after the snipe yesterday, down the hollow along. I'd orders for two dozen for Mrs Mare, and he's fired all away on me. Have ye ere a few ye can spare? I'm thankful to ye, sir."

"Well, Jem, what do you say? shall we take the Flat Rock ground?"

"No better, no better! them barchies over the rise of the hill beyond the pond has eight coveys, if there's one. Down Ponto, down I say; Juno lass shall have a bit. Look at her, gentlemen, there's a skin on her like silk; ye never saw a little pointer with a truer nose. It'll be a grand morning when the sun's up, and we's better be moving along."

"I've brought my setter, Rover, you know," said Wolfe. "Two dogs will be quite enough."

"Well, then, I'll be after taking Juno; a pointer's better on a hot day, though there's plenty of water everywhere. Hie up, lassie. Jack, catch up Ponto, and shut him up. All ready, gentlemen."

Poor Ponto! what a miserable, long-drawn howl it

was which stung our ears as we drove off. He knew just as well as we did that it was the first day of the season, and his true setter's heart had just been beating fifty to the dozen at the thoughts of the sport. It was a mercy to get under the lee of the grove of pines to shut out such distress from sympathising ears, and to urge the steeds fast over the five miles between Jem's house and the steep hill which winds down into the village of Tor Bay. At the bridge, over the noisy stream which bisects the deep valley, the road forks; the left running up into a great barren towards Portugal Cove, and the right, which we followed, leaning still coastwise. Just as we sprung the opposite rise, Jem shouted back from his gig—

"Hark to 'em, sir! hark to 'em! pull up a minute."

The weak report of a gun, and then another, about two miles distant, came murmuring down the glen.

"Hark to 'em, sir! that 's the Doctor's party; they must have camped out on the Cody's Well ground, and they 'll take the Indian-meal Barrens. They can't see yet, but they 're trying the guns, to make all right. Go ahead, sir."

Some fifteen minutes after this we turned to the left into a narrow rutty path, which led up the slope of the hill, thickly fringed with overhanging spruces and brushwood, all dank and dropping with heavy dew. About a mile of this natural shower-bath, brought another signal from Jem for a halt; the word to unharness was given, and we jumped out on a lovely bit of sward among the thickets. The dogs and guns seemed to shake themselves together by magic. Green, my man, had orders to find a camping-ground near a rill of water—no difficult matter in Fish-and-fog-land—and to have the kettle boiling by ten o'clock. Then spoke up Jem Strongback with authority—

"Now, Kiurnal, d'ye see the bare head of the hill above the bushes? we'll take all round that before breakfast; it's all open, lovely ground up there: hie in good dogs; steady, now, Juno lass, steady!"

It might have been a third of a mile through the wood, wetted through and through by the dripping ferns, while every now and then the sharp warning "kiar-kiar," of an old cock bristled every nerve with excitement, when the taller timber began to give place to a smaller more open undergrowth, and the white rock to be bare, save of the blue-berries and raspberries in the little chinks and knolls round its base. "Easy now," cried Jem, "easy now all; let the dogs hunt round a bit."

"Hist!" cried Wolfe, "hist! the dogs are drawing; steady, Rover, steady."

Is there a lovelier sight in all nature than to watch the faithful and intelligent servants of man, true to their instincts, exerting their innate, unseen gifts in his favour? Mark their quivering nerves, stiffening to the tips of their tails as the scent grows hotter, then pausing, thoughtful, or advancing step by step, towards the covey, concealed yet surely felt!

Round the gray rock they led us slowly, with fingers on the trigger, and then stood like the rock itself, a picture for the sculptor; right fore-paw balanced lightly, and every other limb and muscle rigid as a statue. The silence was sepulchral for that long long minute, until the very brain seemed dizzy with the strain; when—

"Whirr, whirr, whirr, whirr," on all sides; and the bang, bang, bang, of six muzzles dissolved the painful spell.

For my part I saw nothing but a cloud of white, rising in the low blue-berries between us and the brush-wood and whirling like lightning round the base of the rock. I fired, but with what result I knew no more than Adam. Not so with Wolfe and Jem.

"I covered one, I 'm certain," cried Wolfe.

"Oh! there must be a brace and a half of 'em in the trees; faith, I saw one tumble," rejoined Mister Jem.

"How many were there?"

"Fourteen, and the old cock, I believe; we ought to have had three brace; a splendid rise!"

"Good dog, Rover," cried Wolfe, as soon as he was reloaded; "seek, find, good dog."

"Hi in, Juno, lassie! seek him out," chimed in Jem; but not a feather could be discovered. The fact is, that the covey in the rise had wheeled suddenly round the rock, and we had all fired behind them. There was, of course, a great deal of protestation about birds lost, and then we thought it best to move on.

Quietly over the open behind the rock, stealing, crunching down the low fruit-laden bushes, and watching every sign of the dogs; suddenly, about two hundred yards on, Juno pointed to the right, and instantly again to the left.

"Hist!" cried Jem; "spread out a bit; the covey 's scattered here, and may be we 'll pick 'em all up. D'ye hear the old cock bawling?"

"Whirr!" from beneath his very feet, as he spoke, rose a bird, which he tumbled over; and at the report of his gun another, and another, which all fell to our mark; I missing my second barrel, and Wolfe wiping me neatly in a long shot. Just as the lower limb of the red sun rose over the horizon, our first birds of the season were stowed in our bags.

Over the woody crest of the hill, from knoll to knoll, we beat the ground carefully, rising four more coveys within a mile or so, and picking eight or ten birds out of them; when Rover, stopping short beneath a clump of birches on the edge of the copse, began circling round and round, until Juno took up the hot scent in the same way, without making anything of it. At last Jem called them off, "Gone, gone, Juno lass—gone I say. Captain, you call off Rover—he wont mind me." But not a bit of it; the dogs began increasing the circle of range, the scent if possible growing hotter, when suddenly Rover started straight off at right angles to a clump of raspberries, fifty yards away, and there stood like a rock. At the sound of our approach, a magnificent old cock rose to wing, with a "Ca, ca, ca," and was tumbled over by Wolfe or Jem, both claiming the bird. It was worth claiming, for a more splendid handful was never picked up. The scarlet tips over his eyes glistened like rubies, and his rich brown and purple plumage, with a tip of white here and there, from the glossy head to the spray feathers on his toes, bespoke the fine condition of the noble game. With what a thud the fellow came to mother earth, and what a handful he was to pick up! Stuff him into the bag over your broad shoulders, Wolfe, my friend; three or four brace of those beauties will make you smile again, as you breast the hill when the sun is up.

"Where the deuce and all is Juno?" cried Jem. "She 's on a bird, and I 've never se'ed her since Rover pointed the old cock. I'll tell you what it is, that old varmint has led us away from the covey, and Juno 's on 'em."

"Hi in, Rover, good dog! hark back here; seek 'em out."

We were standing in an "open" of low ankle-deep shrubs, mingled with seed-grasses, mosses, wild strawberries, and creeper-covered stones, all surrounded by knots of firs and lady birches, thickly fringed with drooping dewy ferns; and the dog, after snuffing around with nose high in air, led us through the thickest of the screen towards a rock, whose gray head was just visible over the highest branches. The boughs of the spruces were so close and tough that it was difficult to follow the dog; but at last we had our reward. On the nether edge Jem stopped with finger up, pointing with intense admiration to his beauty Juno, transformed into a marble Niobe. In and out among the stones and small brushwood ran a number of grouse-chicks, about a fortnight old, following the eager call of the mother, whose feathers shone like frosted silver in the slanting beams of the rising sun. It was as pretty a sight as one might well see on a shooting-tramp, and not the least to watch the eye of the dog, doubtless puzzled at our inaction at what, no doubt, she thought a wonderful chance. Probably the first brood had perished from wet or vermin, and the brave parents had set to work to rear another. The little ones ran round our feet quite fearlessly, and chirupped there, until the mother, hopping from stone to stone, wooed them away into the thicket; while we, whistling to the dogs, turned away in another direction, with a sad regret that the sapient old cock had fallen a victim to his paternal love and instinct.

Delicious as was the work and walk while the sun remained low, yet, when the dew was fairly lapped up from the grasses and ferns, the thermometer of our enjoyment gradually subsided, and at the same rate the birds disappeared. Wise in their own way, they sought the thick impenetrable spruce covers for shelter; and the light open birches and brushwood, their favourite haunts morning and evening, were deserted. After ten o'clock, by which time the heat was almost insupportable, we never saw a feather. The dogs began to flag visibly; and the moment we stopped to consult about our way among the tangled paths of the thicket, lay down at our feet with heaving sides and panting tongues.

"It's no good any more now," cried Jem. "Gentlemen, if ye'll stop here a minute I'll climb up that bit of a hill and look out for Green's fire."

Three minutes after we saw him on the top of the rock looking eagerly around seawards; then came a holloa to us, while his hand pointed the direction we were to take. In half an hour, from the crest of a bluff, we saw the blue smoke curling out of that vast sea of bush, and soon reached the little camping-ground, which had been well selected by Master Green. It lay under the lee of a huge moss-covered boulder, above which the spruces and lady-birches trembled in the breeze; while round its base there curled the clearest of rills, springing out of the ferns on the rise above. Before us the eye swept over hill and barren, meadow, copse, and loch, to the fishing-hamlets on the bluff coast, where the white-washed cottages confused themselves in the burning haze with the fishers' sails out on the opal sea beyond. Our little baskets of prog—hard-boiled eggs, cold tongue, fowl, and sandwiches, with a screw of salt—lay ready open, and the kettle on the embers gave out the fragrant essence of tea. We allowed no beer or wine on these expeditions until the sun was gone down; and Green had as much as he could well do to get a mouthful in the intervals of passing round the hissing kettle to us three hungry and thirsty hunters. But as all things come to an end, so did this luxury. Wolfe and Jem began to load their pipes, and, of course, to fight the morning's work over again. Every bird that had risen was discussed amid a little friendly jeering and jealousy. Amid that clatter, my head resting on a mossy stone, somehow one began to fancy that, across the haze of the burning air, the white boats of the fishermen, in the far distance, were wheeling together in a mazy dance. That was the last idea, ere the drowsy god passed his hand across the scene and shut it out of view.

One, two, three, four hours! impossible to believe, yet, looking at the sun, it must so have been. What was it startled us in our doze? for Wolfe was leaning on his elbow, looking eagerly about, and Jem, with his hand across his eyebrows, was peering right and left across the horizon. Ah! is that it? With a wild scream a flight of curlew, following their leader in wedge-like flight, dashed past almost over our heads; then wheeling here, there, and round and round as they distanced, pitched on the bare brow of a barren hill about half a mile off.

"My stars!" cried Jem; "catch up the dogs, Green; hold 'em tight, and don't let 'em stir. Come on, sir,—come on; we'll 'count for some of them chaps. Bully for me, but there's a flock of turkey ones!"

Down the hill we rushed full tear, and through the matted brushwood, until brought up sharp by the stream which roars and tumbles through the gorge. It was something to consider how to pass the whirling waters—deeper than the knee, and maddened by obstructing boulders. While we hesitated, glancing round for a good spot, Jem was on the grass clutching at his stockings.

"Faix," cried he, "I wish we had the Bishop here, to give us a hoist over."

"The Bishop! what on earth do you mean?"

"I mane the Bishop, gentlemen—Bishop Field—and nothing but him. I heard of one of my friends, who was out with him and the clargy, down the coast, on a confirming business; they was walking across from one station to another, when suddenly they comes to a stream like this, I take it. None of the parsons would cross. It looked nasty. So down went the Bishop on the stones, whips off his gaiters and socks, and turns round quite gaily—'Now then, gentlemen,' says he, 'which of ye will I lift over first?' They had to face it after that; and it very nigh swept them all off."

Could we do less than the Bishop? or follow the example of Jem's happy hit? In two minutes, with linked arms, we were battling amid the boulders, and in five more breasting the opposite slopes, until at last, pretty well blown, we stand steaming under the spot on which we guess the quarry had pitched.

"Easy, gentlemen; down on your knees—creep up—don't show," whispered Jem hoarsely, as he glided from stone to stone and from bush to bush, until he reached the very crest of the brow. His head was just on a level, and he was drawing the gun up stealthily to the poise, when away they all went about seventy yards ahead with a scream and a joyous whistle, contemptuous as it was shrill. Jem wiped his streaming forehead, and "darned 'em all" heartily in true colonial style. Many a chevy after the wary beggars I had afterwards, and never bagged one—no, not one. I could never manage to get within range, although about this time they are plentiful on the high barrens, flying from their breeding-grounds in the north of Newfoundland and Labrador to the swamps of Louisiana and Florida. But the boys of the town would sometimes stalk them successfully, for the little scamps could creep behind stones and stumps, which were "foolishness" to me or Wolfe. They generally found their way then to the hospitable table of the Governor. "Colonel," I fancy I hear the old gentleman saying now, "Let me send you one of these; ye ne'er tasted a better, I'll be sworn." Heigho! for the past; those were great birds, indeed, and so were the days when we ate them.

The word was given to go back for the dogs, and we faced the dense thickets again with parched mouths, after our useless climb. It was heavy work casting aside the tough branches; the sun was hot enough still to make such exertion unpleasant; yet, for all that, it made a little surprise, which there befell us, all the sweeter. Suddenly we burst through into a little clearing, not more than twenty yards across, in which there stood two or three wild cherry-trees loaded with fruit—perhaps such fruit as might have been despised in Covent Garden by the side of May-dukes or Morellas, but to us inexpressibly grateful with its little drop of sharp subacid in each cherry, no bigger than a red currant, and clear as the brightest of Bohemian glass.

"Now, cap'n," said Jem, when he had well cleared

his tree, "we have to make up for this bout; we'll take this side of the pond down to the road, and then to the big hill anent the sea. There's half a dozen coveys I knows of there."

All agreed. The dogs soon got their heads again, a sweet little breeze sprung up, and like giants refreshed we started for our evening's sport. Hard by the road which forks off to Cove and Cape St Francis, a small lake, fringed with alder and willow, and ribboned into little shady bays, receives the waters of the rill of our late bivouac. On the slopes above we were pressing through the dense wood, when Jem, who was leading, stopped, and with a gesture of his hand imposed silence.

"What is it?" cried Wolfe softly.

"Listen, Cap'n, listen!"

"Quack, quack, qua, qua, qua!" faintly heard, yet not very far off.

"Call in the dogs, whistle 'em in! Juno, lie down, down charge! go to heel, good dog!"

"Qua, qua, qua, qua," still more faintly, but the dogs caught it, and cocked their ears perceptibly. Down on our knees we dropped, parting the branches noiselessly towards the lake. Step by step, inch by inch, we crept towards the call. I lost sight of my friends behind a bush, just as we could see the gleam of the waters through the leaves and twigs; when suddenly, "bang" on one side, "bang, bang" on the other, put an end to my prospects of a shot. A terrible splutter, and then the quacking ceased for ever. With the end of a long stick, Jem fished on shore a brace of fine black ducks, with the blue badge on the wing. Except the canvas-back of the Potomac, there is no wild fowl equal to this fellow. They are highly prized in Newfoundland, not being over plentiful, and rarely seen except in pairs. Our prize was a great addition to the bag, and almost made amends for the fruitless chase after the curlews.

Across the road, laughing and talking, then down into a lane winding through the tall overhanging brushwood for nearly a mile, until, just at the ford of a little brook, where a few big stones were dotted here and there for crossing, almost beneath our feet sprang a covey, the gleam of their white wings being seen but for an instant as they topped over the low wood.

"Mark! mark! mark!" cried out one and all. "I see them," said Jem; "pitched just in a little hollow over them lot of firs."

"Humph!" said Wolfe, "that comes of talking, with dogs at heel, and not hunting."

"Who would have thought of meeting them here, right in the track?"

"You never can tell where they will be of an evening, they come out into walks and by-paths after the droppings, and especially where there's running water. Look out now," pursued Jem; "let the dogs go ahead a bit."

They led us up the side of a hill, at an angle of about 60°; and although it was evening, rivers ran from our faces ere we had breasted the top fairly. Here, among the fir copses, intersected with paths,

Rover and Juno tracked warily, noses to ground, but on the scent. Up one of these dark tracks, carpeted with generations of brown fir leaves, Wolfe and I followed the dogs; but as the scent soon grew less warm, I turned back quickly to try another, when, in a little clearing round a leafy corner, what should I see but Master Jem, the cunning old fox, gun to shoulder, in the very act of "potting" a magnificent covey, about fifty paces in front of him. Off went his barrels, and as it was too late I held my tongue, rejoicing, nevertheless, to see that only one bird out of twenty rose at the report with drooping wing; the shot had glanced off the well-protected coats of the others. Down bustled Wolfe with the dogs, and we quickly picked up three brace of the scattered tribe; the scent gradually leading to an open on the very edge of the cliff, whence we saw the long line of iron-bound coast towards St John's, dotted with the white fishing-hamlets, and their neat edgings of field and copse. As we circled round back towards the hill again, Jem stopped to listen, and backed the dogs with eager gesture.

"Look, Cap'n! don't you see 'em? there they hop; two, five, seven, ten—there!"

Wolfe strained his eyes, so did I, but all in vain.

"Where?" we whispered; "where? What are they?"

"Look!" said Jem; "do you see that grey, mossy stone, about a hundred yards ahead? the big one, just to the right of it,—there they hop."

Now we made them out, though not easily, so similar

was the colour of the birds to the ground they select to feed on. Warily we moved towards them, guided as much by the whistling of the plovers as anything else.

"Wait," whispered Jem, "wait; they'll clump up together, and then we'll fire; it's a long shot yet."

In about ten seconds more, bang went all the guns together. Four of the birds lay on the ground, and two or three of the rest flew away with trailing wing. Wolfe dashed after one; I after another, which disappeared suddenly behind a low boulder. Almost stumbling in my haste over the spot I expected to find the bird, I barely had time to draw up shuddering to see the stone projected half its short breadth over the perpendicular sea-cliff of four hundred feet, where, at the base beneath my amazed eye, true as a plummet-line, broke the hoarse Atlantic breakers. Some great landslip must have occurred here to undermine the guardian escarp of earth; one step more forward and the hand now holding the pen would have been hidden for ever beneath that boiling foam.

It was time to turn homeward; edging the woods as we walked, and picking up several birds among the open glades, to which towards sunset they always resort. By this time, after several smart shots between Wolfe and Jem, the former had bagged nine brace of grouse, and the latter eight-and-a-half. So when we crossed the road towards our shooting-ground of the morning, Master Jem said, carelessly enough as it were—

"Now, Cap'n, I tell you what, that's a desperate heavy wood to the right. If you take the road, and walk on about half a mile, the Kiurnal and I'll turn down into this bit of a path, and meet you round. Maybe we'll pick up a bird or two as we go."

"All right," said Wolfe, as he went off leisurely up the road to the left.

The moment he was out of sight, Jem dashed into the jungle path, and walked more than a quarter of a mile at the top of his speed. "Come on, Kiurnal," he cried; "we'll circumvent 'em this time." Beneath a sharp rise on our left he dashed head foremost into the thick wood, tearing through it, and climbing over the close-set obstacles as if his very life depended on it. All I could elicit was, "Come on, Kiurnal, come on; push up now, we're close on." At length, as he was grasping the trunk of a tree for a lift to a higher spot, not fifty feet from the brow above us went the "bang, bang," of a gun, and Jem dropped as if shot himself, crying—

"There's that d—— Cap'n a bin and got among the barches."

He looked as if he had been dipped into a bucket of water, yet up he jumped and sprang again at the saplings. "Come on, Kiurnal, or we won't get a shot at all,"—when again came the report of Wolfe's gun, as we struggled out of the confounded thickets, and, half-dead, half-blind, stood upon the edge of the open birch copse. Here it was that cunning Master Jem had intended to arrive first, for he knew that this was a favourite haunt of the birds at this time; and Juno took up the scent at once, first here, then there, now under this clump, now under that tuft; but all in vain, for the scent was blind; the birds had just left. To add to Jem's disgust, which served him right enough, there came farther off the crack of Wolfe's piece again; and Jem, wiping his flushed visage with a groan, exclaimed, "Oh, that cute old cuss of a Cap'n! who'd a thought he'd a been an' got in among the barches first?"

However, we did manage to pick up a few odd birds before the curtain of night became too thick to see; about which time we hit off to a nicety the spot where the lane and road met, and saw Green with the trap all ready for a start. I gave Jem a good nip from my flask,—not only allowable now, but very advisable; then, while I sat down to change wet shoes and socks, to my surprise away he started again, and in less than five minutes I heard him firing as hard as he could for several minutes. It was useless attempting to follow, as I could have seen a bird against the lighter part of the sky, and that was all. In a few minutes more he returned with two brace and a half of grouse. "Ah," said the old coon, "I guess I've done the Cap'n. I knowed there'd be a sprinkling in that old potato-garden. They often comes up close to the road just about now." As he spoke he fired off the blank charges of his gun, when at the report, from the ditch almost touching the nag's feet, up sprang a whacking old cock, and whisked away with a wag of his tail beyond ken in the gloaming. It was enough to make one dance with disgust to think of the hours we had tramped without seeing a feather, and now, with gun unloaded and only darkness visible, they were buzzing like mosquitoes all about one.

Ah! on the brow just above, there go the charges of Wolfe's gun as a signal to know where we are. We give him a hail, ringing loudly through the still night, and very soon, preceded by Rover, we hear him lumbering through the brushwood. While he takes off his wet toggery we count the birds and make up the day's sport. Seven and twenty brace of grouse, a brace of black duck, five plovers, with five brace and a half of snipe, make up the bag; of which the greater share fell to the superior skill of my friend. In spite of the luck of the old potato-garden, Wolfe had just managed to keep one bird ahead of Jem, though the latter said nothing about the failure of his dodge at the "barches." How Wolfe laughed as I told him the story; it was almost worth enduring that climb through the wood to see Jem's disgust, and Wolfe's sides shaking with the story after.

Twelve miles after a heavy day over a hilly road is weary work enough. When I had changed my shoes, and had taken a nip at the flask, I felt I could have started again and walked for hours. But long before we had reached the crest of the hill, whence Fort Amherst's light gleamed behind the city, now eclipsed by the tower of St Thomas' Church as we turned to the left, and now mingled among the long row of lights in Government House as we echelloned to the right, both

Wolfe and I were far in the realms of dreamland. I remember only a voice of welcome at the gate, with a hurried tale of our sport, before I was fast asleep again on the bear-skin spread before the hearth. And so ended the first day's shooting in the breezy woods and over the barrens of bright evergreen Newfoundland.

CHAPTER XV.

AUTUMN—A "WITLESS" EXPEDITION.

FREQUENT during the next few weeks were the meetings at Bakehouse Corner, and many other corners as well, for the comparing of bags, in which transactions all dozens were no doubt bakers' dozens, and something over. Anyhow, so completely riddled of game were the ten miles round the city by the end of that time, that in as many days we hardly got as many shots. No matter whether we tried a long trot round over the Three Barrens, or a tramp over the treadmill of Broad Cove, round the Virgin's Bosom or Petty Harbour bogs, it was all the same story in the end,—lots of dry bread to digest with precious little sack to moisten it. Thus it was that one evening, as we walked in Indian file across the bogs of the White Hills, Wolfe propounded the solemn verdict "that it wouldn't do at all." "The continual worry has driven the birds into the woods," said he; "we'd better try some other ground, and keep this for the end of the season again."

"What line do you propose?"

"I have heard that about thirty miles down towards Cape Race, beyond the Bay of Bulls, there is good open ground and plenty of birds."

"Good! why not make a three days' excursion and try it?"

"When can you start?"

"Say Wednesday, returning Saturday evening; it's moonlight."

Thus agreeing, home we jogged, tired and muddy, but better contented; for it is always a consolation, after an unlucky day, to cut out fresh prospects for quick realisation, and the more pleasant when unknown ground and scenery has to be explored. So it came to pass, that one o'clock on the next Wednesday afternoon found the well-laden shooting-trap before the door, while Rover and Ben, circling round the wheels with stiffened tails, defied each other with muttered growls. The good mare swept us out by the lovely road which aligns the river towards Waterford Bridge. We can trace its course for many miles on our way towards the Bay of Bulls by the woody banks running through an undulating country but half reclaimed on our right; while on the left the slopes stretch up to the breezy headlands, beyond which there is nothing but sea and cloud from this to Europe. We pass the turning to Petty Harbour, with its many lakelets running from one to the other through rocky gorges, not far from which, upon the sea-coast, one of the most curious natural phenomena existing is well worth going to see. It was after an easterly blow upon the lee-shore that I had the good fortune once to pass in a steamer and see the "Spout" in full blast. A perpendicular funnel through the cliffs, some twenty yards or so inland, and bent like a syphon towards the sea, receives the waters of each wave breaking upon the rocks. The waters rush up the orifice, in a shower of spray in the air, re-descending with a crash upon the rocks around. With astonishing regularity, at half-minute intervals, the spout blows like a petrified whale, forming a natural landmark for mariners impossible to mistake. Indeed, so jealous at one time were the pilots of their beautiful rival, that exclaiming, like the Ephesians of old, their craft was in danger, the excitement drove them to make an expedition to destroy it. It is supposed they did some injury to the funnel; but, nevertheless, when we saw it, "There she spouts again," was a sight as wondrous as novel. From this we ran gaily along a country road, winding in and out among lochs, fringed with rocks, and dark firs bending over the reeds lovingly wherever the waters shallow into little lonely bays. These are great places for duck and trout, and our wistful eyes followed Rover's movements, as he hunted in and out among the scrub along the water's edge.

Of a sudden, Green, my man, looking round, cried—

"And by the japers, is it Rover pinting there? and as stiddy as a rock he is."

A hundred yards or so back stood the dog looking straight into the ditch by the roadside.

"And there's Ben a drawing over the little bog

yonder, sir," cried the excited Green; "there's a covey there by the Holy ——"

"Bah!" said Wolfe, rising up and looking back, "we should have roused them as we drove past: it must be a musk-rat." So he began whistling and calling "Rover, Rover," but Rover never stirred, though I fancy his head bent a little towards the voice.

"It's birds," cried Green, "it's birds, sir; I see one now a-flying over the bush into the little bog."

Down jumped Wolfe, his barrels were loaded, and a very few seconds sufficed to fix them into the stock. As he drew up to the dog, ten or twelve birds rose out of the little ditch, Wolfe taking a brace out of them before they alighted on the further edge of the adjoining bog. I felt half crazy thinking that my own gun was not get-at-able, and the more when Wolfe began to draw on Ben's point at the edge of the bog. Up sprung the old cock with a "kur, kur, ki, kur, kur," right over our heads, untouched by the discharge, and then Wolfe followed the dogs again to the covey, not three hundred yards away, where he knocked over a third bird at the rise. He came trudging back with three young birds in his hand, and returned his barrels to the case. "Now, that's what I call a bit of luck," said he, striking a fusée for his pipe, "which won't happen every day. On you go."

Another brace of miles brought us to the top of the steep hill which leads down to the Bay of Bulls, a well-sheltered gap in the wall of sea cliff, of which advantage has, of course, been taken to form a good-sized fishing-settlement. Through the struggling town we drove, beneath the fish flakes, just like raised terraces for vines in sunny lands, stretching across the road, and upon which the whole population were mounted, busy in covering with bark the half dried fish against the dews of night. Beyond the opposite slope we came to another little bay, with another fishing-settlement. Why this should be called Witless Bay cannot be explained; perhaps it was a corruption of some old word; but it was our destination, and not to be despised on account of its appellation. The village lay snugly in a gap in the cliffs, with comfortable cottages promiscuously scattered about it, all with plots of cabbages inside the fences, and pigs and geese without. Above these in condition, on one side of the little bay under the shelter of the cliffs, rose the steeple of the church, while near a dark clump of firs the smoke of the priest's house mingled with the chimneys of the convent quite lovingly. In a few minutes we heard of a little hostelrie kept by Paddy Carey, at the end of a maze of lanes on the opposite side of the bay. I don't know how my trap survived the jolting of the big boulders on the path, but at last we arrived before the cottage, where Mr Carey himself, pipe in mouth and in his shirt-sleeves, was surveying the glories of his cabbage-garden. Behind him, through the open door, we could see a sort of bar filled with fishing-folk over their evening grog. To our demand for accommodation, the man took his pipe from his mouth, and with a long, blank stare said—

"Bee the holy, Barney! just to think, here's a purty, and the missus gone out till to-morrow."

"Well, but," chimed in Wolfe, "I suppose you have the beds all the same."

"Oh, oh!" cried Paddy, "Barney, my boy, what'll I do at all? the missus gone out till to-morrow."

"Never mind the missus, Mister Carey, I dare say we'll do very well."

"Och! come in, come in; bay all manes, gintlemen; we'll do the best for ye."

Inside we found, beyond the bar, a little dusty parlour, and above in a garret two bunks, the whole highly perfumed with cod-liver oil, in which Mister Carey was an extensive dealer. Green was to sleep before the great wood-fire in the bar, and by a good deal got the best of it. Ten minutes made us pretty snug under the circumstances, and rejecting Mr Carey's offer of salt cod and cabbage, we made out some tea with buttered toast, looked well to our guns, and turned in early.

There were ominous looking clouds coming up from the south-west when we roused at five o'clock. By six we had fairly started, with two native guides, to breast the steep hill beyond which our ground was said to stretch. Both took their "davies" to plenty of birds, predicting great sport on arriving at a certain "yellow mash" about eight or ten miles off. Over the crest of the hill on the cliffs the tract lay straight along the edge of little lochs, bordered by wood or bog; and we had not gone half a mile when, in the middle of a little brown barren, right from under our feet, up sprung a glorious covey of at least twenty birds. Before we could say "knife," they were over the brow and gone.

"That comes from talking," said Wolfe, taking his pipe out of his mouth, and putting it away; "serve us all right; what a covey! Oh yes, master Rover, you 're very busy now it 's too late; gone away, boy, gone away."

Away rattled the dogs ahead, and very soon I heard the crack of Wolfe's piece among the scattered covey, getting a shot myself at a good point from Ben among the brushwood. About a mile farther on, we flushed a covey, taking a brace out of it, and then two brace of old birds successively, knocking the whole of them over. It was now nearly eight o'clock, and we had done pretty fairly; but to our dismay the mist from the southward was steadily increasing, making the ferns and birches through which we passed terribly wet. Just as we were passing round the edge of a loch, a "Cra, cra, cra, cra," wild and piercing, brought us to a sudden halt. Peeping through the bushes, on a spit of sandy mud, about two hundred yards off, were five magnificent geese, calling to some of their acquaintance with outstretched necks, and telling them, no doubt, what a delightfully moist day it was. "Cra, cra, cra, cra, cra," screamed again the wild challenge over the wavelets of the dark loch, as anxiously we debated whether by any means we could get within shot. But not a particle of shelter was to be seen, and we watched them for mere fascination's sake, until, of a sudden, with louder screams, they rose in the air, and straight as an arrow, in long Indian-file, disappeared behind the misty woods of the far side of the loch. They were most likely young birds bred in the marshes about here, waiting by instinct for a signal from some flock passing down south from Labrador to the mighty swamps of Florida or Louisiana.

A miserable walk through driving mist, guns under arm, and head to ground, brought us to the edge of the "yallow mash," a great inland bog covered with a short jaundiced grass, extending for some eight miles on towards Killigrew's Barren, once across which, we were to fall in with game in any abundance. It looked uninviting, but manfully we pushed into the inland sea, often fetlock deep in mud and ooze. At this time, about eleven o'clock, there was not a breath of wind, and the misty atmosphere felt quite stifling; when, at a glint or struggle of the sun to make his number for the day, the bog became alive—literally alive—with the accursed black-fly. The more gallant the effort to pierce the gloom, the worse the pests became. Guides and all, it was nothing but muttered curses, with flap, flap, at each step or tumble forward; while very soon, necks, hands, and faces, ran down small rivers of blood. An hour's struggle at this horrid work was as much as any one could stand, the very tough-skinned guides themselves looked done up, and I caved in altogether. As to shooting, had a hundred coveys risen all round, not a trigger could have been pulled. Oh! for a breath of air! Oh! for a breeze to blow the accursed little devils away. But more stifling than ever came the atmosphere, and worse in proportion the attacks of our bloodsuckers.

"Where are we?" I cried at last to the guide; "how far now have we to go along this awful marsh?"

"Och! the sorrow o' me knows, yer honner; 'tis the flies is awful."

I could just see the burly figure of Wolfe looming along, head bent well down, some fifty yards to the left, and hailed him.

"Holloa! I can't stand this; I shall lay down and die soon; let's get out of it, for heaven's sake."

A minute after, as the mists on the right rolled up together like a folded curtain, we caught the glimpse of a high peak. "We must climb that, yer honner," said the guides, "to get rid of these bastes; 'tis the Boatswain's Look-out." With drooping heads we made for the bottom of the ascent. Up that horrid climb of three hundred feet, with rivers of red and white flowing from cheek, temple, brow, and neck, the demon flies followed us. The guides suffered just as much as we did, and the instant we reached the culminating point, a flattish rock surrounded by shrubs, rushed to make a fire and search for water. Thankfully we all sheltered under the lee of the smoke as it rose from the damp embers, and agreed that we had never enjoyed a cup of tea such as the kettle produced ten minutes after.

Before we had finished breakfast, a blast of wind swept across our elevated parlour, driving off the mists, and, to our joy, the flies as well. But the guides cried to hurry up, as we should have a deluge of rain upon us before long. It was decided to turn homewards, and give up shooting that day as a bad job. Before we had scrambled down the side of the hill to the "yellow mash" again, the rain, condensed from the fogs by the cold current of air, came down in a steady lash—bad enough, but paradise compared to the flies. Forming Indian-file, locks under arms, dogs with slouched ears and drooping tails, we tramped over bog and hill, those slushy, weary miles, back to the village of Witless Bay, after a very witless day's work—consisting of no sport, a precious mauling from the flies, and as honest a drenching as a man need well soak in. However, when we had peeled our soaking garments, and gotten within the embouchure of Mr Paddy Carey's kitchen-chimney, there to sniff up (like the famous Tom Codlin) the dinner preparing, our hearts revived. Mrs Paddy had, to Mr Paddy's great content, returned and effected a marvellous change for the better—concocting, moreover, a fragrant stew of fowl, potatoes, and cabbage, which went down uncommonly well. After that the guns had to be thoroughly taken to bits, wiped, and oiled. Then we enjoyed our tobacco inside the chimney, half-roasted by the huge logs of pine and birch; while villagers dropped in and out on the chance of a word of gossip, or a drop of rum *frigidum sine.* Thus we consoled ourselves for defeat, and pleasantly prepared to do good battle on the morrow.

It was well we did so; for, from beneath the eastern

horizon, to our joy, the morn broke gloriously upon nature, refreshed with the copious bathing of the previous day. In spite of oleaginous counsels, we decided dead against that accursed "yellow mash," and took the crests of the hills at once. Here we found open barrens, sprinkled every hundred yards or so with little copses of birch, fir, larch, and brushwood; and, as the run followed the contour of the cliffs, it dipped and rose into alternate little hills or dells. Before twelve o'clock we flushed among them eight coveys, and, with a fair sprinkling of scattered birds, picked out fourteen brace to our credit, reaching at last the extremity of a bluff, commanding a wide plain between us and the cliffs of the coast. The Atlantic, dotted here and there with a white sail, stretched north and south in one grand unbroken level—the sheen of the midday sun glistening on its face. The surface of the bluff was carpeted with blueberries, so thickly that one lifted the foot in vain to find a spot where the little plum-like fruit might not be crushed; anon sweeping into the hollow of the palm a hundred or so, with the pearly bloom on each berry, we fling them into our mouths as a stoker shoves coals into his furnace. Vast are the quantities of wild fruits, raspberries, cranberries, strawberries, quashberries, partridge-berries, stoneberries, found on the hills, barrens, and bogs of Fish-and-fog-land. They are brought into the city and villages to be jammed down roughly with molasses—a capital substitute for butter for the little ravenous fishers, during the long months when grass is not and milk itself is scarce.

Here we emptied the bags and proposed a halt for refreshment, when Wolfe, turning a sort of professional eye on the open broken ground below us, would have it that we ought to explore there first. "Chacun à son gout." I was dead beat, and, as a matter of course, the guide was of my opinion. "There 's sorra little in it," said he, throwing his bags on the ground with a welcome sigh.

"H'm," replied Wolfe, "it looks to me a promising bit, and it wouldn't take us half an hour; besides there's no woods for the birds to sneak into."

"Away you go, then, while Green and I make up the fire and boil the kettle—doubt if you get a shot."

Down stumped Wolfe and Rover, followed by the disgusted guide; while we, first carefully putting the game under a bush and covering it with ferns, began tearing up by the roots the rotten stumps of trees which had covered these hills many many years ago, and had probably perished by a conflagration. Of this tinder-dry wood there was any quantity at hand, and a glorious pile of it was soon heaped on the very brow of the bluff. Then Green, making a little scientific aperture underneath, opposite the breeze, stuffed the hole with dried grasses, little twigs, with a bit of paper "afore all," as he styled it; and now, striking a match with the heel of his boot, touched the tender spot, fanning the first weak kindling with his own natural bellows. Crack went the twigs; crack, crack, responded the thicker boughs inside; and Green soon rose from his knees with "Faix, it'll be a glorious foire; an' it's a pity we have niver a pertaty to put into it!" He filled the kettle from the little rill in the bushes, while I piled on stump after stump until the smoke rose into a very cloud overhead, to cause, it may be, many a sailor far out at sea to wonder then at the great fire which sprung up suddenly on the blue hills of the distant coast.

Ay! it was delicious, this hour of utter *abandon* on the sunny hills, free from dust, or dirt, or sign of weary toil. The very crackling of the flame tickled the ear with an idea of independent comfort, as if home in its best enjoyment could easily be set up here. It lasts too short a time, and is too dependent on such weather, this Crusoe luxury; but the brief hour of its lasting is a compensation to balance the miseries of many longer periods in the grind of daily life, as most men have it.

"Pop," faintly from the distant plain below, and yet another "pop." Out ran Green from behind the lee of the fire, and pointed out the two little puffs of blue smoke which marked Wolfe's presence in the bushes.

"He's missed him, sir;—be the holy! he's missed him. I sees him a-wheeling down to the firs to the right. Och! look at him now; he's a wheeled off this way;—look at him, sir; here he comes: thunder! how he's rising."

I caught sight of the bird at last, as Green said, rising over the bush about half a mile off. Up he towered, up, up, up; until at last, with a gentle flap or so of his wings, he dropped like a parachute among the dense brushwood, and was lost to view.

"Go and get him, Green; you see where he fell, just by the big white stump: anyhow I'll guide you when you're down there."

"Sure, sir, an how'll I git him at all? shall I take the gun and have a drive at him?"

"Pick him up, man, he's dead."

"And is he dead at all! sure he flew well enough."

"You'll find him dead enough; look alive, and we'll surprise the Captain when he comes up."

Down tumbled Green over the rocks, till he got among the scrub on the level, when, guided by my handkerchief, I heard a faint triumphant shout, and soon after he was climbing the hill again, with a splendid old cock in his hand.

"Sure, sir," said he, "it's a mishtery to me what's killed him, for his wings and body is as roight as the day he was born."

Separating the fine feathers at the back of the head, I showed him the smallest trace of blood. A pellet, only one, had struck the bird somewhere near the brain, its action not felt until some seconds had elapsed as he flew away from the fusillade. Then he began to tower, up, up, until consciousness and strength ceasing, he fell gently back to earth. It was a wonder there was no hawk on the watch to snap him off before the sportsman's eyes, as is often the case, they understanding the law of the thing by the flight of the quarry just as well as we do.

"Hang him on the stump, Green; here comes the Captain, and we'll hear what he says. Well, what luck?"

"H'm," replied our friend, "a precious climb; and I was never more deceived in my life with ground."

"What! did you bag nothing after all that tramp? We thought we heard your bark several times. Here, take this mug of tea. Eh?"

"Did you? H'm, then it was some one else shooting, I suppose. I only fired twice; knocked a bird over as dead as a door nail, but though I searched till I was sick of it, the place was so thick I couldn't find him."

Just then Green, the gaffer, laughed with a sly glance at the bird on the tree. Wolfe guessed at once how it was, and coughed over his tea as he said—

"H'm, you picked him up, eh? Did he tower? I thought he might; how far did he fly?"

"About a moile, or a moile and a half, sir; and you might have been looking for him all day where you thought you knocked him over."

"H'm," growled Wolfe.

"Yes, sir; and you see it's us as lighted the fire and bagged the bird after all."

So then we all laughed, ate and drank like hunters, lay back for a chat over our morning's work, and cantered gaily into the region of happy dreams, while the soft sea-breeze sighed over our heads, and curled the smoke as it rose from our fast lessening fire. Too swiftly sped the time of that rude outspanning, with all wants, to make us equal to princes of earth, around us in mock simplicity.

Too short, too short, such minutes. A colder whisper of the breeze roused us to business again. The dying embers of the fire were scattered in safe places, and the guides told to take us a good round homewards. We were jealous of losing a moment of that delicious autumn afternoon, or a yard of that springy barren, covered with wild flowers, leading on through thickets to other little barrens, where the presence of man was noted only by a worn thread across, and otherwise just as nature made it. Here we were sure of a point or two, and always rose a covey at the sunny corners of the dwarf juniper thickets, almost stiff enough to walk over.

At last, with just sufficient light to tumble down the slopes, we reached Paddy Carey's hostelrie again, and turned out some weighty bags upon the kitchen table. We counted over five-and-twenty brace of grouse, besides other sprinklings, by far the lion's share of which belonged to Wolfe. We had intended to double our bag the next day, now that we had our hands in; but, before turning in, a look out from Paddy's cabbage-garden over the sea told of a cloud of driving mist gathering in the south; a warning to all who had had experience of the "yellow mash," not to be neglected. So, thankful that we had nicked one glorious day out of the ruck, we packed the bags, and harnessed for St John's, not the worse or sorry for our adventures amid the hills and mists of Witless Bay.

Shall I go on, or is the reader wearied of our joyous days over the countless barrens and thickets which surround St John's on all sides? Alack! day by day the line of light grew narrower, and bid us turn our steps homeward sooner and sooner. There is neither time nor space to tell a thousandth part of these bright beads strung on memory's chain. As eyes grew surer, and wind stronger, so the days and the birds decreased together; though each white feather, dyed for winter's fashion, added weight and plumpness to the noble game. Still about the beginning of November they were very scarce indeed; a point from Ben or Rover was a point indeed then not lightly to be missed. Rarely then we heard the plaintive cry of the American robin, "Oh! poor Captain Kennydy—Kennydy! oh! poor Kennydy—Kennydy!" And bitter cold were our drives home ere, twinkling in the far distance, we caught the first glint of Fort Amherst light, the herald of approaching warmth and comfort.

And yet there was a reprieve in store for us we could little have expected. Suddenly at this time spring appeared to break again upon the desolation of nature. The cold moist grays dissolved into tints of beauty, almost worthy of Naples. The cattle left the close stalls to browse the scanty herbage, and the birds of passage, in flocks along the shallows of the lakes, might be seen at sunset preening their wearied feathers. Sweet are the words of a modern poet singing of these fairy moments of the Indian summer:—

"What visionary tints the year puts on
When falling leaves falter through motionless air,
Or numbly cling and shiver to be gone!
How shimmer the long flats and pastures bare,
As with her nectar Hebe Autumn fills
The bowl between me and those distant hills,
And smiles and shakes abroad her misty, tremulous hair!

. . . .

"How fuse and mix, with what unfelt degrees,
Clasp'd by the faint horizon's languid arms,
Each into each, the hazy distances!
The soften'd season all the landscape charms;
Those hills, my native village that embay,
In waves of dreamier purple roll away,
And floating in mirage seem all the glimmering farms.

"Far distant sounds the hidden chickadee
Close at my side; far distant sound the leaves;
The fields seem fields of dream, where Memory
Wanders like gleaning Ruth; and as the sheaves
Of wheat and barley waver'd in the eye
Of Boaz as the maiden's glow went by,
So tremble and seem remote all things the sense receives.

"The cock's shrill trump that tells of scattered corn,
Passed breezily on by all his flapping mates,
Faint and more faint, from barn to barn is borne
Southward, perhaps to far Magellan's Straits;
Dimly I catch the throb of distant flails;
Silently overhead the henhawk sails,
With watchful, measuring eye, and for his quarry waits.

"The sober'd robin, hunger-silent now,
Seeks cedar berries blue, his autumn cheer;
The squirrel on the shingly shagbark's bough,
Now saws, now lists with downward eye and ear,

Then drops his nut, and with a chipping bound,
Whisks to his winding fastness underground ;
The clouds like swans drift down the streaming atmosphere.

" O'er yon bare knoll the pointed cedar-shadows
Drowse on the crisp, gray moss ; the ploughman's call
Creeps faint as smoke from black, fresh-furrow'd meadows ;
The single crow a single caw lets fall ;
And all around me every bush and tree
Says Autumn's here, and Winter soon will be,
Who snows his soft, white sleep and silence over all."

What more? One thing, a little word on health, that chief of blessings. When, on a bleak, snow-threatening afternoon about the beginning of December, after many a feeble day's work latterly, we made up our minds that all was over for this season, and gave the guns their final oiling, we could have walked from sunrise to sunset without a thought of fatigue. Those glorious rises over the boundless hills, breathing in from their tops the pure Atlantic breezes day after day, had toned us down into a first-rate fighting trim. One could see by Wolfe's clear blue eye, elastic step, the tone of his handsome face, and the grasp of his hand, that all was well within. Long may it be so, old friend, now far away! and if you ever read these recollections, pat Rover on the head for my sake. As I write these last words Ben is sitting at my feet: I look down into his hazel eye, pass my hand over his big silken head, and cry for fun, "Kur, kur, kur, kur; seek him out." Ah! how his eye glistens, and his tail moving slowly to and fro intimates in his own way, "I know, I know." And I love him all the more that his spirit can pass with mine back upon those misty, sea-girt barrens which we have often trod so patiently, so lovingly together. "Down charge, old boy! down charge!"

CHAPTER XVI.

"THE ODD TRICK AND THE RUBBER"—
SOCIAL AND POLITICAL.

WE were now called upon to enter a widely different campaign to the one which had so pleasantly concluded. One morning, about the beginning of December, the first spat of snow was on the ground, and over its pure surface we tramped down Water Street to the bank, to do a little business and pick up the news. As the red-baized guardians noiselessly swung behind, the brave banker himself left off a consultation with his cashier in a brass netted bird-cage, and came forward to greet us.

"Walk into my parlour, do; glad to see you. His Excellency is inside; Mr Green will draw out the forms; pray walk in."

Doffing our caps to the fine old British gentleman who represented Her Majesty in England's Ancient Colony, we entered the sanctum replete with the fate of almost every man of note in it. Little flies and big flies, mosquitoes and blue-bottles, all had to come sooner or later to the presiding spider behind the green table here, when he sucked a drop or two from each *en passant*, and so grew more genial and pleasant daily. It was thus he picked up all the gossip, and knew the interest of the community *seriatim;* no small matter professionally, and not the less convenient socially, in a place to which the mail only came in winter once a-month. But the spider, as I said, was a genial spider, and if he sucked, as his duty bid him, he always did it pleasantly to his victim's feelings.

Pleasantly! shall I tell you how pleasantly? Surely as the hand of the clock daily passed the mark of eleven, the towering form of the noble old Governor would be seen gaining inch by inch down the steep hill from St Thomas' Church, halting nowhere until he reached the one small chair in the banker's little parlour. There, no matter what was going on—what monetàry convulsions were exciting change — what domestic anguish was racking his upper stories—what calls pressed, or messages awaited urgent replies—the banker gave up that hour to the amusement of his aged friend. That unselfishness and sacrifice (and it was no light one either) on the banker's part, was simply life to the old gentleman. The remaining twenty-three hours of his existence he passed in a great uncongenial residence, half palace, half work-house, in look at least, where a cricket chirping in the kitchen might easily have been heard in the attics. Few can understand, except men who have lived in colonies, the desolation of spirit which (in the very midst of society) the Queen's representative may feel;

always fearful, while seeking natural and social sympathies, of stepping out of the uncompromising path so indistinct between dignity and urbanity. Very guarded in choosing his society must he be; and many a one, after the first mistake is discovered, are driven back into their own solitary thoughts during the remainder of their prætorships. God speed the banker that thus it was not with our own much-valued chief.

"I was just remarking to his Excellency," quoth our friend, "when you came in, that I expected a good many of the whist-club would drop in on me to-day; the first snow, sir, is our signal to commence."

"I wish, wi' a' my heart, I were young enough to join ye, gentlemen. Where do ye begin yere meetings?"

"Well, sir, we ought to offer the President of the Council the first chance."

"He 'll plead to a certainty his poultry 's too young."

"And there 's none arrived yet from Halifax, or I 'd offer my own house," said the banker.

"If that 's a', banker, I 'll send ye a turkey and a dozen of port," said the Governor; "some of that cask Walter Grieve imported for us. It 's vera fine."

There was no getting out of this, and we clinched the bashful banker on the spot with much clapping of hands. Next morning, Michael, our trusty old waiter, who was anxiously expecting a summons, might have been seen with a slip of paper in his hand tramping round the town and its suburbs to sound the welcome note that our jolly winter gatherings were fairly launched again.

Certainly to be lost amid the fogs, and quartered amid the silence of eternal snows for a stretch of four or five months at a time is a part of his education which an Englishman seldom calculates on. To have society, among men at least, one must have something to meet upon common ground as it were, even though it be but an excuse for joining a social gathering. No doubt, there are many more sensible and elevating things than a sixpenny rubber. The study of chemistry, readings from Shakespeare, chess, *cum multis aliis*, may each have its votaries; but none of them combine that happy mixture of the *otium cum dig.* with that demand on skill and memory combined, which so rapidly develop themselves during each encounter. There was always a certain amount of groaning and pious exclamation among the ladies when the club was about to open; but the sensible among them rejoiced at the possibility of banishing ennui from brows which, now and again, after hard work for daily bread, needed the wholesome relaxation.

So, in spite of the frowns of worthy wives, the club was formed of sixteen members, heads of families, sober and substantial, good fellows every one of them, and good neighbours one to the other. Each Monday during the snow-bound months the meet took place at the house of a member drawn by lot, until each had had his turn; when, if the snow would not melt, there was another draw for an extra night or two. Punctual as the clock struck seven, the lobby of the host steamed with the evaporations of our half-frozen wrappers;

thence we were duly ushered into a side parlour for an attack *en passant* on tea and its pleasant belongings. Not always, in truth, was the attack a slight one, for we were all early diners, *selon le coutume ici.* They have still good old-fashioned ways in the Ancient Colony, one of which is the manner of giving that tea. "Fair Margaret, in her tidy kirtle," presided behind the hissing urn, or the kettle hummed on the hob of the cheery fire. Mrs Joslyn, of the lake-farm, always knew when the club met; her orders through the winter always running, "for Mondays of a sure, sir," for the best of cream, butter, and chickens. Then, besides, one lady was famous for her coffee, another for her brown bread, and another for her pound-cake; and the host would be sure to observe the affront to his wife if the well-merited attention to each was neglected. Truth to say, there was little need to press his guests, most of whom would dally round the pleasant table until one of the elders called us to order. "You 're wanted to cut in, sir," was the awful summons from our senior magistrate to the last lagger, until all were round the green cloth; the four highest playing together, than the four next; when from that moment until eleven, except in the shifting of partners, or a burst of indignation at some outrageous play, silence worthy of a nest of conspirators was the rule. But about that hour a manifest uneasiness began to prevade the assembly. An appetising fragrance to one-o'clock-diners has begun to steal in from unknown parts of the house; while sundry clinking noises about the passages, suggest the possibility of trumping your partner's best card in the confusion of ideas. Michael, the waiter, rushes in and collars the chairs of the first quartette who finish their *parti*, and then whispers a mysterious word to our host, which being interpreted means, "that the cook is ready to dish up." Gradually the cards are thrown up, and we gather round the fire to await the grand signal; while with much dignity our senior member passes his snuff-box to such as are on his list for enjoying that honour. To him, of course, all honours are in return paid, when the folding-doors are thrown open; and the well-lighted room, with a long table right royally spread, bursts into welcome view, groaning beneath the weight of a substantial British supper, concerning which our rules were impartially strict. No kickshaws, or champagne, or sweets, were ever permitted. "Four dishes with vegetables," was the rule; but the rule was not without elasticity in its operations. The four dishes were dishes indeed worthy of a general's inspection-dinner, and a soldier's ideas of good fare need go no further, if indeed they could. A noble turkey, never under sixteen pounds, generally faced the president, while a splendid wild-goose did the same graceful homage to the vice; we had, nine times out of ten, roast ducks and chicken-pie as sidesmen; a real York ham and stewed oysters just to balance the table; and two pyramids of mashed potatoes browned to perfection. Stilton cheese and celery followed as a proper incentive for the "materials," with a kettle straight from the hob in better tune than ever, and lemons, if procurable.

Now, what think you of that for a supper, my friend? and, mind you, all of the best—of the very first chop quality, and no country in the world to beat it? But yet of all the dishes the *chef par excellence* was the "wild goose," and many an extra night did we nick during the season on the strength of discovering one of our members still possessed a specimen of that *rara avis, nigroque simillima cygno;* literally true. In other lands my experience of the bird had been decidedly fishy; so not less was my amazement to see the carver draw his knife across a breast of the depth of an aitch bone, and with slice after slice help his sixteen friends generously off the same. It was even come and cut again with a lucky few, until he offered the skeleton to the last hungry inquirer. To taste was to be satisfied at once of its merits, and to drop your fork with a sigh to your neighbour as you whisper, "A royal bird, sir! a royal bird, indeed!"

The fact is, that these noble, swan-like bipeds are wild in their breeding, but farm-yard in their rearing. When fledgings, with the soft down blossoming thickly, they are taken from the nest in considerable numbers. The vast bogs and marshes round Cape Race yield the greatest harvest, where they are chiefly reared by the farmers for the St John's market. So highly are they valued, that in the spring time the village girls make regular excursions to the reeds in search of the eggs, which are brought home with glee for a novel kind of incubation. By day, wrapped in wool, they are suspended in the bake-pots near the open fires; and by night, transferred to the ladies' stockings, they enjoy the warmth of their virtuous couches, smuggled away in unmentionable corners. The little gobbler babes, thus strangely invited to life, are diligently hand-fed by the maidens, and each autumn exchanged into bright ribbons and shawls, or it may be luxuries for Christmas cheer. About the beginning of October the boats from the south and south-west begin to haul in to the metropolitan wharfs of the merchants, laden with ocean spoils; and not a boat but what brings up its tribute of wild geese as well, the birds about three-quarters grown. They are eagerly purchased for 7s. 6d. to 10s. a bird, and soon become domiciled in the poultry-yard, whence many a time the hoarse sunset screams of the gander, on our return homewards from autumnal strolls, have suggested pleasantly the approach of those social gatherings over which the owner was honourably to preside. With a sharp lemon sauce and proper roasting, there is nothing in the feathered tribe to excel this noble game; and at his sacrificial festivities we may heartily drink success to the fair damsel who nursed him to maturity, in a generous libation of that whisky-toddy with which our merry party always concluded.

But stop, not too fast; before the kettle steams on the table, we have to discuss our cheese, port, and celery, the two last items in Fish-and-fog-land as important as Johannisberg or Tokay to a scion of the house of Hapsburg. Ah! you may smile, gentle reader, in more favoured climes. Your smile is not unnatural; yet if you lived in a place where the green herb was hidden for months at a time, you would relish the crispness of a bite of celery as much as if you were a cow turned out on spring grass, after a winter's stabling on musty hay. It is the more precious here because it is rather a chary thing to grow, arising partly from grubs, partly from want of skill. Just after the first snow has fallen, the produce is dug up and carefully replanted in sand in a frost-proof cellar, whence it comes to table as fresh as from a market-garden at home. Towards the end of spring it is indeed a treat; and it was always a point of honour with those who had gardens to see that the host of the whist-club-night was amply provided. "Gentlemen," cried he at the head of that social table, often enough, "Gentlemen, I need hardly tell you where that celery comes from, I am sure. Nothing but Rostellan could produce its equal." It was but a natural consequence to take an extra half-glass of port to the health of the jovial owner of that property, as a vote of thanks, on such a hint.

And port—good genuine port merits a word of notice *en passant*, does it not? They vow it is not the same port in quality which used to reach them thirty years ago. I cannot say, but generally the tap was good, often very fine. Not that strong, heavy clerical fluid which does duty on nine out of ten dining-tables in England; but rather a lighter, less fruited, and more delicately-bodied vintage; yet as true a port as would satisfy the requirements of the old Royal Duke.

Formerly this wine, coming over from Portugal in the returning fish-vessels, could be had here for eighteen shillings a dozen; in these degenerate days it runs from fifty to sixty shillings! There was a good trade then from St John's to many other ports with this return produce for their fish, but it has entirely disappeared, and only enough is introduced for the small demands of the colony itself. Newfoundland port was once a byword in the world, as well known as Cliquot or Allsopp. In Newfoundland alone now are its virtues still cherished.

Enough of the "choicest" of our merry suppers, and enough. See Michael has the glasses round, while the rosy wine itself is thrust ignominiously to the centre of the table. The kettle sings a "charge your glasses, gentlemen, quick, quick, quick! while the water's hot, hot, hot, gentlemen!" in a tune which loosens all tongues to a chorus with him. For twenty brief minutes there is a babel of jokes and laughter round, while sly shots upon weak points, whether of fish or potatoes, fly like hail across the table. Ehew! our grey-bearded senior member has finished his one magisterial rummer, precisely as the silver tongue of the pendule behind him notes the first half hour of a new day gone; he is slipping silently away behind our host's chair, with his hand deprecating the syren's call for "just another thimblefull, sir." It is a signal for departure, as little to be neglected as the order for a well-disciplined regiment to "lodge arms" and break-off on parade; so there is a scramble into pea-coats, goloshes, and mufflers on the spot. Ah! what a blast of cold is that which searches through the door, as the outer porch opening reveals just a glint of the eternal white covering of earth. It must be faced, there is no use shirking it. Wolfe and I, with any one else going our way, plunge heavily into it head downwards, chatting the evening over again as we slowly plough homewards. Never by any chance in the streets of the town do we ever meet a living creature, hear the bark of a dog, or the whine of a restless child. The houses are sealed by double windows, and animal life is deep under shelter from the pitiless breath of nature. By the Baker's Corner we say "Good-night! good-night!" Sometimes in the deep silence around I have fancied the dark South Side Hills across the frozen harbour have whispered solemnly again those friendly farewell words.

Once during the gusty political winter of 1863, when parties, pretty evenly balanced, were trying their strength together in the Assembly, our little club was nonplussed by the absence of its members, many of whom wrote M.P.P. after their sponsorial titles. Dissension ran so high that they could rarely slip away before nine or ten o'clock; while one Monday night Michael had actually announced the supper without the M.P.P.'s putting in an appearance. This might be nothing extraordinary in Westminster; but in Fish-and-fog-land, where primitive and seasonable hours for business matters still prevailed, it certainly was. So, on leaving our entertainer's roof, we voted that we should go up to the House and find out what was stirring. It must surely be a matter of deep and vital importance as could warrant the half of such a goose as we had just left being discussed in the kitchen; and yet, prepared as we were for something picturesque, the imagination fell short of the reality as the great scarlet folding-doors silently relapsed behind us. In front we beheld a large well-lighted hall, railed off for about one-third of its length from the *oi polloi*, whose chosen representatives, divided into ministry and opposition, or ins and outs, by the simple test of religion, were ranged at little desks on either side, with a long table for the lawyers in the centre. Above all, at the far end, raised three steps over the floor, sat the black-gowned Speaker in a commodious arm-chair, his face gazing intently at the ceiling, and his thoughts far away in the land of dreams, probably fancying that he was cleaving the clouds on the back of a wild goose,—a natural suggestion caused by the noisy declamations on his right, and the pleasant supper he had missed. Down beneath the hollow of his little desk, where his knees usually had refuge, the Premier, leader of Responsible Government, was snugly stowed away with a candle reading "Aurora Floyd;" while the nearest member had his feet on his desk far above the level of his head, in an attitude very tempting to any one with a flexible cane "handy to him." The rest of the honourable members on both sides of the House were asleep in the various attitudes usually adopted when enjoying that luxury in a chair, with one notable exception on the opposition benches. This gentleman, gifted with stentorian lungs of about a thousand horse-power, aided by the bass of a tremendous fist upon his desk, resounding in strokes of about thirty to the minute, like the booms of a distant gun, was doing his best to weary out the Government by a side-wind in speaking against time upon some unimportant motion. It was on the proposition that in future, to prevent imposition, no further reward should be paid for the skins of wolves (which it was shrewdly supposed were purchased and brought to the colony), that this chosen lawmaker thus held forth during the first five minutes of our entrance:—

"And now, sir" (this to the snoring speaker), "I ask you, I ask you (thump) to put this momentous question to this Honourable House, whether, under the mighty considerations submitted to them (thump) by honourable members, whose voices, silent now, may still be heard in other forms (thump); whose voices have been heard, I say, in defence of this amendment; I ask, sir, shall it be said, shall it go forth to the world through the press, through the talk and scandal of this amphibious community, nay, through the medium of the gallant officers (here he winked at us) who, I perceive, have just entered the strangers' gallery, that we, the responsible Parliament of this colony, ever consented to the wolf wearing his own skin (thump), when the poor out-harbourman, the starving fisherman (thump, thump), the slave, the victim (thump) of the present rotten (thump), nefarious (thump), undermining system (thump) of the Government, sir, now in power (thump, thump, thump), requires that skin for his own use and that of his little ones (thump)? And, sir, I will maintain before these unprejudiced strangers, I will call upon them hereafter to bear me witness (thump), nay, I will call upon high heaven itself to record its testimony (thump), that nothing that I have heard from the cringing lips of any honourable member of that Government (thump) has given me the faintest idea, or left a particle of wisdom on my mind (thump), that the wolf would prefer wearing his own skin, when that instinct, which nature has engrafted in the bosoms of all wild animals, is teaching it that its warmth, its comfort, are necessary during the rigours of our winter to the children of the poor starving fisherman (thump). Howl, howl, ye winter winds! weep, nature, weep! Vain man it is alone who outrages thy solemnity! vain man who, dressed in a little brief orthodoxy, plays such artistic tricks before his idols as makes the—the—very angels smile in pity! Ah! the honourable member starts, he twists, he writhes, he is uneasy in his dreams; what mean those hollow moans? does he think the angels are bending over him, and taking his confession? And is he lamenting, as well he may, how he, a veritable wolf in sheep's clothing (thump), year by year at the head of the long processions of temperance bands, on the first of May, loudly proclaims the sin of touching a drop of honest liquor, which is not in the commandments, and yet if a stray ship comes in of a Sunday, and wants her coals quick, sets to work with a will for the dollars—the dollars, sir (thump), regardless of the holy day, which I believe *is* (*thump, thump*) mentioned in the Commandments? I ask you, sir, would the wolves do this? Do they strain at camels, and swallow gnats? or *vice versa*, whichever it is, for it comes to the same in the end. Would the very ourang-outangs who take the young negresses—but what do I see? Ah! something rotten in the state of Denmark! does the good lady wish to know where her liege lord is? Ah! a message from the Upper House, which he knows too well to refuse! Is the honourable member sleepy, and is he about to retire to his domestic happiness? will he really not stay a little longer! Alas! poor Yorick! Ah! what sight is this which meets my gaze? Horatio, did his highness say—angels and ministers of grace defend us!"

The bold speaker checked his torrent of wordy nonsense for half a minute, fairly bewildered by astonishment, as well he might be. A boy had brought a note to the Premier, but not a summons home as the wild orator hoped. It was to inform the leader of the government that his mattress and blankets, for which he had sent, were outside. Forthwith the Premier closed the fascinating pages of Miss Braddon's clever story, blew out his candle, and released himself from the little cupboard under his desk. Whispering to an honest, old, white-bearded, wintry member, who, stroking that beard and laughing, followed him out; in a few minutes they were seen returning into the House with mattresses over their shoulders, which were thrown down by the little desks, and prepared for a night's occupation. Several other Government members followed their example, which plainly said to the silly tactics of the Opposition, "talk away as much as you like now, we're very comfortable, and mean to see you out, my bucks." And see them out they did with a vengeance. We of the whist-club went home to our quiet beds, with a joke or a sigh over the folly of Responsible Government in a community of a hundred thousand souls, or thereabouts, three quarters of whom were ignorant, superstitious fishermen. We thought an hour or so more at most would finish up the wolves, and their butchers too. But next day, at one o'clock, on passing by, the doctor's merry voice, as he rattled along in his gig, cried out—

"That fellow is still speaking. Go up to the House and look at the sight!"

"What! the same member still at it? impossible!"

"Fact! never stopped since yesterday four o'clock!"

"Is it possible! well, there'll be pickings for you out of this."

"Ah! ah! likely enough; good morning;" and away went the cheery gleaner of five-pound notes from young husbands at a swinging pace round the Baker's Corner.

We went up to the House at once. The area in front was half filled with the rowdies of the city, while the people's gallery was crammed with that ilk. They more than fancied the Government was to be beaten; and the out-harbour folks would see it recorded in large capitals that the reaction had set in at last. He of the giant lungs, whom we had left speaking at midnight, was still hammering away his incoherent stuff; not with the force of Nasmyth smashing at a coil of iron at a white heat, but now rather with the still, deliberate, measured blows by which the same ponderous engine will drive a nail slowly into a beam. The hand which imitated the hammer was now leaning heavily on the desk for support, and the whole framework of the man seemed loosened. Still he talked, talked, talked, though no one listened. The mattresses of the members were rolled up under the desks ready for another night if necessary; and the Premier's unshaven face wore a look of invincible determination. He certainly had the best of it. He had had his sleep and breakfast after a fashion, and the odds were heavy against his antagonist. We nodded to our friends among the members, looking miserable enough at their desks, and smiling as they cast up their hands and eyes in disgust at the situation. However, two hours after that, passing by the House again, we saw a stream hurrying out of the doors, and learnt, as they rushed past, that it was all over at last. The giant had just caved in from pure exhaustion, and the Speaker instantly calling a division, the matter was settled in a trice. The wolves saved their skins, so far as the reward for them was henceforward to be *nil*;

and, no doubt, he of the hammer-lungs would have had a hardish fight to save his own had he been left to the mercies of the indignant matrons whose last night's rest he had so unceremoniously disturbed, and who received now the extraordinary explanation of the cause from their disgusted spouses.

This was a farce, a miserable farce, played to annoy the Ministry by an Opposition, many of whom were heartily ashamed afterwards of their share in the transaction. But it was followed very soon by another rumpus, which demonstrated in a more serious way the low ebb to which sound public opinion had fallen (if, indeed, respect for such a thing existed at all), and placed the legislators of Responsible Government in a far from enviable position. The story may briefly be told thus:—

The Upper House of the Colony is composed, let us say, of Messrs A, B, and C, and called the Legislative Council; the lower section, styled the Assembly or the Commons, we will call Messrs D, E, and F; and note, that all the members inclusive, from A to F, are merchants, lawyers, and business men of Fish-and-fog-land. We may further note that, as a general rule, A, B, and C do ten or twenty times as much public work as D, E, or F. But it came to pass that on the formation of Responsible Government the Lower House claimed and received a certain amount of sessional pay to cover expenses of travel, time lost, &c. &c.; and further, that in process of time the

Council, or Upper House, claimed the same gratuity. Then the Assembly said, "No! no! no! you represent the Lords, and must work for nothing but honour." "That's all very fine," replied the Lords; "we are nothing but business-men, the same as yourselves; we give a great deal more time to the public service than you do, and if you are paid, so ought we to be." Then cried the Commons again, "No! no! no! we'll see you pretty well confounded first; not a halfpenny will we vote you." So it went on for several years, until at last A, B, and C said to D, E, and F, "Now, take heed, gentlemen, we will stand no more of this nonsense, if you do not vote our money with your own, we will throw out the Contingency Bill *in toto;* you shall swim in our boat for the future, and do the public work for honour and glory alone." But D, E, and F laughed, saying, "They will never dare do it; we will bring the whole country down on them." However, to their unbounded astonishment, A, B, and C kept their promise, threw out the Contingency or Salary Bill to the Parliament in 1859, and caused D, E, and F to return home to their desks and fish-flakes blue with disgust. In spite of the loud and angry denunciations of the stump oratory in the out-harbours, the Council quietly did the same the following year, making the Commons blue, doubly distilled. They felt it was time to compromise; and to save their dignity, in 1861 they agreed with the Council to submit the matter to the Duke of Newcastle, the

Colonial Secretary in England, by whose judgment they consented to be bound. A few months later the Governor received the Duke's reply as follows:—

"DOWNING STREET, 10*th February* 1862.

"NEWFOUNDLAND. No. 146.

"SIR,—I do not feel that it would become me to undertake the office of an actual arbitrator between two branches of the Legislature; but, since they have desired to know my sentiments, I have inquired into the practice in the principal neighbouring Provinces, and I find that in Canada, Nova Scotia, and in New Brunswick the members of the Legislative Council receive precisely the same personal allowance as the members of the Assembly. In Canada this course is fixed by a permanent Act; and in New Brunswick it is at the commencement of each Parliament enacted for the whole duration of that Parliament, so as to extend to the Council the courtesy of settling the matter once for all, and preclude its annual discussion.

"Seeing such powerful and uniform precedents, and considering that a perfect equality in respect of personal allowances of the present nature would seem best calculated to maintain the desirable harmony of feeling between co-ordinate branches of the Legislature, I am bound to say that my opinion would be in favour of following the same course in Newfoundland. —I have, &c.,

(Signed) NEWCASTLE."

"Governor Sir A. BANNERMAN, &c. &c. &c."

Well, gentle reader, what do you suppose was the course of the representatives of the people under Responsible Government upon receipt of that letter? You may probably reply that, as between gentlemen the matter was settled, not admitting of a doubt; but in truth you will be sadly mistaken—sadly mistaken. There is not much to crow over in such an error, for even the old Governor, long accustomed as he was to certain gross feeders on political offal, could hardly credit his ears, on the common principle of fair-play, when he was told that the matter was again going to be treated in the Lower House as if the appeal to the Duke as umpire had never taken place! It turned out to be quite true. Man after man had the unblushing bad taste to rise and vote against the Council, on the plea that the Duke had given only an opinion, and not a decision; though they were perfectly aware that in law he had no right to decide such a question; and that, moreover, they had desired his sentiments on the open right or wrong of the question. In vain the Premier pointed out this view of an arbitration as the only honourable course for them to adopt; in vain the Speaker nobly supported his friend and old colleague; in vain did four other members raise their voices against a storm of chicanery and unworthy pleadings which, chequered with personalities, fell like a hail-storm from the majority. It was not a ministerial question, so that all creeds were free to vote as they pleased, and it resulted that the Council's just demand was again thrown out. The division left it on record, upon the great photograph of the strange deeds of the world, that, as it was well said, there was but one sun in Asia, two kings of Brentford, three tailors of Tooley Street, four snobs of Liverpool, five heads of John the Baptist (all original), so now to this famous numerical roll shall be for ever added (and to be mentioned with all honour and distinction) the *six gentlemen* of Fish-and-fog-land! *

Did they gain by all this unworthy chicanery? Nothing, absolutely nothing, but utterly lost in the end of the game both the "odd" trick and rubber; for the Council quietly stood their ground, and threw out the bill for the salaries of the Commons again and again, until these needy legislators were starved into equity. If the noble Colonial Minister kept a diary, some future Macaulay may find perchance amid its notes strange comments on the wisdom of entrusting small unfledged communities, unfettered by any fear of a wholesome public judgment on their acts, with the cares of self-government, in these complicated times of rapid progress and maturing civilisation.

* The Attorney-General, The Speaker, The Colonial Secretary, The Receiver-General, Dr Winter, and Mr Leamon.

CHAPTER XVII.

FAREWELL.

"GLORY to God in the highest, peace on earth, good will toward men," so rung out, clear, musical, and pleasant, the bells of the Catholic Cathedral, on a New-Year's morn, which sun and wind had both agreed to bless. At least so many of us interpreted the distant harmony, as we made ready to give that greeting to friends and neighbours after the good old French custom, possibly introduced from Canadian sources here. Pity that it is rapidly fading out; left, indeed, principally to younger men, who take that opportunity of introducing their merits or wishes for future acquaintance to the ladies of their class. Yet there were still the official visits of ceremony which we, as in duty bound to our elders and superiors, prepared to pay; no great tax upon one's patience to such pleasant friends; to say nothing of the merry gliding over the crisp white mantle of earth to the music of a thousand bells, crossing from house to house on the same errand as ourselves. Crossing too over the chequered marble in the hall of Government House, in our visits of respect to the venerable chieftain, who, in his red morocco chair of state, looked like one of the Northern Vikings, a tower of strength and power, come back in the form of a rare old British gentleman.

"Thank ye, thank ye, gentlemen," said he, as we offered our congratulations; "I'm pretty weel for an auld man; but I'll throw a line with ye, Maister Wolfe, after the trout at Cape Race, if this confounded cough will leave me strength enough in May. Ye see, I'm just treating it mysel' with a little plain water, and a squeeze of orange in it. Have you seen her ladyship? Weel, then, go and see her, and ye'll find a glass of something better to drink our gude Queen's health; and be sure you admire her ladyship's hyacinths, for she's vera proud of them. Good-bye, good-bye."

So we passed out, giving place to others, to the brighter parlour of Lady Bannerman, where, as the Governor said, the flowers in the gay sunny windows claimed due admiration; though by no means casting in the shade the grandeur of her ladyship's new cap and velvet dress, before which we bowed with all solemnity and respect.

Our own good Bishop gave us next his word of good-will, and we soon found ourselves under the portico of his honour the Chief-Justice, elbowed by a troop of young Irish aspirants for legal honours, with a few who had already made their footing on the slippery bar. Like his friend the Governor, Sir Francis sat in his big morocco chair, doing full dignity to the ermine, spite of the merry twinkle of his eye, when he whispered—

"Be off now with your blarney, and get a glass of something with Lady Brady. You see," he continued, "I've a bad cough, and I'm just after moistening my throat with a little water, with a squeeze of orange in it."

Singular identity of beverage! fragrant too with a delicate aroma; but I fancied rather that of the lemon than of the orange, and the light colouring due to the distilled juice of the cane. A mistake on our parts, no doubt.

And yet it was singular again—very singular, it must be confessed—when we stood in the parlour of the jolly old President of the Council, that he, with his gouty feet swathed in flannel, should have remarked—

"And what will ye be taken, mee dear fellows? is it poort? You're right, there is worse than that in the world. You see, I'm just moistening mee lips with a drop of water, with a squeeze of orange in it; help yourselves." The Marchioness's make-believe with Dick Swiveller was quite a joke to this!

Our last visit—last but not least—was to *the* great man of Fish-and-fog-land,—the hearty, excellent, yet warlike Roman Prelate, at his palace under the shadow of his great cathedral, on the heights commanding the city. As it happened, we were just in the nick of time to see him in all his glory. Yes, there on the steps of his front door, in long, black robes, adorned with the massive gold cross and chain, with attendant priests around, the Bishop stood—a fine, genial, well-favoured man—about to receive the address of congratulation from the "Sons of Fishermen" or the Irish Society. These, at the time, were defiling with flags and banners, music and symbols, in long snake-like procession before him. As the leaders reached the presence, a halt was called, and, for a moment, silence reigned; while we, beneath a buttress of the cathedral, watched rather curiously the proceedings. At length his Lordship (the first Fisherman of the colony) thus spoke: "Well, boys, I'm glad to see you all. I hope God will give us a good year; and this day year I'll see you all as well as I do now, and all that."

Procession.—"Ay, my Lord, that's it. God bless your Lordship!"

Then came a pause for at least a minute, during which not a sound could be heard.

Bishop.—"Well, we've a fine day, boys; and, perhaps, that's a sign we are going to have a fine year; and I'll tell you what, boys, we want a good fishery this year; we do, boys, and all that."

Procession.—"Ay, ay, my Lord; we do, we do. God bless your Lordship!"

Another pause: now for the address no doubt.

Bishop.—"I think, boys, God will send us a fine year, for He knows we want a good fishery, and all that."

Procession.—"We do, my Lord, we do; true for you, my Lord! God bless your Lordship!"

Pause again: silence deeper than ever.

Bishop (at last).—" Well, boys, I 'm glad to see your band 's in fine tune; and I'm glad to hear it, and all that."

Procession.—" Thank your Lordship. God bless your Lordship!"

Another pause: silence supreme. Both parties evidently exhausted of what they had to do or say. At length, to our infinite relief, a man with a banner cried with startling suddenness—

" Three cheers for our Bishop!"

The long, human serpent wriggled and roared accordingly, with good-will and heartiness; yet it wanted the true ring for " all that."

But the Bishop smiled, dangled his gold cross, and bowed three times graciously.

Now, thought somebody, they are going on. No; there was another terrible pause.

At last another bannerman cried—

" Three cheers for our priests! Hooray! Hooray!"

Then the priests bowed very low and solemnly; the band struck up, and the tail of the procession alone was left on the white snow.

Well, it was not very edifying; indeed, there was a touch of the ludicrous in the affair; neither was the Bishop oratorical, or apt to seize the passing opportunity for good advice, or even flummery with his people. But it was exactly what was expected and desired between both parties. They simply wanted to recognise each other in the flesh, and so pass on. His people knew the Bishop was their master, and, moreover, that he loved them; the good Bishop knew he was their master, and was happy in the knowledge. What need of mere waste of words in a state of such perfect understanding and satisfaction. How many a public man, to be on such terms with his constituents, would gladly put his oratory and "all that" in his pocket!

Then to his Lordship (John Thomas, ✠), we paid our respects and congratulations as was right and proper. A hearty reciprocation and a glass of champagne were his return for the compliment, to say nothing of taking us round his noble library, the finest room in the colony. His reception-room was handsome, adorned with statuary from Italy; but for himself and the priests who lived with him, the little room below with its deal chairs and common delf, would have probably been scorned by a bagman. So strange is the contrast which he presents in the attributes of his daily life and the profession he upholds. Utter self-denial of personal luxuries, with the uttermost farthing of power and authority in all temporal matters with his fellow-men; a good man in his own private path; an unscrupulous antagonist to all political opponents. He is but true to his order after all; the man himself we may sincerely respect, but the pride of priestcraft we must equally deplore.

Alack! for pleasant friendships formed by a soldier in his varied service; alack! for the new faces he is ever meeting when he would willingly keep the old.

Before the revolving cycle of the new year came round again, our orders carried us suddenly away from scenes we had now learnt to love so well, to begin another act in the great drama of life. The young man setting out in a military profession, in the first burst of eager youth, anticipates with joy all the friends he will make, all the countries he will visit, all the varied aspects of nature which will change before him. It is very pleasant for a few years; but as the fire of youth cools the pleasure palls, until at last, when sober manhood crowns the edifice, the order to change is generally, even in a bad station, a signal for regret; pain to bid adieu to old familiar features and friends, pain to think of the irksomeness of removing these necessary duties elsewhere. One may think, besides, that the good things present cannot be replaced at all. The broad blue expanse of ocean opening out at Logie Bay; the bubbling trout-streams trickling between the hills; the broad breezy barrens, fruit-ladened and fringed with copse; the glorious heathy walks over hill and dale; the sport without fear or license, not to be beaten in its own way any where; the very dogs who follow us with love, with love returned; the plants we have raised and tended; the voices we have been accustomed to so many years; our Sunday strollings round the margin of the dark blue lake; the great fleecy clouds condensing on the hills, like armies drawn out for battle array; the Indian summer, with its sober sad reflections; our genial gatherings in winter: are all—

and many, many more—associations which we scarcely hope to renew. Brighter skies and brighter scenes may await us in other lands; fruits and flowers spread their choicest temptations before thirsty admiring eyes; but nowhere else can man grasp the hand of his fellow man with greater trust, or with greater confidence in a hearty welcome eat his neighbour's bread. This it was which smoothed down every rough path for us, and lighted up the dreariest days of winter with gleams of gladness, towards which brighter suns or happier climes, by these unaided, might have wooed and charmed in vain.

It came at last, that fatal order to "move on." All our little belongings passed into other hands; and one bright morning in June we stood on the deck of the steamer, gazing up to the noble cliffs as she passed through the Narrows out to sea. From the corner of the little battery, far far up directly over our heads, some men waved a flag; and a woman held up a baby in token, I suppose, of love to another woman who had done her, and many others, some silent deeds of kindness. The bluff shoulders of the rocks soon shut out from sight the harbour, the city, our own house, the landmarks of past years; while before us spread the mighty Atlantic, like an unknown page in our future lives. Far out at sea the great white clouds from the Gulf Stream came rolling up before the gentle wind; and when, about an hour afterwards, we entered their chilling folds, the purple cliffs of Fish-and-fog-land passed for ever out of sight; lost amid the eternal mists which, as the smoke of a battle-field, proclaim the silent conflict of the vast elements of nature, striving together under mysterious immutable laws for the cycles of change, and the progress of earth towards a never-to-be-attained maturity.

BALLANTYNE AND COMPANY, PRINTERS, EDINBURGH.

A LIST OF BOOKS

PUBLISHING BY

SAMPSON LOW, SON, AND MARSTON,

CROWN BUILDINGS, 188 FLEET STREET.

TWO YEARS BEFORE THE MAST, AND TWENTY-FOUR YEARS AFTER: a Personal Narrative. By RICHARD HENRY DANA, junr. An Entirely New and Copyright Edition, with Notes by the Author. Crown 8vo, cloth, 6s.

OUR NEW WAY ROUND THE WORLD. By CHARLES CARLETON COFFIN. 8vo, cloth, with numerous Illustrations, 12s.

The volume is handsomely printed, and enriched with upwards of one hundred engravings and maps, reproduced from photographs and original sketches, made upon the spots which they are intended to illustrate. Mr Coffin's "New Way Round the World" is not only valuable because of the light it throws upon people and countries really little known to us, and with which we are likely to be brought in contact, but it is an engaging and picturesque narrative, and would attract popular attention under any circumstances.

Two New Volumes of the Bayard Series, 2s. 6d. each.

THE ROUND TABLE: the Best Essays of WILLIAM HAZLITT. With Biographical Introduction.

BALLAD STORIES OF THE AFFECTIONS, from the Scandinavian. By ROBERT BUCHANAN.

*** The BAYARD SERIES comprises Works that may be termed Pleasure Books of Literature, produced in the choicest style, at a popular price: printed at the Chiswick Press, on toned paper; bound by Burn, flexible cloth extra, gilt leaves, silk head-bands and registers. Volumes now ready, each complete in itself, price Half-a-Crown.

THE STORY OF THE CHEVALIER BAYARD.
DE JOINVILLE'S ST LOUIS THE KING.
THE ESSAYS OF ABRAHAM COWLEY.
ABDALLAH. By EDOUARD LABOULLAYE.
TABLE-TALK OF NAPOLEON.
VATHEK. By WILLIAM BECKFORD.
THE KING AND THE COMMONS. By Prof. MORLEY.
RASSELAS. By Dr JOHNSON.
WORDS OF WELLINGTON.
HAZLITT'S ROUND TABLE.
BUCHANAN'S BALLADS.
COLERIDGE'S CHRISTABEL. *Just ready.*

LATIN PROVERBS AND QUOTATIONS, with Translations and Parallel Passages, and a copious English Index. By ALFRED HENDERSON. Fcap. 4to, 530 pages, 16s.

"The book is, we should imagine, the best of the kind that has yet been issued from the press."—*Examiner.*

THE SHAKSPERIAN TREASURY OF WISDOM AND KNOWLEDGE. By CHARLES W. STEARNS, M.D. Post 8vo, cloth, 8s. 6d.

LYRICAL PIECES, Secular and Sacred, from the Home Circle of a Country Parsonage. Edited by the Rev. ABNER W. BROWN, M.A., Vicar of Gretton and Hon. Canon of Peterborough. With numerous Illustrative Vignettes, and with Archæological and other Notes. Crown 8vo, 7s. 6d.

THE AUTHORISED ENGLISH VERSION OF THE NEW TESTAMENT; with Readings from the Sinaitic, the Vatican, and the Alexandrine MSS., in English. With Notes by the Editor, Dr TISCHENDORF. Revised and carefully collated for the Thousandth Volume of Baron Tauchnitz's Collection. Cloth flexible, gilt edges, 2s. 6d.; cheaper style, 2s. *New Edition now ready.*

THE SPEECHES OF SIR J. D. COLERIDGE, H.M. Solicitor-General, combining all that may be considered of importance in the lengthened Examination of Witnesses in the Case SAURIN *v.* STARR. 8vo, 5s.

MAURY'S PHYSICAL GEOGRAPHY OF THE SEA AND ITS METEOROLOGY. A New and Revised Edition, with copious Index. 8vo, 6s.

LEOPOLD THE FIRST, King of the Belgians. With Notes and Memoirs of Contemporary Events and Persons from authentic and unpublished Documents. 2 vols. 8vo, Portraits, 28s.

THE BYEWAYS OF EUROPE. Visits by unfrequented Routes to Remarkable Places. By BAYARD TAYLOR, Author of "Views Afoot." 2 vols. post 8vo, 16s.

A NEW AND REVISED EDITION OF MRS PALLISER'S BOOK OF LACE; with 169 Illustrations and Coloured Designs, including some interesting Examples from the Leeds Exhibition. By Mrs BURY PALLISER. 1 vol. 8vo, cloth extra, £1, 1s.

DOMESTIC EDITION OF THE ROYAL COOKERY BOOK. By JULES GOUFFÉ, Chef-de-Cuisine of the Paris Jockey Club. Translated and adapted for English Use by ALPHONSE GOUFFÉ, Head Pastry-cook to Her Majesty the Queen. A Household Edition, in one handsome large-type book for domestic use. 10s. 6d.

THE BLACKBIRD OF BADEN, and other Stories. BY ROBERT BLACK, M.A. 6s.

EDELWEISS. A Story by BERTHOLD AUERBACH. Translated by ELLEN FROTHRINGHAM, Small post 8vo, cloth, 5s.

THE GATES AJAR. By ELIZABETH S. PHELPS. Royal 32mo, cloth, 1s.

CONTINUATION OF THE STORY OF FOUR LITTLE WOMEN: Meg, Joe, Beth, and Amy. By LOUISA M. ALCOTT. With Illustrations. 16mo cloth, 3s. 6d.; or, complete with the previous volume, 2 vols. 7s.

KATHRINA: Her Life and Mine. In a Poem, by Dr J. G. HOLLAND.—Just ready. Forming the New Volume of "Low's Copyright Cheap Editions of American Copyright Authors." 1s. 6d. stiff cover, or 2s. cloth. Also Ready,

1. HAUNTED HEARTS. By the Author of "The Lamplighter."
2. GUARDIAN ANGEL. By the Autocrat of the Breakfast Table.
3. MINISTER'S WOOING. By the Author of "Uncle Tom's Cabin."
4. VIEWS AFOOT. By BAYARD TAYLOR.

PEAKS AND VALLEYS OF THE ALPS. From Water-colour Drawings by Elijah Walton. Chromo-Lithographed by J. H. Lowes, with Descriptive Text by the Rev. T. G. BONNEY, M.A., F.G.S. Folio, half morocco, with 21 large Plates. Original subscription, 8 guineas. A very limited edition only now issued at £4, 14s. 6d.

ARTISTS AND ARABS; or Sketching in Sunshine. By HENRY BLACKBURN, Author of "The Pyrenees," &c. Numerous Illustrations. Demy 8vo, cloth, 10s. 6d.

THE PYRENEES; 100 Illustrations by Gustave Doré, and a Description of Summer Life at French Watering Places. By HENRY BLACKBURN. Royal 8vo, cloth 18s.; morocco, 25s.

Also, by the same Author,

TRAVELLING IN SPAIN. Illustrated, 16s.; or Cheaper Edition, 6s.

THE ROYAL COOKERY BOOK. By JULES GOUFFÉ, Chef de Cuisine of the Paris Jockey Club. Translated and Adapted for English use. By ALPHONSE GOUFFÉ, Head Pastrycook to Her Majesty the Queen. Illustrated with large Plates beautifully printed in Colours, and 161 Woodcuts. Super-royal 8vo, cloth extra, £2, 2s.

⁂ *Notice—Household Cheaper Edition.* The unanimous welcome accorded to "The Royal Cookery Book" by all the leading reviews within the short time that has elapsed since its appearance, and the conviction that it is *the cookery book for the age*, induce the Publishers to issue for contemporaneous sale with this sumptuous presentation volume a Household Edition in one handsome large type book for domestic use. Price 10s. 6d., strongly half-bound.

A DICTIONARY OF PHOTOGRAPHY, on the Basis of Sutton's Dictionary. Rewritten by PROFESSOR DAWSON, of King's College, Editor of the "Journal of Photography;" and THOMAS SUTTON, B.A., Editor of "Photograph Notes." 8vo, with numerous Illustrations, 8s. 6d.

DR WORCESTER'S NEW AND GREATLY ENLARGED DICTIONARY OF THE ENGLISH LANGUAGE. Adapted for Library or College Reference, comprising 40,000 Words more than Johnson's Dictionary. 4to, cloth, 1,834 pp., price 31s. 6d. well bound.

"The volumes before us show a vast amount of diligence; but with Webster it is diligence in combination with fancifulness,—with Worcester in combination with good sense and judgment. Worcester's is the soberer and safer book, and may be pronounced the best existing English Lexicon."—*Athenæum.*

THE LIFE OF JOHN JAMES AUDUBON, the Naturalist, including his Romantic Adventures in the Backwoods of America, Correspondence with celebrated Europeans, &c. Edited, from materials supplied by his widow, by ROBERT BUCHANAN. 8vo. With Portrait, 15s.

"A readable book, with many interesting and some thrilling pages in it."—*Athenæum.*

"From first to last, the biography teems with interesting adventures, with amusing or perilous incidents, with curious gossip, with picturesque description."—*Daily News.*

"But, as we have said, Audubon could write as well as draw; and while his portfolio was a cause of wonder to even such men as Cuvier, Wilson, and Sir Thomas Lawrence, his diary contained a number of spirited sketches of the places he had visited, which cannot fail to interest and even to delight the reader."—*Examiner.*

THE VOYAGE ALONE; a Sail in the "Yawl, Rob Roy." By JOHN M'GREGOR. With Illustrations. Price 5s.

Also, uniform, by the same Author, with Maps and numerous Illustrations, price 5s. each,

A THOUSAND MILES IN THE "ROB ROY CANOE," on Rivers and Lakes of Europe. Fifth Edition.

THE "ROB ROY" ON THE BALTIC. A Canoe Voyage in Norway, Sweden, &c.

FREDRIKA BREMER'S LIFE, LETTERS, AND POSTHUMOUS WORKS. Edited by her sister, CHARLOTTE BREMER; translated from the Swedish by FRED. MILOW. Post 8vo, cloth, 10s. 6d.

THE RISE AND FALL OF THE EMPEROR MAXIMILIAN: an Authentic History of the Mexican Empire, 1861–7. Together with the Imperial Correspondence. With Portrait. 8vo, 10s. 6d.

MADAME RECAMIER, Memoirs and Correspondence of. Translated from the French and edited by J. M. LUYSTER. With Portrait. Crown 8vo, 7s. 6d.

SOCIAL LIFE OF THE CHINESE: A Daguerreotype of Daily Life in China. Condensed from the Work of the Rev. J. DOOLITTLE, by the Rev. PAXTON HOOD. With above 100 Illustrations. Post 8vo, 8s. 6d.

THE OPEN POLAR SEA: a Narrative of a Voyage of Discovery towards the North Pole. By Dr ISAAC I. HAYES. An entirely new and cheaper edition. With Illustrations. Small post 8vo, 6s.

CAPTAIN HALL'S LIFE WITH THE ESQUIMAUX. New and Cheaper Edition, with Coloured Engravings, and upwards of 100 Woodcuts. With a Map. Price 7s. 6d. cloth extra. Forming the cheapest and most popular Edition of a work on Arctic Life and Exploration ever published.

THE BLACK COUNTRY AND ITS GREEN BORDER LAND; or, Expeditions and Explorations round Birmingham, Wolverhampton, &c. By ELIHU BURRITT. Second and cheaper Edition, post 8vo, 6s.

A WALK FROM LONDON TO JOHN O'GROATS, AND FROM LONDON TO THE LAND'S END AND BACK. With Notes by the Way. By ELIHU BURRITT. Two vols., price 6s. each, with Illustrations.

SAMPSON LOW, SON, AND MARSTON,

CROWN BUILDINGS, 188 FLEET STREET.

www.ingramcontent.com/pod-product-compliance
Lightning Source LLC
Chambersburg PA
CBHW021213270326
41929CB00010B/1115

* 9 7 8 3 3 3 7 3 4 0 7 5 9 *